RETURN FROM EXILE

Daymond Duck
Larry Richards, General Editor

THOMAS NELSON
Since 1798

NASHVILLE DALLAS MEXICO CITY RIO DE JANEIRO BEIJING

Return from Exile
The Bible Smart Guide™ Series

Published in Nashville, Tennessee, by Thomas Nelson. Thomas Nelson is a trademark of Thomas Nelson, Inc.

Thomas Nelson, Inc. titles may be purchased in bulk for educational, business, fundraising, or sales promotional use. For information, please e-mail SpecialMarkets@ThomasNelson.com.

General Editor: Larry Richards
Managing Editor: Michael Christopher
Scripture Editor: Deborah Wiseman
Assistant Editor: Amy Clark
Design: Diane Whisner

ISBN 10: 1-4185-1004-1
ISBN 13: 978-1-4185-1004-6

Printed in the United States of America
08 09 10 11 RRD 9 8 7 6 5 4 3 2 1

Introduction

Welcome to *Return from Exile—The Smart Guide to the Bible*™ series. This series is designed to present the wonderful message of the Bible in a format that respects the Source while endeavoring to be accurate and easy-to-follow. We want you to understand God's message!

To Gain Your Confidence

Return from Exile—The Smart Guide to the Bible™ is for those who don't have the inclination, resources, or time to research a lot of hard-to-decipher material. The apostle Paul told the Corinthian believers, "And I, brethren, when I came to you, did not come with excellence of speech or of wisdom declaring to you the testimony of God" (1 Corinthians 2:1 NKJV). He wanted people to understand his message so he tried to avoid a vocabulary that only the scholars could understand. The author has endeavored to use a straightforward message with an educational approach that puts learning the Bible first. Complicated language that hinders one's study and understanding is deemed an unnecessary and unwanted weakness.

A Word About *Return from Exile The Smart Guide to the Bible*™

This book is a commentary on the writings of four Old Testament authors. Two authors, Ezra and Nehemiah, wrote books found in the Bible subsection called History. The other two authors, Haggai and Zechariah, wrote books found in the Bible subsection called the Minor Prophets.

For hundreds of years the Hebrew Bible treated the writings of Ezra and Nehemiah as one book. But a Latin translation of the Bible called the Vulgate came out in the fourth century and separated these writings into two books. Since then, they have been treated as two separate books. Almost everything known about the history of the Jews from 538 BC to 425 BC comes from these two books.

Three groups of Jews returned to the Promised Land during this time. The first main wave of returnees went back under the leadership of Zerubbabel and rebuilt the altar used for sacrificing burnt offerings. About two years later these people laid the foundation of the Temple, but due to great opposition did no more work on it. The Temple languished for the next sixteen years. Then, Haggai and Zechariah stirred them up and the project was completed. After that, Ezra led the second main wave back, taught the Law of Moses, and started a revival. Nehemiah then came along and supervised the rebuilding of the wall around Jerusalem. Zerubbabel was a member of the old royal family. Ezra was a priest in the restored land and Nehemiah eventually became the land's new governor. The following chart will help:

Return from Exile

	First Wave	Second Wave	Third Wave
Year	536 BC	458 BC	445 BC
Leader	Zerubbabel	Ezra	Nehemiah
King	Cyrus	Artaxerxes I	Artaxerxes I
Scripture	Ezra 1–6	Ezra 7–10	Nehemiah 1–13
Primary Task	Rebuild the Temple	Teach the Law of Moses	Rebuild Wall of Jerusalem

Haggai and Zechariah were prophets who urged the returning Jews to rebuild the Temple. Both are mentioned in the writings of Ezra (5:1; 6:14). Both returned to the land in the first wave of returnees led by Zerubbabel. Both were in the land when Ezra and Nehemiah arrived. And both prophesied in the second year of Darius the king (Haggai 1:1; Zechariah 1:1).

Which Return

It is important to know that the Jews have been off the land on three different occasions. The first was when the descendants of Abraham moved to Egypt. The second was when the Babylonians destroyed the nation. And the third was when the Romans destroyed the nation.

Moses led them back from Egypt after the first exile. Zerubbabel, Ezra, and Nehemiah led them back from Babylon in three main waves after the second exile. (See the chart called "Three Main Waves of 2nd Jewish Return" on page 4). Last, the nation was officially reborn a third time in 1948.

This book primarily concerns the three waves of Jews that returned from Babylon. The first two waves are recorded in the book of Ezra. The third wave is recorded in the book of Nehemiah. However, readers need to know that some of the prophecies given by Haggai and Zechariah envisioned the regathering of modern Israel. It is important to distinguish between what has been fulfilled and what is being fulfilled today.

Some Helpful Dates

When events start in one year (say in December) and they are completed a few weeks later in another year (say in January of the next year) there is always a problem deciphering when the events took place. For this reason, some commentaries vary by one or two years on the dating of certain events. Even though you will find some slight differences among writers, here are some important and widely recognized dates to help you understand most of the events discussed in this book:

605 BC—Babylon attacked Judah the first time.

586 BC—Babylon attacked Judah the third time and destroyed her.

539 BC—Babylon was attacked and defeated by the Medes and Persians.

538 BC—King Cyrus said the Jews could return home.

536 BC—Zerubbabel led the first wave of Jews back and started work on the Temple.

534 BC—Due to opposition, work on the Temple is stopped.

520 BC—Haggai and Zechariah caused the work on the Temple to resume.

516 BC—The work on the Temple was completed.

458 BC—Ezra led the second wave of Jews back and started a revival.

445 BC—Nehemiah led the third wave of Jews back and rebuilt the walls of Jerusalem.

Why Study *The Return from Exile*

There are many reasons why a person should study *Return from Exile—The Smart Guide to the Bible*™, and here are seven important ones:

1. It will answer many questions people have about God and the Bible.
2. It will help people understand many issues that make the daily newspapers and television reports.
3. It shows why the restoration of Israel was important to the Jews and how that affects us.
4. It reveals important information about what the future holds.
5. Studying the Old Testament books enhances people's understanding of the New Testament books.

6. "All Scripture is given by inspiration of God, and is profitable for doctrine, for reproof, for correction, for instruction in righteousness" (2 Timothy 3:16 NKJV).

7. Valuable lessons are learned from the real-life experiences of those who went before us.

How to Study *Return from Exile—The Smart Guide to the Bible*™

This book is divided into four main parts:

- ***Part One*** is a commentary on the **book of Ezra**. This historical segment presents a record of the events that led to the restoration of Israel as a nation. The first six chapters concern the first main wave of returnees who were led by Zerubbabel. The last four chapters concern the second main wave of returnees who were led by Ezra. Rebuilding the Temple is a major subject.
- ***Part Two*** is a commentary on the **book of Nehemiah**. This historical segment presents a record of the third main wave of returnees who were led by Nehemiah. Rebuilding Jerusalem's walls is a major subject in the first six chapters. Reforms that led to a fresh commitment to the Lord and a restoration of traditional worship are major subjects in the last seven chapters.
- ***Part Three*** is a commentary on the **book of Haggai**. This prophetic segment presents four short messages God gave through Haggai. Essentially, these messages are a call to rebuild the Temple and are also promises of help from God.
- ***Part Four*** is a commentary on the **book of Zechariah**. This prophetic segment presents a series of visions God gave to Zechariah. It accurately predicts many things about the first coming of Jesus, the modern restoration of Israel, the modern problems of Jerusalem, the Battle of Armageddon, the eventual conversion of the Jews to Christ, and the second coming of Jesus. It contains amazing revelations that should interest all.

A Word About Words

Originally, Israel was one nation, but after King Solomon died the nation split into a Northern Kingdom called Israel and a Southern Kingdom called Judah. Both kingdoms were eventually destroyed, but when the Jews returned they went back as one nation. So the terms Israel and Judah are used interchangeably in this book.

About the Author

Daymond Duck is the best-selling author of *On the Brink, An Easy-to-Understand End-Time Bible Prophecy*; *The Book of Revelation—The Smart Guide to the Bible*™; *The Book of Daniel—The Smart Guide to the Bible*™; and *Prophecies of the Bible—The Smart Guide to the Bible*™. He is the coauthor of *The End-Times Survival Handbook.* And he is a contributing author to *Forewarning—The Approaching Battle Between Good and Evil; Foreshadows of Wrath and Redemption*; *Piercing the Future—Prophecy and the New Millennium*; and *Prophecy at Ground Zero.*

Daymond graduated from the University of Tennessee with a B.S. in agricultural engineering. In 1979 he entered the ministry and became a bi-vocational pastor. He completed the program at Emory University for United Methodist pastors. He has twice served as honorary state chaplain for the Tennessee Rural Carriers, is a prophecy conference speaker, and is a member of the Pre-Trib Study Group in Arlington, Texas. Daymond and his wife, Rachel, make their home in Dyer, Tennessee. They have three children and five grandchildren.

About the General Editor

Dr. Larry Richards is a native of Michigan who now lives in Raleigh, North Carolina. He was converted to Christianity while in the Navy in the 1950s. Larry has taught and written Sunday school curriculum for every age group, from nursery through adult. He has published more than two hundred books that have been translated into twenty-six languages. His wife, Sue, is also an author. They both enjoy teaching Bible studies as well as fishing and playing golf.

BE SMART • BE INSPIRED •

Understanding the Bible Is Easy with These Tools

To understand God's Word you need easy-to-use study tools right where you need them—at your fingertips. The Smart Guide to the Bible™ series puts valuable resources adjacent to the text to save you both time and effort.

Every page features handy sidebars filled with icons and helpful information: cross references for additional insights, definitions of key words and concepts, brief commentaries from experts on the topic, points to ponder, evidence of God at work, the big picture of how passages fit into the context of the entire Bible, practical tips for applying biblical truths to every area of your life, and plenty of maps, charts, and illustrations. A wrap-up of each passage, combined with study questions, concludes each chapter.

These helpful tools show you what to watch for. Look them over to become familiar with them, and then turn to Chapter 1 with complete confidence: You are about to increase your knowledge of God's Word!

Study Helps

The thought-bubble icon alerts you to commentary you might find particularly thought-provoking, challenging, or encouraging. You'll want to take a moment to reflect on it and consider the implications for your life.

Don't miss this point! The exclamation-point icon draws your attention to a key point in the text and emphasizes important biblical truths and facts.

death on the cross
Colossians 1:21–22

Many see Boaz as a type of Jesus Christ. To win back what we human beings lost through sin and spiritual death, Jesus had to become human (i.e., he had to become a true kinsman), and he had to be willing to pay the penalty for our sins. With his death on the cross, Jesus paid the penalty and won freedom and eternal life for us.

The additional Bible verses add scriptural support for the passage you just read and help you better understand the underlined text. (Think of it as an instant reference resource!)

How does what you just read apply to your life? The heart icon indicates that you're about to find out! These practical tips speak to your mind, heart, body, and soul, and offer clear guidelines for living a righteous and joy-filled life, establishing priorities, maintaining healthy relationships, persevering through challenges, and more.

This icon reveals how God is truly all-knowing and all-powerful. The hourglass icon points to a specific example of the prediction of an event or the fulfillment of a prediction. See how some of what God has said would come to pass already has!

What are some of the great things God has done? The traffic-sign icon shows you how God has used miracles, special acts, promises, and covenants throughout history to draw people to him.

Does the story or event you just read about appear elsewhere in the Gospels? The cross icon points you to those instances where the same story appears in other Gospel locations—further proof of the accuracy and truth of Jesus' life, death, and resurrection.

Since God created marriage, there's no better person to turn to for advice. The double-ring icon points out biblical insights and tips for strengthening your marriage.

The Bible is filled with wisdom about raising a godly family and enjoying your spiritual family in Christ. The family icon gives you ideas for building up your home and helping your family grow close and strong.

something significant had occurred, he wrote down the substance of what he saw. This is the practice John followed when he recorded Revelation on the **Isle of Patmos.**

Isle of Patmos
a small island in the Mediterranean Sea

What does that word really mean, especially as it relates to this passage? Important, misunderstood, or infrequently used words are set in **bold type** in your text so you can immediately glance at the margin for definitions. This valuable feature lets you better understand the meaning of the entire passage without having to stop to check other references.

the big picture

Joshua

Led by Joshua, the Israelites crossed the Jordan River and invaded Canaan (see Illustration #8). In a series of military campaigns the Israelites defeated several coalition armies raised by the inhabitants of Canaan. With organized resistance put down, Joshua divided the land among the twelve Israelite

How does what you read fit in with the greater biblical story? The highlighted big picture summarizes the passage under discussion.

what others say

David Breese

Nothing is clearer in the Word of God than the fact that God wants us to understand himself and his working in the lives of men.[5]

It can be helpful to know what others say on the topic, and the highlighted quotation introduces another voice in the discussion. This resource enables you to read other opinions and perspectives.

Maps, charts, and illustrations pictorially represent ancient artifacts and show where and how stories and events took place. They enable you to better understand important empires, learn your way around villages and temples, see where major battles occurred, and follow the journeys of God's people. You'll find these graphics let you do more than study God's Word—they let you *experience* it.

Chapters at a Glance

PART THREE: The Book of Haggai

PART FOUR: The Book of Zechariah

Part One
THE BOOK OF EZRA

Introduction—Ezra 1-6: The First Wave Returns

Not everyone agrees, but most commentators say Ezra wrote the book bearing his name. He, or some unidentified person usually called the chronicler, compiled the first six chapters of the book from historical records. Then, Ezra appeared on the scene in chapter 7. He was a teacher well versed in the **Law of Moses**, a descendant of the chief priest named Aaron who served under Moses, and a priest to the Jews in **exile**. He led the second main wave of Jews that returned to the land and was instrumental in starting a great **revival** there.

teacher
Ezra 7:6

chief priest
Ezra 7:1–5

priest
Ezra 7:21

Law of Moses
all the rules God gave to Moses

exile
Jews living in foreign lands

revival
renewed zeal to serve God

chronological
in the order they happened

The amazing events in Ezra's book are not in **chronological** order. As a historian, Ezra knew that the sequence of events is very important, but, probably to be more helpful, he arranged some items by subject. It should also be noted that there is a 58-year period of silence in his book that runs from 516 BC to 458 BC, but the book of Esther covers part of the period he skipped over.

Also, it should be remembered that the nation of Israel existed as twelve individual tribes before it became a united kingdom. Under pressure from the threat of enemies, the people clamored for a king. Israel's first king was Saul, her second was David, and her third was Solomon. Following Solomon's death, around 922 BC, the united kingdom was divided into a Northern Kingdom called Israel and a Southern Kingdom called Judah. The Northern Kingdom consisted of ten tribes and was destroyed by Assyria around 721 BC. The Southern Kingdom consisted of two tribes and was finally destroyed by Babylon around 586 BC.

Some commentators refer to the Jews from the Northern Kingdom called Israel as the Ten Lost Tribes of Israel. These writers do not believe that any of the Northern Kingdom Jews retained their Jewish identity so that they could survive and return. These writers say that all of the returning Jews were exiles from the Southern Kingdom called Judah. But, because modern DNA analysis disputes this, not many people accept it anymore. Even though most of the Jews from the Northern Kingdom probably did lose their Jewish identity or get killed, there is wide agreement that a few did survive

Jeremiah
2 Chronicles 36:21

seventy
Jeremiah 25:11–12; 29:10

make known
Isaiah 46:10

remnant
the few within Israel who trust God

Promised Land
another name for the land of Israel

and eventually wind up in the Babylonian Empire. A small number of them probably relocated a second time during one or more of these three returns. Nevertheless, most of the returnees were from the Southern Kingdom of Judah. There is no known record of an organized return of Northern Kingdom Jews, however.

It is interesting to note that the great prophet Jeremiah predicted that God would exile the Jews in the Southern Kingdom called Judah to a foreign land for seventy years because of their refusal to turn from their sins. In 605 BC, King Nebuchadnezzar of Babylon removed a group during the first of three destructive raids on Judah and Jerusalem. Almost seventy years later, in 536 BC, the first main wave of Jews joyfully returned. God was right on schedule with Jeremiah's seventy-year prediction, and he really does make known the outcome of things before they happen. Even the Jews recognize this seventy-year period. In fact, they recognize two seventy-year periods: The first is called the servitude and is the seventy years between Nebuchadnezzar's first attack and the first wave return; and the second is called the desolation and is a seventy-year gap between Nebuchadnezzar's destruction of the Temple and its reconstruction.

what others say

Irving L. Jensen

> There would have been no restoration for Israel were it not for the grace of God. The restoration was surely not deserved. And, before there was even a captivity, the restoration was scheduled on a prophetic timetable by a gracious God who, in the forthcoming captivity period, would be calling out of the communities of Jewish exiles in Babylon a **remnant** of believers whom He could bring back to the **Promised Land**. With these He would perpetuate His covenanted blessings for the generations to come.[1]

Three Main Waves of 2nd Jewish Return

Situation	Events
Jews in exile	Babylon's 1st attack in 605 BC Babylon's 2nd attack in 597 BC Babylon's 3rd attack in 586 BC (Judah completely defeated, 586 BC)
Temple rebuilt	1st wave led by Zerubbabel in 536 BC
Revival begins	2nd wave led by Ezra in 458 BC
Walls of Jerusalem rebuilt	3rd wave led by Nehemiah in 444 BC

When Moses led the Jews from Egypt to the Promised Land, their return was called the Exodus. The return of the Jewish exiles from Babylon is sometimes called the second Exodus. Perhaps the return of Jewish exiles from nations all over the earth during the past one hundred years of modern-day history should be called the third Exodus.

Nebuchadnezzar headed the Babylonian army and his father was the king of Babylon when the first attack on Jerusalem began. He soon captured Daniel, Shadrach, Meshach, and Abednego along with other Jewish youths. But he received word that his father had died while the attack was still underway, so he broke off the siege and returned home to be crowned king of Babylon. His army attacked twice more before all of Judah and Jerusalem fell.

Ezra 1
The Decree of Cyrus

Chapter Highlights:
- The First Year
- Decree of Cyrus
- People's Response
- The King's Gift
- Treasure in Jerusalem

Let's Get Started

When Israel first became a nation, God offered to make a special covenant with the chosen people. If they would try to fully obey him, he would make them a treasured possession of his. As a group, the people responded, "All that the LORD has spoken we will do" (Exodus 19:8 NKJV). They often lapsed into failure, but God was very patient and forgiving. He quickly accepted their halfhearted efforts most of the time. Then, after several generations, the Jews stopped being faithful. They even stopped trying. They went from barely pleasing God to outright opposition to his rule.

God responded by raising up several great **prophets** to let the straying Jews know they were on the wrong track. These brave men of God urged the wayward people to change their ways. They repeatedly warned the rebellious Jews that God would destroy their nation if they refused to **repent**. The people steadfastly stopped their ears, so God allowed the destruction of the beautiful Temple Solomon had built and the captivity of the wicked nation to occur.

As the book of Ezra begins, the nation of Judah has been destroyed by Babylon, and the seemingly indestructible empire of Babylon has been conquered by the empire of Medes and Persians. At this point the Jews who were at one time subject to Babylon were now subject to the Medes and Persians. In summation, the king of the Medes and Persians had all the power.

covenant
Exodus 19:1–8

Persians
Daniel 5:1–30

covenant
an agreement between two or more parties

prophets
people who are inspired by God

repent
turn away from sin and turn toward God

Yahweh
This English translation of the Hebrew word YHWH refers to God.

what others say

The New Harper's Bible Dictionary

When Israel, "God's holy people" (Exodus 19:5f.), failed to keep her covenant with **Yahweh**, disasters, viewed as divine judgment, followed (Judges 2:1–23; 2 Kings 17:7–23; Nehemiah 9:6–31). For the chosen people were not exempt from punishment when they were guilty of wandering from their covenant relationship with God. Prophet after prophet protested, warned, and interpreted Babylonia and Assyria as instruments of judgment.[1]

The Assyrian Empire destroyed the Northern Kingdom called Israel in 721 BC. The Babylonian Empire replaced the Assyrian Empire and attacked the Southern Kingdom called Judah three times. Babylon finally destroyed Judah in 586 BC. The Medo-Persian Empire took over the Babylonian Empire and assumed control of the Jews in 539 BC. They had a Persian king.

Who's in Charge Here?

EZRA 1:1 ***Now in the first year of Cyrus king of Persia, that the word of the LORD by the mouth of Jeremiah might be fulfilled, the LORD stirred up the spirit of Cyrus king of Persia, so that he made a proclamation throughout all his kingdom, and also put it in writing, saying,*** *(NKJV)*

Ezra's historical record begins with a date: "the first year of Cyrus king of Persia." A very large joint army of Medes and Persians under the able leadership of a wise commander named Cyrus overthrew Babylon in 539 BC. At that time, the king of the Medes and Persians was a man named Darius. He stayed on as king of the newly expanded empire, but was terminally ill and expired after only a few months. He was succeeded by Cyrus, who most experts believe began his first year of reign in 538 BC.

God began to exercise divine influence over Cyrus as soon as he took the throne. In order to fulfill what the Lord said through the prophet Jeremiah, the Almighty caused Cyrus to issue a decree. This decree was a public announcement vocally proclaimed all over the kingdom for all to hear and put into writing for all to read (see chart on page 38 called "Persian Kings").

Lord
Jeremiah 25:11–13; 29:10

what others say

Charles R. Swindoll

Often, when looking upon great kings and great presidents and great governors and great men and women of state, we suck in our breath in awe. Yet God is able to move their hearts like His finger would reach down and retrace the course of a river. It's no problem to Him. He moves as He wills, and He isn't through doing so. Let me add, this isn't limited to kings. It's true of you and me.[2]

The prophet Isaiah prophesied approximately 739–695 BC, thereby foretelling events that stretch from his day to the end of the world. He even foretold the existence of King Cyrus and named him by name almost two hundred years before he became king. The fact that God can identify a king by name almost two hundred years before he takes the throne means he can also reveal other things before they happen, i.e., the **Rapture**, **Tribulation Period**, and the first and **second comings** of Jesus.

Hear Ye! Hear Ye!

EZRA 1:2 ***Thus says Cyrus king of Persia:***
All the kingdoms of the earth the LORD God of heaven has given me. And He has commanded me to build Him a house at Jerusalem which is in Judah. *(NKJV)*

Cyrus began his decree by referring to God as "The LORD God of heaven." This was a well-known expression the Jews started using when God abandoned the Ark of the Covenant in the Temple built by Solomon and returned to heaven. God refused to dwell in Solomon's Temple any longer because the people were involved in so much wickedness. He even decided to allow the Babylonians to destroy it.

But Cyrus was a good king and his decree shows he realized that his great position was a gift from the God of heaven. He knew he did not inherit it from his parents, or obtain it by his own wisdom and power.

Cyrus
Isaiah 44:28; 45:1–4

Seven Temples in the Bible

Temples	Reference
The Tabernacle	Exodus 26:30
Solomon's Temple	1 Kings 5–8; Jeremiah 32:28–44
Zerubabbel's Temple (remodeled and called Herod's Temple)	Ezra 3:1–8; 4:1–14; 6:13–15
Church Age Temple	1 Corinthians 6:10–20
Tribulation Temple	Daniel 9:27; 2 Thessalonians 2:3–4
Millennial Temple	Ezekiel 40–48
Heavenly Temple	Isaiah 6; Revelation 7:15

Rapture
when the Church is removed from the earth

Tribulation Period
seven years of God's wrath against the wicked on earth

second coming
the return of Jesus at the end of the Tribulation Period

In 539 BC, the first year Darius ruled over the newly expanded empire, Daniel **fasted** and prayed, confessed his sins and the sins of the Jewish people, and asked God to look with favor on the destroyed Temple and the city of Jerusalem (restore them). Now, about one year later, God moved upon the most powerful man on earth to issue a decree that would bring about the answer to that prayer. The Bible says, "The effective, fervent prayer of a **righteous** man avails much" (NKJV).

confessed
Daniel 9:1–19

prayer
James 5:16

fasted
denied himself food

righteous
he always does the right thing

sovereignty
supreme power, authority or control

pagan
someone who observes polytheistic religion

Let God's People Go

Ezra 1:3 ***Who is among you of all His people? May his God be with him, and let him go up to Jerusalem which is in Judah, and build the house of the Lord God of Israel (He is God), which is in Jerusalem.*** *(NKJV)*

Cyrus decreed that any Israelite who wanted to return home was free to go. They even had his blessing, He added, "may his God be with him." Where should they go? To their homeland. What should they do? Build the Temple? Whose Temple was it? It was the Temple of the Lord. Who is the Lord? He is the God of Israel.

what others say

Charles R. Swindoll

Talk about the **sovereignty** of God! Here's a **pagan** king who inherits somewhere around two to three million Jewish captives from his predecessor. By now they have bought homes, opened businesses, and blended into society. These Hebrews represent a lot of labor and tax income for Persia. Yet Cyrus says, "Go home; rebuild."[3]

It sounds like King Cyrus was a faithful follower of the God of Israel. He was definitely influenced by God, Daniel, and the Scriptures, but historical evidence also shows that he was tolerant of all religions and that he worshiped all the gods of those under his authority. It could be that he worshiped all these gods to gain the favor of his citizens.

Pass the Plate

Ezra 1:4 ***And whoever is left in any place where he dwells, let the men of his place help him with silver and gold, with goods and livestock, besides the freewill offerings for the house of God which is in Jerusalem.*** *(NKJV)*

Cyrus knew that many Jews would probably not return, so he decreed that all who remained behind, no matter where they lived in his kingdom, should contribute money, supplies, and animals for the support of those who returned. It seems that he did not want anyone to be prevented from going home because they could not afford it. It also seems that he knew it would take awhile for those who returned to get established. He asked all the Jews in his kingdom to share the load. He also directed them to "pass the plate" so everyone could help defray the cost of rebuilding the Temple. This was God's way of providing for his returning people.

ultimate Parent
our heavenly Father

eternal gifts
salvation, heavenly rewards, etc.

Levites
members of the tribe of Levi who assisted the priests

what others say

Clarence H. Wagner Jr.

The Bible shows us that God is the biggest giver of them all! He loves to give gifts and blessings. His gifts to each of us are always just the right gifts since He is the **ultimate Parent** and knows exactly what we need and want. God blesses us, sometimes miraculously, on occasions when there is a specific need, but His **eternal gifts** are the gifts that keep on giving![4]

Let's Pack Up

Ezra 1:5 ***Then the heads of the fathers' houses of Judah and Benjamin, and the priests and the Levites, with all whose spirits God had moved, arose to go up and build the house of the Lord which is in Jerusalem.*** *(NKJV)*

Here is insight into the people who responded to the decree of Cyrus. "The heads of the fathers' houses of Judah and Benjamin" refers to the recognized leaders of several families from the two tribes that made up the Southern Kingdom called Judah. "The priests and the **Levites**" were the religious leaders. "All whose spirits God had moved" refers to all who believed they should leave their adopted country, return home, reestablish their nation, "go up" to Jerusalem, and rebuild the Temple. These are the spiritual ones who made preparations

Ephraim and Manasseh
1 Chronicles 9:1–3

Zion
a poetic name for Jerusalem

religious structure
system of priests and Levites

Gentiles
non-Jews

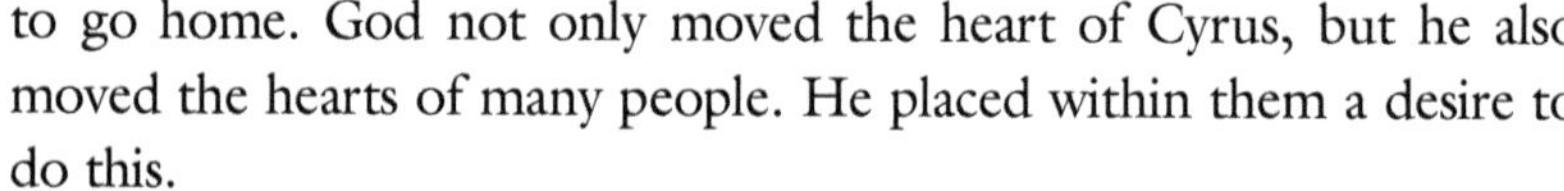

to go home. God not only moved the heart of Cyrus, but he also moved the hearts of many people. He placed within them a desire to do this.

what others say

Sol Scharfstein

The Hebrew word *aliyah* means "going up." In Temple days Jews made "aliyah" by ascending the hills of Judea and climbing the steps of the Holy Temple to offer a sacrifice. The word "aliyah" also refers to the "going up" to the reader's desk in the synagogue to take part in the Torah service. Returning to **Zion** is also designated by the term "aliyah." It too is a form of "going up," for in returning to Zion one ascends from life in exile to the proud Land of Israel.[5]

It's important to notice that the Jews still had family heads, tribal identity, and their pre-captivity **religious structure**. Many of them retained their traditional customs and beliefs even though they were captives in a foreign land for seventy years. Could it be that some knew the Scriptures and actually believed God would set them free and allow them to reestablish their nation? The prophet Jeremiah said it would happen.

The idea that there are Ten Lost Tribes (the idea that the ten tribes that composed the Northern Kingdom called Israel no longer exists) is just a myth. The author of 1 Chronicles wrote that some from the tribes of Ephraim and Manasseh (two of the ten northern tribes) returned and settled in Jerusalem.

A Great Offering

Ezra 1:6 ***And all those who were around them encouraged them with articles of silver and gold, with goods and livestock, and with precious things, besides all that was willingly offered. (NKJV)***

Only about 50,000 Jews returned, but those who stayed behind were very generous in their support. In fact, "all those who were around them" probably includes **Gentiles** as well as Jews. Regardless of nationality, God inclined the hearts of many people to be sympathetic toward the cause of the returning Jews. They voluntarily gave jewelry, commodities, animals, precious things, and freewill offerings. Their great generosity was very encouraging to these returnees who knew that the task of building houses and the Temple would not be easy.

This exodus from Babylon reminds us of the Exodus of Moses leading the Jews out of Egypt. The Jews who left Egypt also took articles of silver and gold, animals, goods, and clothing. It's the same today. Many of the Jews who are returning to the Promised Land are doing so with the help of generous people all over the world. Many people cheerfully give when they think they are giving to God by giving to people or organizations who they believe are fulfilling his plans.

Treasures from Solomon's Temple

> EZRA 1:7 ***King Cyrus also brought out the articles of the house of the LORD, which Nebuchadnezzar had taken from Jerusalem and put in the temple of his gods;*** *(NKJV)*

King Cyrus went all out to do what he believed the Jewish God wanted him to do. In addition to issuing the decree to release the Jews and rebuild the Temple, and in addition to ordering financial support, he located the articles that Nebuchadnezzar had removed from the first Jewish Temple in Jerusalem. Nebuchadnezzar seized those precious articles before he set fire to the beautiful Temple of God. He took them back to Babylon and placed them in the temple of his pagan god.

How did good King Cyrus wind up with these valuable vessels? Following Nebuchadnezzar's death, the crown of Babylon changed heads several times. Then, Nebuchadnezzar's foolish grandson Belshazzar took over. His kingdom was in a war with the Medes and Persians, and Belshazzar wanted to show everyone that he was not afraid of anyone or anything, including the Hebrew God. He threw a big party and sent for the vessels his hotheaded grandfather had stolen from the Jewish Temple. He and his guests drank wine out of them and praised their pagan gods. This was their last big party. Before the night was over, the Medes and Persians captured Babylon with all her treasures, including the precious vessels taken out of the Temple in Jerusalem. God protected the precious articles for seventy years and now he was causing them to be returned.

silver
Exodus 12:35–36

fire
2 Chronicles 36:15–23

god
Daniel 1:1–2

party
Daniel 5:2–4

Nebuchadnezzar worshiped many gods, but his chief god was Bel. This god had several names. Some called him Baal, but others called him **Marduk** or Merodach. A person who worships more than one god is called a polytheist.

A Very Special Gift

EZRA 1:8 ***and Cyrus king of Persia brought them out by the hand of Mithredath the treasurer, and counted them out to Sheshbazzar the prince of Judah.*** *(NKJV)*

The Temple articles that Cyrus was giving back were very valuable. No doubt they were kept in a very safe place. Persia's treasurer was a man named Mithredath, and he was the one that King Cyrus appointed to bring them out. He itemized the Temple articles and officially turned them over to Sheshbazzar.

Not everyone agrees, but most scholars think Sheshbazzar had two names: the Babylonians and Persians called him Sheshbazzar, but the Jews called him Zerubbabel. He was the grandson of king Jehoiachin, the next-to-last king of Judah. This means he was also a descendant of King David and an excellent choice to head the first wave of returnees. He was the legal heir to the next Jewish throne.

what others say

The Wycliffe Bible Commentary

Even as Daniel was known in Babylon officially as Belteshazzar (Daniel 1:7), so Zerubbabel was probably known as Sheshbazzar. We know that Zerubbabel laid the foundation of the Temple (Ezra 3:8; 5:2; Zechariah 4:9); but in an official letter to Darius, "Sheshbazzar" is said to have done this (5:16).[6]

Jehoiachin
1 Chronicles 3:17–19

Marduk
Babylonian god. The Assyrians and the Persians also honored him.

Check Inventory

EZRA 1:9–11 ***This is the number of them: thirty gold platters, one thousand silver platters, twenty-nine knives, thirty gold basins, four hundred and ten silver basins of a similar kind, and one thousand other articles. All the articles of gold and silver were five thousand four hundred. All these Sheshbazzar took with the captives who were brought from Babylon to Jerusalem.*** *(NKJV)*

The inventory lists 2,499 articles and it adds that a total of 5,400 articles were turned over. Why there is a difference is not known, but it seems likely that some articles were not itemized because they were of lesser significance than those that were. But the main point of the passage is not how many items were returned. It is that King Cyrus held nothing back. He possessed a great treasure, but he returned everything. He couldn't give back the Temple that was burned, but he could give back all he possessed that had been taken out of it. This would give the returning Jews a physical connection between the old Temple that was destroyed and the new one that they planned to build. So Sheshbazzar took possession of all these valuable articles and carefully transported them back to Jerusalem to be used in the worship of Israel's God.

Chapter Wrap-Up

- God caused King Cyrus of Persia to issue a decree in the first year of his reign. God did it to fulfill what he said through Jeremiah the prophet.
- The decree stated that God had made Cyrus king and appointed him to rebuild the Temple at Jerusalem. This granted the Jews permission to return and do the work. It authorized an offering to finance the project.
- Many Jews responded, under the influence of God, by making preparations to return. Their neighbors shared in the project with generous, valuable offerings.
- King Cyrus made a great contribution when he returned all the Temple articles that Nebuchadnezzar had stolen from the first Temple.
- The Temple treasures were turned over to the Jewish exiles, who then took them to Jerusalem.

Study Questions

1. What do you think Ezra meant when he said, "God stirred up the heart of Cyrus?" Does God do this today?
2. What does the decree of Cyrus say about how he received his kingdom and what he saw as one of his main responsibilities?
3. After setting the Jews free, what did Cyrus tell them to do?
4. What did Cyrus contribute toward the Temple project and why was this so important?

Ezra 2
The First Census

Chapter Highlights:
- The First Census
- Number of People
- Number of Animals
- Amount of Offering
- Settlements Established

Let's Get Started

Chapter 1 of the book of Ezra first focuses on the release of the Jews and then the focus shifts to those who returned. Here, the first wave of returnees is being named and counted in the first census. Included in this census is a list of servants, musicians, and animals. When they arrived, an offering was taken for the rebuilding of the Temple and there is a report on that. These people made great sacrifices to honor God, and God showed his favor to them by having Ezra compile this sacred list.

knows
John 10:14

gatekeepers
Ezra 2:42

servants
Ezra 2:43

towns
Ezra 2:70

ruler
Micah 5:2

Bethlehem
Ezra 2:21

Several Lists

the big picture

Ezra 2:1–63

This is a list of those who accompanied Zerubbabel (vv. 1–2), a list of those from Israel (vv. 3–19), a list of those from around Bethlehem (vv. 20–35), a list of priests (vv. 36–39), a list of Levites (v. 40), a list of singers (v. 41), a list of Temple gatekeepers (v. 42), a list of Temple servants (vv. 43–54), a list of descendants of Solomon's servants (vv. 55–58), a list of people who could not prove their genealogy (vv. 59–63).

Most people are bored with long lists and genealogies because they do not know what to look for. Notice these things:

- God knows his people by name.
- God's people come from all walks of life (rich, gatekeepers, servants, etc.).
- God's people live in many different towns.
- God's people can endure persecution and remain faithful.

It is prophesied that the One who is to be ruler over Israel (Jesus) will come out of Bethlehem. Here we learn that many people moved back to Bethlehem. Could it be that God was already making

arrangements for a young couple to give birth to the Messiah in Bethlehem? Did you know that Zerubbabel was an ancestor of Jesus?

The prophet Jeremiah was from a place called Anathoth. He was in prison when Babylon attacked Jerusalem. He knew the city would be captured. It seemed like a terrible time to be buying land, but even so, God told Jeremiah to buy some property and put the deed in a safe place because the people would come back and build there again. This was to be a demonstration of Jeremiah's faith in God, and here is recorded the return of the men of Anathoth.

The Nehemiah named here is not the man who wrote the book of Nehemiah, and Mordecai is not the Mordecai mentioned in the book of Esther.

Count the People

> EZRA 2:64–65 ***The whole assembly together was forty-two thousand three hundred and sixty, besides their male and female servants, of whom there were seven thousand three hundred and thirty-seven; and they had two hundred men and women singers.*** (NKJV)

This is a record of the total number of brave souls who left everything beautiful Babylon had to offer and moved to the Promised Land in 536 BC. This first wave of hardy people traveled under the able leadership of Zerubbabel. To some it seems like a large number, but to those who were trying to rebuild the nation it probably seemed like more was needed. The number of servants is large, suggesting that many of the Jews had gained great wealth in Babylon. It also suggests that many of the returnees were wealthy people. The singers were prepared to unify in one voice of joy with instruments of music, stringed instruments, harps, cymbals, and psalms of praise about the coming Temple.

• Number of Exiles	42,360
• Number of Servants	7,337
• Number of Singers	200
Grand Total	49,897

Zerubbabel
Matthew 1:12

Jeremiah
Jeremiah 29:27

captured
Jeremiah 32:1–15

Anathoth
Ezra 2:23

Nehemiah
Ezra 2:2

Mordecai
Ezra 2:2

what others say

Mark D. Roberts/Lloyd J. Ogilvie

The total of 42,360 appears also in Nehemiah 7:66. Unfortunately, it does not sum up the actual numbers of the list (Ezra = 29,818; Nehemiah = 31,089). Although commentators have proposed many solutions to this dilemma, in all likelihood it reflects the awkward Hebrew numbering system along with possible copying inconsistencies. It may also mean that women were included in the total, but not in the constituent numbers indicated above.[1]

months
Ezra 7:7–8

When added up, the figures in verses 1–63 total 12,542 less than the grand total. Some suggest the numbers are erroneous or there is an error in the Bible. Others believe it is more likely that these were children or people who joined the caravan after the lists were compiled. No one knows the real reason for the difference, but this writer sees no reason to believe that the Bible is in error. Ezra said his total is of "the whole assembly."

Count the Animals

Ezra 2:66–67 ***Their horses were seven hundred and thirty-six, their mules two hundred and forty-five, their camels four hundred and thirty-five, and their donkeys six thousand seven hundred and twenty. (NKJV)***

These verses are a record of the total number of animals the first wave of returnees took with them. They had to travel about 900 treacherous miles and the hard trip usually took about four months. They took:

• Horses	736
• Mules	245
• Camels	435
• Donkeys	6,720
Grand Total	8,136

Picture this caravan: almost 50,000 people with more than 8,000 animals on a long, difficult, and dangerous journey. They had to transport the gifts their neighbors had given them, the 5,400 articles King Cyrus had returned for the Temple, several thousand pounds

freewill offerings
No one was forced to give.

according to their ability
The rich gave more and the poor gave less.

of personal treasure (see next two verses), food, clothing, and much more. Historians don't say much about the Jews using horses, mules, camels, and donkeys, but this group sure needed a lot of pack animals. Robbers were a real threat at this time, but this group would have a lot of dedicated defenders.

Count the Offering

EZRA 2:68–69 ***Some of the heads of the fathers' houses, when they came to the house of the LORD which is in Jerusalem, offered freely for the house of God, to erect it in its place: According to their ability, they gave to the treasury for the work sixty-one thousand gold drachmas, five thousand minas of silver, and one hundred priestly garments.*** *(NKJV)*

Following their long hard journey back to the glorious Promised Land, the former exiles gathered at the site where their beautiful gold-adorned Temple once stood. It seems likely that they may have stood there aghast and grieving over the pile of ruins at first. It was a worthless heap of rubbish that had to be removed. Who could believe a loving God would let this happen? They probably read some Scripture, said some prayers, and felt a sense of devotion to God and the honor of their ancestors. Of course, this is just speculation, but we do know that one of the first things they did was to take up an offering. The recognized leaders of some of the families went forward and presented offerings that were specifically designated for the rebuilding of the Temple. But it would not be rebuilt just anywhere. The Temple would be rebuilt in its place on its original site or the same place where Solomon's Temple had stood in Holy Jerusalem. This is the same site that militant Muslims want today.

These family leaders gave **freewill offerings**. They gave cheerfully and they gave **according to their ability**. God had richly blessed them and now they were blessing God. Here is what they gave:

- 61,000 drachmas of gold = approximately 1,100 pounds of gold
- 5,000 minas of silver = approximately 6,000 pounds of silver
- 100 priestly garments

Militant Muslims claim they have a right to the Temple Mount because they believe that Muhammad ascended into heaven from there about 700 AD. But the first two Jewish Temples stood on that site hundreds of years before Muhammad was born. It was a Jewish holy site hundreds of years before the religion of Islam even began.

Nethinim
Temple workers who did menial jobs

Hosea
an Old Testament prophet

End Times
at the close of the Church Age

what others say

Jack W. Hayford

Additional evidence of the spirit of the people is the action indicated here. They "offered freely" and "according to their ability," both of which mind-sets release the power of the Spirit in the kingdom. God never requires us to give what we don't have, yet He does desire that we be willing to give everything that He has given to us.[2]

Settling Down

EZRA 2:70 *So the priests and the Levites, some of the people, the singers, the gatekeepers, and the* ***Nethinim****, dwelt in their cities, and all Israel in their cities.* (NKJV)

Although it's not clear, it seems reasonable to assume that some of the people moved on to the deserted and grown-up towns and cities where their ancestors once lived. It also seems likely that most or all of the priests, Levites, singers, gatekeepers, and Temple servants settled within a reasonable distance of Jerusalem because they needed to be near the Temple Mount. Those who wouldn't be working at the Temple probably settled farther away.

what others say

Zola Levitt

Nobody destroyed the Northern tribes, least of all not a broken-hearted God who loved them. **Hosea** was written to the Northern tribes and prophesied the restoration of those tribes in the **End Times**.[3]

Chapter Wrap-Up

- Ezra took a census and broke it down into categories: families from Israel, families from around Bethlehem, priests, Levites, singers, gatekeepers, Temple servants, descendants of Solomon's servants, and those who could not prove their ancestry.
- Ezra broke the census down into number of people, servants, and singers.
- Ezra counted the animals and broke the list down into number of horses, mules, camels, and donkeys.
- When they arrived Ezra took an offering and reported on what was given.
- Ezra also noted that the former exiles settled in their own towns.

Study Questions

1. What is important about the fact that some of the former exiles were originally from Bethlehem?
2. How many Jewish exiles returned? Do you think this was a large number? What does this tell us about those who were left behind?
3. How many servants returned with the former exiles, and what does this tell us?
4. In your opinion, what did the servants do on the journey?
5. What are two things the Temple was called other than "the Temple"?

Ezra 3
Construction Begins

Chapter Highlights:
- Altar Rebuilt
- Animal Sacrifices
- Feast Celebrations
- Temple Construction
- Joy and Sorrow

Let's Get Started

The verses in this chapter can be summed up with the phrase "humble beginnings." Some of the Jews had to travel from Jerusalem to their ancestral hometown. The fortunate ones didn't have very far to go, but it probably took a few weeks for others to make the trip and get settled in. Few can doubt that the task of clearing shrubs and trees from the untended, grown-up property and the task of starting a new house without much help was difficult. But the returnees didn't spend much time working on their projects at home because they soon returned to Jerusalem with plans to rebuild the altar at the demolished Temple. Three important holidays were coming up: The Feast of Trumpets (Rosh Hashanah), The Day of Atonement (Yom Kippur), and the Feast of Tabernacles or Booths (Succoth). These Jews passionately wanted to offer burnt offerings during the Feast of Tabernacles, and to make these offerings their first step toward reestablishing true worship at the Temple they planned to build.

burnt offerings
Leviticus 1:1–17; 6:8–13

sacred calendar
the calendar God told the Jews to go by

Gregorian calendar
The calendar we use. It was developed by Pope Gregory XIII in 1582.

One Accord

> EZRA 3:1 ***And when the seventh month had come, and the children of Israel were in the cities, the people gathered together as one man to Jerusalem.*** *(NKJV)*

Some might think this verse means the Jews assembled in Jerusalem seven months after they arrived back in the Promised Land, but that's not correct. It actually means the Jews assembled in Jerusalem in the seventh month of the year on the Hebrew **sacred calendar**. The seventh month is called Tishri, and it spans the last part of September to the first part of October on the **Gregorian calendar** (approximately mid-September to mid-October). Not everyone agrees, but it seems likely that the year was 536 BC. An interesting thing about this is the fact that God said the Jews would be off the land for seventy years. King Nebuchadnezzar's first attack was in

Passover
Exodus 12:1–30

Passover
a yearly celebration recounting the night God won Israel's freedom from Egypt

early rains
spring rains

605 BC. He removed Daniel, Shadrach, Meshach, Abednego, and others. Almost seventy years later, slightly less than 50,000 Jews returned home. "The people gathered together as one man to Jerusalem" means they assembled in the Holy City with one purpose.

Hebrew and Gregorian Calendars

Month on Hebrew Sacred Calendar	Month on Hebrew Civil Calendar	Hebrew Name	Gregorian Name
1	7	Nisan (Abib)	Mar.–Apr.
2	8	Lyyar (Ziv)	Apr.–May
3	9	Sivan	May–June
4	10	Tammuz	June–July
5	11	Ab	July–Aug.
6	12	Elul	Aug.–Sept.
7	1	Tishri	Sept.–Oct.
8	2	Heshvan	Oct.–Nov.
9	3	Kieslev (Chisleu)	Nov.–Dec.
10	4	Tebeth	Dec.–Jan.
11	5	Shebat	Jan.–Feb.
12	6	Adar	Feb.–Mar.
13 (Leap Year)*		Adar Sheni	

* Leap Year comes once every three years, Adar Sheni is 29 days long and it means "the second Adar."

The Jews use two different calendars and both are different from all other calendars. One Jewish calendar is called the sacred calendar and the other is called the civil calendar. Both Hebrew calendars are based upon the moon. The first day of the month always falls on a new moon, regardless of the calendar. The sacred calendar was set up to correspond with the Jewish holy days, which start with their preparation for <u>Passover</u>. The civil calendar was set up to correspond with the agricultural seasons, which start with the **early rains**.

Religion and Politics Join Hands

EZRA 3:2 ***Then Jeshua the son of Jozadak and his brethren the priests, and Zerubbabel the son of Shealtiel and his brethren, arose and built the altar of the God of Israel, to offer burnt offerings on it, as it is written in the Law of Moses the man of God.*** **(NKJV)**

The religious leaders, represented by Jeshua and the priests, and the political leaders, represented by Zerubbabel and his brethren, worked together to rebuild the altar of **burnt offerings**. The reason why they built it was to offer burnt offerings according to the instructions written in the **Law of Moses**. This reveals two things. First, the Jews were preparing to resume the practice of offering animal sacrifices, which means they were reestablishing their old religion. Second, the Jews were following the Law of Moses, which means they were going back to the same **Scriptures** they used before the Babylonian exile. Burnt offerings were given by God as a way to atone for their sins. Many Christians believe the ashes that were left after the offering was burned signify the words of Jesus on the cross, "It is finished."

Notice that Ezra called Moses "the man of God." The Jews believed Moses was special. His miracles were wrought by the power of God. He was God's spokesman, and the Ten Commandments and all the other things he wrote were given by God.

what others say

H. A. Ironside

Man as the offerer stood before the priest with his hand upon the head of the burnt offering. He was really identifying himself with the victim [animal) that was about to be slain [and burned). It is the hand of faith which rests upon the head of Christ and sees in Him the One who takes my place. All that He is, He is for me! Henceforth God sees me in Him.[1]

If a society wants to retain its identity, it must retain its language and religion. Thus, Sheshbazzar (Ezra 1:8) had to abandon the name the Babylonians and Persians called him and return to using Zerubbabel, the name the Jews called him (Ezra 2:2). Also, the people had to return to the Scriptures and the way of worship their ancestors had followed.

God said the burnt offering would be "accepted" for the offerer and he would be "forgiven." The burnt offering on the altar was accepted in the place of the Jewish sinner, and Jesus on the cross was accepted in the place of the Christian. By accepting the burnt offering, God was accepting and forgiving the offerer. By accepting the death of Jesus, God was accepting and forgiving the Christian. These offerings teach that obedience pleases God and no matter how bad our sin is, it is still possible to make peace with God.

built
Exodus 38:1–7

Moses
Exodus 24:12; 20:1–18

burnt offerings
an offering the Jews made to show God they were sorry for their sins

Law of Moses
all the rules God gave to Moses

Scriptures
the Word of God

Build Right Here

fifteenth day
Numbers 29:12–16

EZRA 3:3 *Though fear had come upon them because of the people of those countries, they set the altar on its bases; and they offered burnt offerings on it to the LORD, both the morning and evening burnt offerings.* (NKJV)

King Cyrus gave the returnees permission to rebuild the Temple, but they were still afraid of the great number of hostile non-Jews who had moved into the area following the destruction of Jerusalem. The returnees may have believed that they had traveled too far for King Cyrus to protect them. They were apprehensive. Their hearts fluttered with an eerie sense of foreboding, intimidation, and impending danger. But they greatly wanted to reestablish their religion. They probably believed that rebuilding the altar and offering burnt offerings would please their powerful God and invoke his divine protection. So they located the original foundation of the altar and built a new altar on the exact same spot. As soon as the new altar was finished, they resumed the practice of offering burnt offerings at least twice a day: in the morning and again in the evening.

When danger is lurking nearby it is good to have God on our side. He is the only true source of protection. He can speak and make things happen. But if we want him to help us, we need to be obedient.

Celebrating God's Goodness

EZRA 3:4 *They also kept the Feast of Tabernacles, as it is written, and offered the daily burnt offerings in the number required by ordinance for each day.* (NKJV)

The next step in reestablishing their religion was to start celebrating the various feast days God told their ancestors to observe. The first feast day they observed was the Feast of Tabernacles (about 536 BC). This feast began on the fifteenth day of the seventh month (Tishri on the sacred calendar) and lasted seven days. The Jews went by the Scriptures and offered the right number of sacrifices on each day of that holy week (see chart on Jewish Feasts).

what others say

Richard Booker

It was also called the Feast of Ingathering because it was at the end of the harvest season and the Feast of Booths because the Hebrews slept in booths or shelters during the feast (Exodus 23:16; Deuteronomy 16:16).[2]

The Jews celebrated the Feast of Tabernacles to remind them of the forty years their ancestors spent wandering in the wilderness. They built small booths or tabernacles to live in during the week of this feast. These tabernacles had to be: (a) loosely constructed, and (b) have cracks in the roof so they could look up and see the sky above them through the cracks. The loose construction reminded the Jews that their ancestors used temporary housing in the wilderness because they were just passing through. The cracks in the roof let them keep an eye on heaven. God wants us to remember that we are just passing through this life, and to look up toward heaven, toward that city whose Builder and Maker is God.

The Jewish Feasts

Month on Hebrew Sacred Calendar	Hebrew Name of Month	Day of the Month	Feast Name	Gregorian Name, Same Calendar Period
1	Nisan (Abib)	14	Passover	Mar.–Apr.
		15–21	Unleavened Bread	
		16	Firstfruits	
3	Sivan	6	Shavuot (Pentecost)	May–June
7	Tishri	1	Rosh Hashana (Trumpets)	Sept.–Oct.
		10	Yom Kippur (Day of Atonement)	
		15–21	Sukkot (Tabernacles)	

burnt offerings
Numbers 28:1–31

appointed feasts
Leviticus 23:1–44

Let's Keep It Up

Ezra 3:5 ***Afterwards they offered the regular burnt offering, and those for New Moons and for all the appointed feasts of the Lord that were consecrated, and those of everyone who willingly offered a freewill offering to the Lord.*** *(NKJV)*

Starting with this Feast of Tabernacles (about 536 BC), these dedicated returnees obediently offered all of the Lord's required burnt offerings. This included daily offerings, Sabbath offerings, the new moon offerings that fell on the first day of each month, and all the other sacrifices that God told their ancestors to make during the appointed feasts. They also resumed the practice of allowing people to offer burnt offerings at any other time that they desired to do so. Giving was a matter of what God expected on the feast days, but it was also a matter of what each individual wanted to do. Some wanted to do more than what was merely expected. We should give what God asks, but we should also feel free to go beyond what he asks. This is a way of showing him how much we love him. He is the true Giver, and his people can never out give him.

The required daily offerings included a male lamb without blemish being offered each morning and each evening. These spotless lambs pointed to Jesus, the sinless Lamb of God, who would give his life as the ultimate atonement for sin.

They Worked Fast

Ezra 3:6 ***From the first day of the seventh month they began to offer burnt offerings to the Lord, although the foundation of the temple of the Lord had not been laid.*** *(NKJV)*

The first two verses of this chapter state that the Jews started building the altar on the first day of the seventh month. This verse states that they began to offer burnt offerings on the same day. So it took God's people less than one day to rebuild the altar. They immediately started offering sacrifices. And they did all of this before they laid the foundation for the Temple.

Apparently, they offered sacrifices from the first to the fifteenth days of the month, but not on all of the required ones. On the fifteenth of the month, at the Feast of Tabernacles, they offered all of the required sacrifices for the first time. From that point on, they did everything the Law required.

what others say

Warren W. Wiersbe

It wasn't necessary to wait until the temple was completed before offering sacrifices to God. As long as there was a **sanctified** altar and a qualified priest, sacrifices could be given to the Lord. After all, it's not the external furnishings, but what's in the heart that concerns God the most.[3]

We Need Building Materials

Ezra 3:7 ***They also gave money to the masons and the carpenters, and food, drink, and oil to the people of Sidon and Tyre to bring cedar logs from Lebanon to the sea, to Joppa, according to the permission which they had from Cyrus king of Persia. (NKJV)***

The former exiles started making preparations to rebuild the Temple. They hired **masons** and carpenters with some of the money they received to pay for the work. They also hired Phoenician **seafaring** merchants at Sidon and Tyre to float cedar logs from ports in Lebanon to the port at Joppa, which was about thirty-five miles from Jerusalem. The merchants of Sidon and Tyre had to import most of their food, and this probably explains why the Jews paid them with food, drink, and oil. All of these transactions had the approval of King Cyrus.

Kings and queens used cedarwood in their palaces. Religious people used it in their temples. Artisans made statues and musical instruments out of it. It was long-lasting, resisted decay and insects, had an excellent fragrance, and was very beautiful when finished and polished. Very rich people often had buildings made out of stone and had them covered on the inside with cedar paneling so that only the wood showed. The very best is what these returnees wanted for God's house.

Seven Months Later

Ezra 3:8 ***Now in the second month of the second year of their coming to the house of God at Jerusalem, Zerubbabel the son of***

go to

heart
Psalm 51:17

God
Mark 12:28–32

seventh month
Ezra 3:6–7

sanctified
set aside to please God

masons
people who worked with stones and bricks

seafaring
sailors from modern Lebanon

Zerubbabel and Jeshua
Ezra 3:2

Levites
Ezra 2:40

garments
Ezra 2:69

Shealtiel, Jeshua the son of Jozadak, and the rest of their brethren the priests and the Levites, and all those who had come out of the captivity to Jerusalem, began work and appointed the Levites from twenty years old and above to oversee the work of the house of the LORD. (NKJV)

The Jews built the altar and ordered the Temple building materials in the seventh month of their first year back in the land. Five months later they started a new year. Two months into the new year the supplies had probably arrived, so Zerubbabel and Jeshua met again (about mid-April to mid-May of 535 BC). Joining them were the priests, the Levites, and the remainder of those who had returned to the land with them. The entire group assembled in a united effort to start construction on the new Temple. They put the Levites in charge of the project, but required that those who were going to oversee any of the work had to be at least twenty years old. This young age requirement was probably necessary because only seventy-four Levites had returned.

house of God another name for the Temple

Take Me to Your Leader

EZRA 3:9 ***Then Jeshua with his sons and brothers, Kadmiel with his sons, and the sons of Judah, arose as one to oversee those working on the house of God: the sons of Henadad with their sons and their brethren the Levites. (NKJV)***

This verse identifies the three main families that had primary responsibility for supervising the reconstruction. They worked together as a well-organized unit. It is again stated that all those who supervised work on the **house of God** were Levites.

It's Time to Celebrate Again

EZRA 3:10 ***When the builders laid the foundation of the temple of the LORD, the priests stood in their apparel with trumpets, and the Levites, the sons of Asaph, with cymbals, to praise the LORD, according to the ordinance of David king of Israel. (NKJV)***

How much time it took is not revealed, but as soon as the Temple foundation was completed, the group scheduled a worship service. The priests marked the occasion by dressing in the garments they had received when they arrived in the land. They held silver trumpets. The Levites held cymbals. And everyone prepared to worship the Lord. But these faithful Jews did not prepare for anything that did not correspond to their tradition. They planned to worship "according to the ordinance of David king of Israel."

trumpets
Numbers 10:8

cymbals
1 Chronicles 15:16, 19

David
1 Chronicles 6:31–32

good
Psalm 106:1

what others say

H. G. M. Williamson

Just as Moses was believed to have established the patterns of sacrifice, so David was believed to have introduced certain necessary changes into the regulations concerning **Levitical service** when, with the building of the temple, they were no longer required to carry the ark. It is as though our writer wishes to emphasize that despite the exile and despite the fact that the second temple was not physically the same as the first, nothing has changed from the point of view of forms of worship.[4]

Levitical service
the way God told the Levites to do it

Psalms
one of the books of the Bible

Let's Just Praise the Lord

EZRA 3:11 ***And they sang responsively, praising and giving thanks to the LORD: "For He is good, For His mercy endures forever toward Israel." Then all the people shouted with a great shout, when they praised the LORD, because the foundation of the house of the LORD was laid.*** (NKJV)

what others say

Martha Bergen

Music has always played an important role in worship. Before the time of the Temple, it was usually the women who sang and danced in a spontaneous way when the Israelites were victorious in battle (note Exodus 15:20–21; Judges 11:34; and 1 Samuel 18:6–7). With the rise of the Temple, however, music became associated with the singers and players and was done in a more organized way.[5]

Music was an important part of their worship service, but not just any music. The music of choice probably came from the **Psalms** and gave praise and thanks to the Lord. They chose to honor him because he is good and he has an unending love for Israel. They probably divided into groups or choirs because they sang responsively or antiphonally. And

everlasting covenant
Genesis 17:7–8

comparison
Haggai 2:3

because all the people shouted with a great shout, we can probably assume that it was heartfelt. The purpose of this service was the fact that they had completed the task of laying the Temple foundation.

Shouting in a worship service for the purpose of praising the Lord is scriptural. Restoration of the Temple and Jewish worship was a reminder that God was keeping his everlasting covenant with them.

It Depends on Where You Stand at the Time

Ezra 3:12 ***But many of the priests and Levites and heads of the fathers' houses, old men who had seen the first temple, wept with a loud voice when the foundation of this temple was laid before their eyes. Yet many shouted aloud for joy,*** *(NKJV)*

Ezra divided the congregation into two groups: those who were old enough to remember the first Temple and those who were too young to remember it. The older group cried with loud crying, and the younger group shouted with loud shouts of joy and enthusiasm. The question has been asked, did the older group cry because they were happy or because they were sad? The verse does not say. But the prophet Haggai wrote that the older group made a comparison between the two Temples, and they lamented the fact that this one was inferior to the first in glory, magnificence, and splendor. It was a bittersweet experience. They were truly delighted to be a part of this rebuilding program, but they were deeply disappointed and heartbroken because they could not do more.

I Can't Believe My Ears

Ezra 3:13 ***so that the people could not discern the noise of the shout of joy from the noise of the weeping of the people, for the people shouted with a loud shout, and the sound was heard afar off.*** *(NKJV)*

Emotions ran high. The expressions of joy and tears went on with equal volume with a noise that was so loud it could be heard far away. And because one was just as loud as the other, no one could distinguish between the shouts of joy and the sobs of sorrow.

It is difficult to imagine the joy some of these people must have felt over being released from captivity and participating in the rebuilding of their Temple. It is also difficult to imagine the sadness some must have felt when they realized how much that sin had cost their ancestors, themselves, and their children. The chance to start over was a great blessing from God and they were rightly thankful, but they knew they had lost much and would be starting from scratch.

Chapter Wrap-Up

- In the seventh month, the former exiles met in Jerusalem to rebuild the altar and to offer burnt offerings according to the Law of Moses.
- They completed the altar and offered the morning and evening sacrifices.
- They began to observe the feast days, new moons, and other set days.
- They ordered cedarwood to rebuild the Temple. Seven months later they returned to the Temple site and laid the foundation.
- After completing the Temple foundation, the priests dressed in their religious garments and the people held a worship service, sang, rejoiced, cried, and shouted.

Study Questions

1. Why did the Jews rebuild the altar? Did they need a temple to worship God?
2. Identify three reasons why the Jews worshiped God.
3. Name five occasions when the Jews worshiped God.
4. Did the Jews have their priorities straight when they first returned to the Promised Land?
5. Is it necessary to remain silent during a worship service?

Ezra 4
Construction Stops

Chapter Highlights:
- Israel's Enemies
- Opposition to Temple
- Letter About Jerusalem
- The King's Reply
- Construction Stopped

Let's Get Started

This next chapter needs to be treated separately because it does not continue the chronological sequence of events in the lives of the returnees. The historical sequence of events is interrupted to provide two examples of the opposition the former exiles faced. The first example documents the hostility of Israel's enemies who opposed the rebuilding of the Temple. The second example documents the hostility of Israel's enemies who opposed the rebuilding of Jerusalem and its walls. This opposition was spread out over a period of many years under the reigns of Cyrus, Xerxes, and Artaxerxes.

Zerubbabel
Ezra 2:2

Lord God of Israel
Jehovah, also the Christian's God

Jehovah
God

Guess What I Heard

EZRA 4:1 ***Now when the adversaries of Judah and Benjamin heard that the descendants of the captivity were building the temple of the LORD God of Israel,*** *(NKJV)*

The word was out among the enemies of Israel: the Jews had returned and they were rebuilding the Temple. Some of the squatters in the area did not want a Temple of the **Lord God of Israel** in this place. Trouble was on the way. It's a problem that has cropped up over and over again.

The First Tactic: "Let Us Work with You"

EZRA 4:2 ***they came to Zerubbabel and the heads of the fathers' houses, and said to them, "Let us build with you, for we seek your God as you do; and we have sacrificed to Him since the days of Esarhaddon king of Assyria, who brought us here."*** *(NKJV)*

Israel's enemies went to Zerubbabel, the Jewish governor, with a deceptive offer to help rebuild the Temple. They tried to disguise their intentions by announcing that they had been worshiping the Jewish God for many years. They did worship **Jehovah**, but they

gods
2 Kings 17:24–33

angel of light
2 Corinthians 11:14

proclamation
Ezra 1:1–4

proclamation
decree

polytheism
tbelief in more than one God

idolatry
worshiping false gods

materialism
leaving out spiritual things

sensualism
giving pleasure to the senses

mongrel
impure

syncretism
a merging of beliefs

misrepresented the truth. Their worship was corrupt because they also worshiped many other gods. They even claimed that they had been offering sacrifices to Israel's God "since the days of Esarhaddon king of Assyria, who brought us here." This is an important statement because it addresses the false impression some have of the so-called Ten Lost Tribes of Israel. Assyria removed those ten tribes when it conquered the Northern Kingdom. These people are saying that one of the Assyrian kings returned some of us to the land and we have been worshiping Israel's God ever since. Their statement is a reminder that Satan transforms himself into an angel of light.

No Help Wanted

Ezra 4:3 ***But Zerubbabel and Jeshua and the rest of the heads of the fathers' houses of Israel said to them, "You may do nothing with us to build a house for our God; but we alone will build to the Lord God of Israel, as King Cyrus the king of Persia has commanded us."*** *(NKJV)*

Zerubbabel and his associates emphatically refused this phony offer of help. In effect they said, "King Cyrus didn't include you in the **proclamation** to rebuild the Temple. He commanded us to do it. We will work alone. And we will do it for our God." Even though they needed all the help they could get, they wisely recognized this attempt to sabotage the Temple project and corrupt their worship. And so they quickly rejected the offer outright.

what others say

The Pulpit Commentary

The movement was one for the re-establishment of God's peculiar people in their own land, under their own system, as a witness to the nations against **polytheism**, against **idolatry**, against **materialism** and **sensualism** in religion. As the Samaritans [Israel's enemies) had adopted a mixed or **mongrel** worship, uniting idolatrous rites with the acknowledgement of Jehovah (2 Kings xvii 29–41), their admission by Zerubbabel to a partnership in his work would have been equivalent to the abandonment of pure religion, and the acceptance of a **syncretism** inherently vicious, and sure to develop into pronounced forms of impurity and corruption.[1]

The Second Tactic: "Let's Discourage and Scare the Jews"

EZRA 4:4 ***Then the people of the land tried to discourage the people of Judah. They troubled them in building,*** **(NKJV)**

Rejection didn't cause Israel's enemies to give up. When their first tactic failed, they used two other weapons to stop construction of the Temple: discouragement and fear. They strongly criticized the Jews in an effort to frustrate them into giving up. They also tried to scare them away from the site. It is not unusual to find historians who estimate that this went on anywhere between fourteen to twenty years. It is very typical of Muslim efforts to stop modern Jews from rebuilding. They keep threatening to start the Mother of all Battles over possession of the Temple Mount. Why? Because it works.

what others say

Kay Arthur, David Lawson, and Bob Vereen

The important thing is not to understand your circumstances. The important thing is to understand God and what He has instructed you to do. The enemy will come; that's a certainty. The question is, "Will you continue to go on as directed by God?" If you do, you can rest assured that the eye of our God will be on you, and your enemies will not stop you from doing His work.[2]

The Third Tactic: "Let's Bribe People to Work Against the Jews"

EZRA 4:5 ***and hired counselors against them to frustrate their purpose all the days of Cyrus king of Persia, even until the reign of Darius king of Persia.*** **(NKJV)**

Israel's enemies were passionate about this cause. They hired counselors to bribe Persian officials to interfere with Jewish efforts to rebuild the Temple. It was an ongoing effort that began under the reign of Cyrus and extended into to the reign of Darius.

These counselors were like modern-day lobbyists in the United States. They had access to the rulers of their time. They were hired to influence—some say bribe—Persian rulers to work for or against

expeditious
wasted no time

the issues of the day. In this case, counselors were hired to influence Persian officials to slow or stop the construction of the Temple.

Persian Kings

King	Reign (Approx.)
Cyrus	538–530 BC
Cambyses	530–522 BC
Pseudo-Smerdes (Gaumata)	Ten months
Darius I Hystaspes	522–486 BC
Ahasuerus (Xerxes I)	486–465 BC
Artaxerxes I	465–425 BC

The Fourth Tactic: "Let's Get to the New King Right Away"

Ezra 4:6 ***In the reign of Ahasuerus, in the beginning of his reign, they wrote an accusation against the inhabitants of Judah and Jerusalem.*** *(NKJV)*

This verse skips forward about fifty years to the early reign of King Ahasuerus (Xerxes I). Israel's enemies lodged a mysterious complaint as soon as he took the throne. Any attempt to figure out what they complained about is hopeless, but the point of the account is that Israel's enemies were determined, persistent, and **expeditious**. They acted quickly because they thought the new king would be more sympathetic to their cause.

The Fifth Tactic: "Let's Lie and Deceive the New King"

the big picture

Ezra 4:7–16

During the reign of Artaxerxes I, an influential group of Israel's enemies wrote a letter opposing the rebuilding of Jerusalem (vv. 7–8). Several other important people joined them (vv. 9–10). They called Jerusalem a rebellious city; said if the city was rebuilt, the Jews would stop paying their taxes, the Jews would dishonor the king, and the Jews would expand the borders of their nation (vv. 11–16).

These verses skip forward about twenty more years, but notice that they do not record an example of what Israel's enemies did to oppose construction of the Temple. They record an example of what Israel's enemies did to oppose construction of the city of Jerusalem. They lined up a group of sympathetic government officials and sent a misleading letter to the king. They rightly accused Jerusalem of having a history of being a "rebellious and evil city" (Ezra 4:12 NKJV) because the Jews did make several attempts to gain their independence before Nebuchadnezzar destroyed the nation. But there was no justification for suggesting this new generation of Jews would now stop paying their taxes, dishonor the king, or expand their territory. This was simply a list of false accusations designed to deceive Artaxerxes and stop the construction of Jerusalem.

archives
the place where official records are kept

If at First You Don't Succeed, Try, Try Again

the big picture

Ezra 4:17–23

Artaxerxes checked the records and confirmed Israel's history of rebellion (vv. 17–19). He found evidence that Israel had paid taxes to other powerful kings and concluded that he deserved taxes too (v. 20). He wrote a letter to Israel's enemies and told them to issue an order without delay for the Jews to stop rebuilding Jerusalem until he authorized them to resume (vv. 21–22). They immediately went to Jerusalem with a display of force and intimidated the Jews into stopping construction (v. 23).

King Artaxerxes searched his **archives** and found evidence of Israel's past rebellions. He learned that the Jews had paid taxes in the past and concluded that they should continue to do so. He sent a letter to Israel's enemies that authorized them to stop the Jews from rebuilding Jerusalem, but left the door open in case he wanted to change his mind later. Israel's enemies quickly went to Jerusalem with troops and compelled the Jews to stop building.

distinctives
in this case, their special natures or assignments

what others say

Jack W. Hayford

The messages of Ezra are a constant reminder of how easily God's people can lose heart and their **distinctives**. . . . When this happens God's plans are delayed. Erring saints cannot totally thwart God's sovereign plans, but they can delay or frustrate them. God is greater than we, and He does have ways of transcending our shortcomings. However, He wants us to walk in obedience so that His plans can be fulfilled as originally revealed.[3]

Back to the Temple

Ezra 4:24 ***Thus the work of the house of God which is at Jerusalem ceased, and it was discontinued until the second year of the reign of Darius king of Persia.*** *(NKJV)*

The first three tactics recorded in this chapter are about opposition to rebuilding the Temple. The next two tactics are about opposition to rebuilding Jerusalem. The result of the first three tactics was to stop construction on the Temple. The result of the last two tactics was to stop construction on the city of Jerusalem. This verse is a summary of the first three tactics. The persistence of Israel's enemies brought construction on the Temple to a standstill until the second year King Darius was on the throne (about 521–520 BC).

Chapter Wrap-Up

- When Israel's enemies heard the Jews were rebuilding the Temple, they misrepresented themselves and tried to join the Jews.
- When the Jews refused their help with the Temple reconstruction Israel's enemies tried to discourage them, scare them, and bribe people to frustrate them.
- Israel's enemies also opposed the reconstruction of Jerusalem. They wrote a letter to King Artaxerxes that pointed out Jerusalem's historical rebellion and suggested the Jews would oppose him in several ways.
- King Artaxerxes considered the letter that Israel's enemies had sent and issued an order to stop construction in Jerusalem.
- This is a record of what Israel's enemies did to halt construction on the Temple and on the city of Jerusalem.

Study Questions

1. Can people worship God and offer sacrifices to him even though they are not saved?
2. What two tactics did Israel's enemies use to stop construction on the Temple? Did they work?
3. In the letter to Artaxerxes, how did Israel's enemies try to butter-up the king?
4. In the letter to Artaxerxes, what three things did Israel's enemies say the king would lose if he didn't stop the construction of Jerusalem? Did this work?
5. In his reply to Israel's enemies, what "out" did the king leave himself concerning the construction of Jerusalem? Is it important? Why?

Ezra 5
A Request to Resume Construction

Chapter Highlights:
- Who's in Charge?
- A New Start
- Tell Me Something
- God Sees You
- Is It Time?

Let's Get Started

The returnees rebuilt the altar and celebrated (about 536 BC). Supplies were ordered and construction was started on the Temple foundation the next year, but how long it took is not revealed. Eventually the Temple foundation was laid and the former exiles celebrated again. By this time strong opposition was on the scene and the workers became discouraged and afraid. Some lost interest. The work stopped. The Jews turned their attention to their own houses and neglected the house of the Lord for about fifteen years. They had their priorities out of kilter, but the Lord would not let this project die. He had sent the Jews back to the land to rebuild his house and he intended for them to do just that.

altar
Ezra 3:1–4

foundation
Ezra 3:8–13

afraid
Ezra 4:1–5

work
Ezra 4:24

houses
Haggai 1:4

Lord
Haggai 1:7–11

Iddo
Zechariah 1:1

Haggai
Haggai 1:3–11

rebuilt
Zechariah 1:16

prophet
a person through whom God speaks and guides

Who's in Charge Here?

> EZRA 5:1 ***Then the prophet Haggai and Zechariah the son of Iddo, prophets, prophesied to the Jews who were in Judah and Jerusalem, in the name of the God of Israel, who was over them.*** *(NKJV)*

God needed someone to put life back into the Temple building project, so he raised up two prophets for the job: one **prophet** named Haggai and another named Zechariah. Nothing is said about Haggai's ancestry, but Zechariah was the grandson of Iddo. These two godly messengers appeared on the scene around 520 BC. They started proclaiming the Word of God to the Jews in Jerusalem and the surrounding area. In the name of the God of Israel Haggai chastised the Jews for their failure to rebuild the Temple. And in the name of the God of Israel, Zechariah declared that the Temple would be rebuilt. These men could say this because they spoke for the sovereign Ruler of the Jewish people.

Zerubbabel
Ezra 3:2

prophesy
speak the word of God

what others say

F. Charles Fensham

In Zechariah 1:1 we have "Zechariah the son of Berechiah, the son of Iddo": in other words "the son of Berechiah" is left out here. Some scholars have taken pains to explain this, but "son of . . ." does occasionally in the OT refer not to a direct son, but to a descendant.[1]

A New Start

EZRA 5:2 ***So Zerubbabel the son of Shealtiel and Jeshua the son of Jozadak rose up and began to build the house of God which is in Jerusalem; and the prophets of God were with them, helping them.*** *(NKJV)*

Zerubbabel, the political leader, and Jeshua, the religious leader, were stirred to action by the prophesying of Haggai and Zechariah. They did not have permission from Darius to resume construction on the Temple, but they immediately started back to work. And these two powerful prophets did more than **prophesy**. They rolled up their sleeves and helped with the construction.

Tell Me Something

EZRA 5:3–4 ***At the same time Tattenai the governor of the region beyond the River and Shethar-Boznai and their companions came to them and spoke thus to them: "Who has commanded you to build this temple and finish this wall?" Then, accordingly, we told them the names of the men who were constructing this building.*** *(NKJV)*

Word quickly spread that the reinvigorated Jews had resumed work on the long-delayed building of the new Temple. Probably in response to a complaint, Tattenai, a Persian regional governor who ruled Syria and part of the Promised Land, soon investigated the site with several other government officials. These inspectors asked Zerubbabel and Jeshua two questions: "Who gave you the authority to restart this project" and "What are the names of the men working with you?" God's servants responded with the requested information.

God Sees You

Ezra 5:5 ***But the eye of their God was upon the elders of the Jews, so that they could not make them cease till a report could go to Darius. Then a written answer was returned concerning this matter.*** *(NKJV)*

eyes
Psalm 34:15

righteous
those who do the right thing

elders
leaders

King David said, "The eyes of the Lord are on the **righteous**" (NKJV). And, here, God was watching over the Jewish **elders**. He was in favor of their rebuilding efforts, so he paved the way for them to continue the project while Tattenai sent a letter to Darius to find out how he wanted this matter handled.

what others say

Mervin Breneman

God so guided Tattenai's attitude that he allowed the Jews to continue the construction until he could check with King Darius. In order to fulfill his purpose, God used and coordinated the preaching of the prophets, the work of the leaders, the determination of the whole community, and the decisions of "pagan" government officials.[2]

Is It True?

the big picture

Ezra 5:6–17

Israel's enemies sent a letter to King Darius, told him they visited Jerusalem, saw the Temple being rebuilt, questioned the Jews about their authority, and asked the names of those doing the work (vv. 6–10). They said the Jews replied that they serve God, the God their ancestors angered, the God who let Babylon destroy the Temple (vv. 11–12). They said the Jews told them King Cyrus issued a decree for them to rebuild the Temple. He returned the articles King Nebuchadnezzar took from the first Temple, and told them to put those articles in the rebuilt Temple (vv. 13–16). They asked the king to search the archives to see if the Jews told the truth, and to give them instructions on what to do (v. 17).

Tattenai and his companions told King Darius that they had toured the Temple site and discovered that the Jews were making significant progress on the reconstruction. They already had several

asked
Ezra 5:3–4

King Cyrus
Ezra 1:2–4

articles
Ezra 1:7–11

large stones and wooden beams in place. These Persian officials repeated the two questions they had asked the Jews and told the king how the Jews had answered them. They also told him that the Jews said King Cyrus had issued a decree for them to do this and had given them articles from the first Temple to put into the Temple they were building. They recommended that King Darius check this out to see if the Jews had told them the truth about the decree and asked him for instructions on how to respond.

The decree of Cyrus gave the Jews legal standing. It would have been risky for Tattenai and his associates to force them to stop the construction. Before they got in over their heads, they asked Darius to see if the project had been authorized.

Chapter Wrap-Up

- The prophets Haggai and Zechariah spoke in the name of God and urged the Jews to rebuild the Temple. Construction started and the prophets joined in.
- Tattenai and some of his companions visited the site and asked who had authorized the construction and what were the names of the workers.
- Construction continued while Tattenai wrote King Darius to explain the situation and to tell him the Jews said King Cyrus had issued a decree for this. He urged Darius to check this out and asked Darius to tell him how to respond.

Study Questions

1. What two prophets encouraged the Jews to rebuild the Temple? Where did these men get their authority?
2. What did the Jews say was the reason the original Temple was destroyed? Whom did the Jews say they were serving by rebuilding the Temple?
3. What part did the Jews say King Cyrus played in their efforts to rebuild the Temple?

Ezra 6
Construction Completed

Chapter Highlights:
- The Great Search
- What the Record Shows
- Completed and Dedicated
- It's Feast Time

Let's Get Started

Tattenai's letter to King Darius prompted a search of the royal archives to see if King Cyrus did, in fact, issue a decree for the Temple to be rebuilt. It appears that a copy of the exact decree was not found, but a royal memorandum that confirmed the Jewish claim was discovered, and that was enough for King Darius to reach a decision.

letter
Ezra 5:6–17

archives
Ezra 5:17

Temple
Ezra 1:2–4

Where Is It?

EZRA 6:1–2 ***Then King Darius issued a decree, and a search was made in the archives, where the treasures were stored in Babylon. And at Achmetha, in the palace that is in the province of Media, a scroll was found, and in it a record was written thus:*** **(NKJV)**

King Darius followed Tattenai's recommendation and ordered a search of the **archives** in Babylon, but nothing was found in the treasuries there. However, that was not the end of the search. Those looking for a record decided to check the **citadel** at Achmetha (Ecbatana) in Media. They did not find a copy of the original decree, but they found a very important **memorandum**.

archives
the house of the books

citadel
the king's summer palace

memorandum
note for future reference

what others say

Jack W. Hayford with Joseph Snider

In Jerusalem, Zerubbabel and Jeshua may have dreaded the prospect of hearing the imperial court's response to Tattenai's inquiry. What they did not know was that the Lord was using the vast and intricate machinery of the Persian bureaucracy to guarantee the fulfillment of the prophetic words of Haggai and Zechariah.[1]

laid
Isaiah 44:28

This Is What the Memorandum Said

EZRA 6:3–5 ***In the first year of King Cyrus, King Cyrus issued a decree concerning the house of God at Jerusalem: "Let the house be rebuilt, the place where they offered sacrifices; and let the foundations of it be firmly laid, its height sixty cubits and its width sixty cubits, with three rows of heavy stones and one row of new timber. Let the expenses be paid from the king's treasury. Also let the gold and silver articles of the house of God, which Nebuchadnezzar took from the temple which is in Jerusalem and brought to Babylon, be restored and taken back to the temple which is in Jerusalem, each to its place; and deposit them in the house of God"—(NKJV)***

The royal memorandum noted that during his first year on the throne, King Cyrus had issued a decree to rebuild the Temple and to make it a place for offering sacrifices. His edict specified the height and width of the new building—probably to control the costs. It called for three stories to be built with massive stones and one story to be built with new wood. The edict specified that the costs were to be paid out of the royal treasury, and it authorized the return of the Temple articles.

Notice the words in this memorandum: "Let the house be rebuilt," and "Let the foundations of it be firmly laid." These words are similar to those the prophet Isaiah used almost two hundred years before King Cyrus wrote this memo. It seems almost certain that the king had the Scriptures in front of him when he was ordering this to happen.

Tough Talk

the big picture

Ezra 6:6–12

King Darius wrote to Tattenai and his companions and told them to stay away from the Temple site, to leave the Jews alone, and to let them rebuild the Temple on its original site (vv. 6–7). He also ordered them to help the Jews by paying the expenses of the workers, by providing animals for the sacrifices, and by providing whatever other items the priests requested so they could please God (vv. 8–10). He closed by threatening to severely punish anyone who did not obey him (vv. 11–12).

Discovery of the royal memorandum prompted a sharp reply from King Darius to Tattenai and his companions. The king emphatically told them to get away from the Temple site and stop hindering the Jews. He explicitly said the Temple should be rebuilt on its original site. Furthermore, he not only ruled that the decree of King Cyrus would stand, but he also decided to back it up with a decree of his own that would ensure the completion of the project. He ordered Israel's enemies to pay the expenses of the Jewish workers out of the tax revenues generated from that province. He also ordered them to provide the Jews with sacrificial animals, wheat, salt, wine, and oil for their daily sacrifices "that they may offer sacrifices of sweet aroma to the God of heaven, and pray for the life of the king and his sons" (Ezra 6:10 NKJV). He then closed with an ominous warning that anyone who disobeyed him would be treated like a criminal: he would be killed and his house would be destroyed without delay.

edict
Ezra 6:11

elders
Ezra 5:2–9

zeal
religious enthusiasm

Israel's enemies made a serious mistake by requesting Darius to search the archives. Otherwise, he would not have known about the decree Cyrus had issued. Could it be that this was why God allowed them to oppose the project this time? Notice that their interference put the king squarely on Israel's side and provided the Jews with money, protection, and a constant supply of items to be sacrificed.

The Temple Is Completed

EZRA 6:13–15 ***Then Tattenai, governor of the region beyond the River, Shethar-Boznai, and their companions diligently did according to what King Darius had sent. So the elders of the Jews built, and they prospered through the prophesying of Haggai the prophet and Zechariah the son of Iddo. And they built and finished it, according to the commandment of the God of Israel, and according to the command of Cyrus, Darius, and Artaxerxes king of Persia. Now the temple was finished on the third day of the month of Adar, which was in the sixth year of the reign of King Darius.*** *(NKJV)*

The king's written threat to execute anyone who disobeyed his edict got the full attention of Israel's dedicated enemies. They readily complied with his orders to provide funding and sacrifices for the Temple. The elders of the Jews charged forth and worked hard. The timely prophesying of Haggai and Zechariah bore fruit, and the Word of God filled the Jews with **zeal** and inspired them to con-

Artaxerxes
Ezra 7:21–28

grace
the undeserved favor of God

children of Israel
all the descendants of Israel who were under the covenant with God

worship
praise to God for who he is and what he has done

tinue. So with the powerful help of God and the backing of this important decree, the beloved Temple was completed about four years later, on the third day of the month of Adar (February/March) in the sixth year of the reign of King Darius. This was about 516 BC and exactly seventy years after the Temple had been destroyed by King Nebuchadnezzar.

> what others say
>
> **Union Gospel Press**
>
> Life was not easy for those who returned. The task of rebuilding their temple and towns was overwhelming, and their oes were persistent; yet through God's **grace** they gradually reestablished themselves.[2]

Because the Temple was completed approximately fifty years before Artaxerxes became king, some critics say they have found an error in the Bible. But others argue that Ezra properly gave Artaxerxes credit because he played a major role in maintaining and remodeling the Temple during his reign. In one sense the Temple was completed before Artaxerxes became king, but in another sense the final touches were not added until after he became king. Ezra completed his book during the reign of King Artaxerxes, and it seems likely that he tried to go back and give the current king credit for his part in the finished project.

The Temple Is Dedicated

Ezra 6:16–18 ***Then the children of Israel, the priests and the Levites and the rest of the descendants of the captivity, celebrated the dedication of this house of God with joy. And they offered sacrifices at the dedication of this house of God, one hundred bulls, two hundred rams, four hundred lambs, and as a sin offering for all Israel twelve male goats, according to the number of the tribes of Israel. They assigned the priests to their divisions and the Levites to their divisions, over the service of God in Jerusalem, as it is written in the Book of Moses.*** *(NKJV)*

When the long-delayed Temple was finally completed, the **children of Israel** decided to celebrate what God had done for them and to dedicate their wonderful new place of **worship**. The dedication included the sacrifice of 100 bulls as an offering for the sins of the priests, 200 rams as an offering for the sins of the rulers, 400 lambs as an offering for the sins of the common people, and twelve male goats as an offering for the sins of each of the twelve tribes of Israel. They also divided the priests and Levites into specific groups so they would be serving in the proper capacity at the Temple, according to the writings of Moses.

Scriptures reveal that there were twenty-four divisions, with each division serving for one week. The father of John the Baptist, a priest named Zacharias, was serving his term when an angel of the Lord told him that he would have a son.

The Jews sacrificed twelve male goats, one for each of the twelve tribes of Israel. This is significant because there are those who believe that ten of the tribes have been destroyed. Since it is doubtful the children of Israel would sacrifice animals for the sins of nonexistent people, we can assume they believed people from every tribe existed.

Some have rightly noted that it was King David who divided the priests and Levites, and it was King Solomon who adopted the divisions when the first Temple was built. However, their assigned duties, privileges, and rights go back to the writings of Moses.

priests
Leviticus 4:3

rulers
Leviticus 4:22–23

common people
Leviticus 4:27–35

Zacharias
Luke 1:5–25

King David
1 Chronicles 23:6–23; 24:1–19

Levites
Numbers 3:5–10; 8:5–22

Moses
Exodus 29:1–46; Leviticus 8:1–36

Passover
Exodus 12:1–3

The Feast of Passover

Ezra 6:19 ***And the descendants of the captivity kept the Passover on the fourteenth day of the first month.*** (NKJV)

The fourteenth day of the first month is the fourteenth of Nisan on the Hebrew Sacred Calendar (see chart on the Jewish Feasts). It is the day God set aside for the Jews to celebrate the Feast of **Passover**. God had decreed that all the firstborn of Egypt would die. He told the Jews in Egypt to kill a lamb without blemish, catch the blood, and sprinkle it on the doorposts and lintels of their houses. He said he would pass over those homes where he saw the blood had been sprinkled. The Jews obeyed, and their firstborn males were spared from death. The returnees remembered this event about five weeks after the dedication of the Temple in 516 BC. This was the first Passover celebrated at the rebuilt Temple. It is interesting to note that God told the Jews they would be off the land for seventy years. Then, seventy years after Nebuchadnezzar's attack in 606 BC, they returned. To be more specific, exactly seventy years after

Passover
a yearly celebration reliving the night God won Israel's freedom from Egypt

Nebuchadnezzar's third and final attack, in which he destroyed the Temple, it was rebuilt and the Jews celebrated their first Passover.

The Hebrew Sacred Calendar has seven feast days: three in the month of Nisan (the Spring Festival), one in the month of Sivan (the Summer Festival), and three in the month of Tishri (the Fall Festival). These are sometimes called Pilgrim Festivals or Pilgrim Feasts because the male Jews were required to visit Jerusalem three times a year to offer sacrifices during these celebrations.

Passover always comes in the spring season (March/April), during the week Christians celebrate Easter. The Passover lamb without blemish prefigures Jesus, God's Lamb without blemish or sin. Jesus was crucified on Passover (Matthew 26:2). He turned his last Passover celebration into the Lord's Supper. Paul called Jesus the Christian's Passover (1 Corinthians 5:7). He made his triumphal entry into Jerusalem on Palm Sunday, which is the day the Jews chose the Passover lamb. He was crucified on Passover and was raised from the dead on Easter.

Passover Celebrations in the Old Testament

Celebration	Scripture Reference
The First Celebration (in Egypt)	Exodus 12
The Second Celebration (in the wilderness)	Numbers 9
The Third Celebration (at Gilgal)	Joshua 5
The Fourth Celebration (at Jerusalem under Hezekiah)	2 Chronicles 30
The Fifth Celebration (at Jerusalem under Josiah)	2 Kings 23

three times
Exodus 23:14–19

water
Exodus 29:4

ceremonially clean
Numbers 8:5–7

Sin Water

EZRA 6:20 ***For the priests and the Levites had purified themselves; all of them were ritually clean. And they slaughtered the Passover lambs for all the descendants of the captivity, for their brethren the priests, and for themselves.*** *(NKJV)*

Before performing religious ceremonies the priests and Levites purified themselves by sprinkling their bodies with the water of cleansing. This is a **ritual** God told the Levites to go through to make themselves **ceremonially clean**. After doing this the Levites killed the Passover lambs for everyone, including themselves.

ritual
having to do with worship practices

ceremonially clean
authorized to perform certain religious duties

Christians believe these Passover lambs pointed to Jesus. John called him the Lamb of God who takes away the sin of the world. The Jews could not break any of the perfect Passover Lamb's bones, and the Roman soldiers did not break the bones of Jesus while he was hanging on the cross. The Jews were required to consume the entire Passover lamb. They were forbidden to leave any of it for the next day, and likewise, Jesus was not left on the cross until the next day. His body was taken down and buried on the same day he was crucified. Pilate tried to release Jesus, but the crowd called for the release of Barabbas instead. It is clear that God didn't want Jesus released. Why? Because God's timetable dictated that Jesus would die on Passover.

immoral
sinful

Gentiles
non-Jews

The water of cleansing was sometimes called "sin water" or the "water of sin." The Levites called it this because God required them to use it for the removal of their sin. We do not know how it was prepared, but God would forgive the Levites' sins when they were sprinkled with it.

Seek and Ye Shall Find

> Ezra 6:21 *Then the children of Israel who had returned from the captivity ate together with all who had separated themselves from the filth of the nations of the land in order to seek the Lord God of Israel.* (NKJV)

Two groups of people took part in the Passover feast: (1) The Jewish returnees, and (2) All the Jews who had remained in the land during the Exile and had abandoned the **immoral** practices of the **Gentiles** because they wanted to lead a new life of service to God.

Only circumcised Jews could participate in the Passover feast. Likewise, Christians who intend to lead a new life in Christ are the only ones who should take Communion, which is sometimes called the second ordinance of the church. Christians differ on how often it should be observed, but most take Communion more often than once a year (sometimes weekly, but usually monthly or quarterly).

It Was an Act of God

> Ezra 6:22 *And they kept the Feast of Unleavened Bread seven days with joy; for the Lord made them joyful, and turned the*

joy
merriment, happiness

leaven
yeast

heart of the king of Assyria toward them, to strengthen their hands in the work of the house of God, the God of Israel. *(NKJV)*

The Feast of Unleavened Bread begins on the day after the Feast of Passover. These two feasts plus the Feast of First Fruits combine to make up the Spring Festival. Their closeness on the Hebrew sacred calendar makes them one big weeklong celebration (see comments at Ezra 6:19; also, see chart "The Jewish Feasts" on page 27).

The feast originally began as a memorial to remember the fact that the death angel passed over Egypt, changing Pharaoh's heart and causing him to release the Hebrew slaves. Moses led them out of Egypt, but they were in a hurry to leave because they feared Pharaoh would change his mind, chase them down, and force them to return. They did not have time to stop, make dough, mix leaven in it, let it rise, and bake it. Instead, while they were on the run, they ate unleavened bread to nourish themselves and celebrate their release from Egypt. When they settled down in the Promised Land forty years later, they celebrated the feast on an annual basis.

The returnees from Babylon had added reason to celebrate with **joy** the Feast of Unleavened Bread: God had changed the king's heart and inspired him to help them rebuild the Temple. This is a good summary of the whole project. The successful reconstruction of the Temple was God's doing, and he deserved the glory.

In preparation for the Feast of Unleavened Bread, the Jews carefully cleaned their whole houses to be sure they removed every speck of **leaven**. They understood that leaven is a symbol of evil, or sin, and their getting rid of the leaven symbolized their desire to clean up their lives. In essence, they had a spring housecleaning. Could it be that Christians need period revival that brings about a spiritual housecleaning? Doesn't it make sense that people need to be holy if they intend to worship a holy God?

Christians believe the Feast of Unleavened Bread points to Jesus, who called himself the Bread of Life. Since leaven is a symbol of sin in the Bible, and Jesus was without sin, he is the unleavened or sinless Bread of Life. Jews call unleavened, not risen bread the "bread of affliction" (Deuteronomy 16:3 NKJV). The afflicted, beaten, crucified, unleavened Bread of Life was in the grave and not yet risen on the day after Passover when the Jews were celebrating the Feast of Unleavened Bread.

Chapter Wrap-Up

- Upon the recommendation of Tattenai and others, King Darius ordered a search of the archives to see if King Cyrus ordered the rebuilding of the Temple. He found a memorandum in Ecbatana at the summer palace of King Cyrus.
- The memorandum confirmed King Cyrus's decree that granted the Jews certain worship privileges and financing.
- King Darius issued a new decree that ordered Israel's enemies to stop interfering and to start providing help. He also threatened the life and house of anyone who disobeyed his order.
- The Jews completed the Temple and held a dedication service. Sacrifices were offered for the sins of the priests, the Levites, and the common people.
- On the Feast of Passover the priests and Levites purified themselves, offered sacrifices, and asked many others to join them in their celebration. The following day they started joyfully celebrating the Feast of Unleavened Bread.

Study Questions

1. What did King Darius find when he searched the archives for the decree of King Cyrus? What did this prove?
2. What important things did King Cyrus put in his memorandum?
3. In his decree, what did King Darius tell Tattenai and his companions to do? What did he say would happen if they refused to do it?
4. What did King Darius want the Jews to do for him after they rebuilt the Temple?
5. What did the Jews do after the Temple was dedicated? What holy days did they celebrate shortly thereafter?

Introduction—Ezra 7–10
The Second Wave Returns

The first main wave of exiles returned in 536 BC, and the second main wave returned 78 years later, in 458 BC. There are 58 years of silence between chapters 6 and 7. Although Ezra is the likely author or compiler of the first six chapters, he didn't actually arrive on the scene until chapter 7. And most of those mentioned in the first six chapters were dead by the time chapter 7 was written.

Those who returned in the first wave that was led by Zerubbabel got off to a shaky start in their relationship with God. They had times of great faith, but the years spent in Babylon were difficult to overcome. Their spirituality never reached the consistent level God wanted. The priesthood had been established, but the new generation that was growing up needed help. God responded through a priest named Ezra, who led a second wave back to Israel. Ezra was inspired to teach the Law of Moses to God's people and to restore true worship in the land. He is often credited with starting a spiritual revival among the Jews because of the outstanding job he did.

Ezra 7
The Decree of Artaxerxes

Chapter Highlights:
- Ezra's Family Tree
- Ezra's Qualifications
- The Second Wave Returns
- The King's Letter
- Praise the Lord

Let's Get Started

Of course, God is the divine Author of the book of Ezra, but it is time to meet the likely human author and learn a little more about what went on in the fledgling Jewish nation (see the chart "Three Main Waves of 2nd Jewish Return" on page 4).

family records
Ezra 2:61–63

Aaron
the chief priest when Moses led the Hebrews out of Egypt

pedigree
ancestry

Ezra's Family Tree

EZRA 7:1–5 ***Now after these things, in the reign of Artaxerxes king of Persia, Ezra the son of Seraiah, the son of Azariah, the son of Hilkiah, the son of Shallum, the son of Zadok, the son of Ahitub, the son of Amariah, the son of Azariah, the son of Meraioth, the son of Zerahiah, the son of Uzzi, the son of Bukki, the son of Abishua, the son of Phinehas, the son of Eleazar, the son of Aaron the chief priest—**(NKJV)*

The text skips forward from the reign of King Darius to the reign of King Artaxerxes and a man named Ezra. When the first wave of exiles left Babylon there were some who had no family records to prove their ancestry. This was not the case when Ezra came on the scene. He could trace his family tree all the way back through sixteen generations to **Aaron**. He was going to change things, so it was important to establish the fact that he had the right **pedigree** or recognized authority.

This is one of two places where Ezra's genealogy is recorded in the Scriptures. The other is found in 1 Chronicles 6. This one is shorter, but the two places in Scripture do not contradict one another. Both are accurate.

what others say

Martha Bergen

Genealogies were important in Israelite society. They helped establish a person's credibility and indicated his significance within the community. The larger one's genealogy, the more

letter
Ezra 7:11–26

credible and significant he was. The person the Bible records with the longest genealogy is Jesus Christ. He can be traced through seventy-six generations back to Adam (see Luke 3:23–38).[1]

What's That on Your Shoulder?

Law of Moses
all the rules God gave to Moses

EZRA 7:6 ***this Ezra came up from Babylon; and he was a skilled scribe in the Law of Moses, which the LORD God of Israel had given. The king granted him all his request, according to the hand of the LORD his God upon him.*** (NKJV)

When King Nebuchadnezzar destroyed Israel many of the Jews were deported to Babylon. This is where Ezra lived when he decided to move to Jerusalem. He was very knowledgeable in the **Law of Moses**. He knew that God was the source of these Holy Scriptures. Everything that Ezra requested is not known, but it is evident that since God had his hand upon Ezra, King Artaxerxes was inspired to look upon him with great favor.

what others say

Tim LaHaye

For all practical purposes, reading is the foundation of all learning. Someone has said, "If you can read, you can learn anything." If you are going to learn the Bible, you will have to develop the habit of reading large portions of the Scriptures. Bible study is essential to become "approved unto God" (2 Timothy 2:15).[2]

King Artaxerxes gave Ezra everything he asked for, but what did he ask for? No one knows for sure. But one important item was a letter granting him permission to move to Jerusalem, take other exiles with him, take up offerings, perform other activities.

A Long, Hard Trip

EZRA 7:7–10 ***Some of the children of Israel, the priests, the Levites, the singers, the gatekeepers, and the Nethinim came up to Jerusalem in the seventh year of King Artaxerxes. And Ezra came to Jerusalem in the fifth month, which was in the seventh year of the king. On the first day of the first month he began his journey from Babylon, and on the first day of the fifth month he***

came to Jerusalem, according to the good hand of his God upon him. For Ezra had prepared his heart to seek the Law of the LORD, and to do it, and to teach statutes and ordinances in Israel. (NKJV)

priests
Ezra 2:36–39

These verses present an overview of Ezra's difficult and dangerous trip to Jerusalem. Some of the details are given in later passages, but Ezra was not alone on this treacherous trip. Several priests, Levites, singers, gatekeepers, and Temple servants joined him. They left Babylon in the seventh year of King Artaxerxes (458 BC) on the first day of the first month (Nisan/March–April), traveled about nine hundred miles, and arrived in Jerusalem four months later on first day of the fifth month (Ab/July–August). God was with him, guiding him, caring for him, and protecting him. Why? Because Ezra had done three things:

- Determined to be a seeker of God,
- Observed or practiced what he learned from the Word of God, and
- Prepared to teach the Word of God in Israel.

He was an avid scholar who tried to find God, practice God's will in his own life, and teach it to others.

what others say

Charles Colson

If the church is the Body, the holy presence of Christ in the world, its most fundamental task is to build communities of holy character. And the first priority of those communities is to disciple men and women to maturity in Christ and then equip them to live their faith in every aspect of life and in every part of the world.[3]

A Love Letter

the big picture

Ezra 7:11–26

King Artaxerxes gave Ezra a letter recognizing his status as a priest, scribe, and expert in the Word of God (vv. 11–12). The letter authorized any Jew who wanted to return to Israel to do so and it directed Ezra to determine if the Jews in Israel were fol-

restore
Daniel 9:25

pagan
a person who does not worship the true God

lowing the Law of Moses (vv. 13–14). The king gave a contribution to Ezra, gave him permission to collect offerings along the way, told him to carefully see that the money was used to purchase or make sacrifices to God, and granted him permission to withdraw money from the king's treasury at his discretion (vv. 15–20). King Artaxerxes also decreed that all treasurers in the Trans-Euphrates region where Jerusalem was should provide large sums of money, wheat, wine, oil, salt, etc., for the project and told them they could not require those who serve at the Temple to pay taxes (vv. 21–24). The king commissioned Ezra to appoint magistrates and judges for the Jews, told him to teach the Word of God to the people and authorized him to punish those who disobeyed the Word of God (vv. 25–26).

Obviously, King Artaxerxes had great respect for Ezra as a priest, scribe, and scholar. He allowed the Jews to freely decide whether they wanted to stay or return. He made a generous personal contribution to Israel's God, allowed Ezra to collect freewill offerings, made provision for other Temple support as needed, and exempted the priests and Levites from taxes. He told Ezra to teach the Word of God to his people and said anyone who violated the Word of God was transgressing against the Persian government.

what others say

Lyle P. Murphy

One of the institutions that evolved in the Captivity was the synagogue. Jewish history and legend suggest that Ezra brought the institution to Jerusalem. The synagogue in Babylon was a sad substitute for the temple, but it was an important place for Jewish prayer, study, and fellowship. Bringing the synagogue system to Israel signaled the opening of Jewish spiritual life, placing it in the hands of the people.[4]

King Artaxerxes was a **pagan** king. He is a good illustration of the fact that people can be good to others, do good deeds, give to God, give mental assent to the existence of God, and yet not be saved. Being good and doing good are very important, but faith in Jesus is the one essential characteristic King Artaxerxes lacked.

The king's letter provided for Temple support only. Nothing is said about rebuilding the walls of Jerusalem. This will come at a later date. But it is important because Gabriel had predicted that a command would be given to restore and build Jerusalem 483 years before the **Anointed One** comes. Obviously, this letter did not do that.

God Did It

Ezra 7:27–28 ***Blessed be the Lord God of our fathers, who has put such a thing as this in the king's heart, to beautify the house of the Lord which is in Jerusalem, and has extended mercy to me before the king and his counselors, and before all the king's mighty princes. So I was encouraged, as the hand of the Lord my God was upon me; and I gathered leading men of Israel to go up with me.*** *(NKJV)*

Ezra showed humility and thanksgiving by giving the glory to God for influencing King Artaxerxes to do these wonderful things for the Temple. He also believed it was God's **good favor** working in the good king's heart that caused the king to elevate him to such an exalted position. This heavenly power encouraged Ezra to choose several faithful leaders from the Jewish community to join him in this worthy endeavor.

Should Christians really love their enemies? Should Christians really turn the other cheek? Can God really make unbelievers a blessing to his people? The answer to all of these questions is, "Yes!" God can cause an unbeliever to do good deeds. That is what he did with King Artaxerxes. We need to make sure that our own activities do not interfere with the ways in which God wants to move on the hearts and lives of unbelievers.

go to

enemies
Matthew 5:44

cheek
Matthew 5:39

Anointed One
Jesus

good favor
the grace of God

Chapter Wrap-Up

- Ezra's genealogy shows that he came from a long list of prominent Jews who were direct descendants of Aaron. It is designed to show that he was fully qualified to assume the position he was being appointed to.
- Ezra was an expert in the Scriptures that God had given up to this time, and he received the full cooperation of King Artaxerxes.
- Ezra led a group of Jews on a difficult four-month journey from Babylon to Jerusalem. He was a man who studied, kept, and taught the Word of God.
- King Artaxerxes wrote a letter to Ezra that recognized his qualifications, granted other Jews permission to return with him, and provided funding for the Temple. It also authorized Ezra to appoint political leaders, teach the Word of God, and punish those who refused to obey.
- Ezra glorified God for influencing the king to do all he did on his behalf. God's help with this encouraged Ezra to do the things the king commissioned him to do.

Study Questions

1. What statement is repeated three times in this chapter? What does it mean?
2. How did Ezra prepare himself for the teaching assignment he would be given in Jerusalem and who was he supposed to teach?
3. How did the king support Ezra financially?
4. Name two sets of laws the Jews would be required to keep. What would be the punishment for disobedience?
5. What does this chapter teach about the separation of religion and politics?

Ezra 8
The Second Census

Chapter Highlights:
- The Second Census
- A Prayer for Help
- A Charge to Keep
- The Trip
- Getting Started in Jerusalem

Let's Get Started

This chapter provides a more detailed account of the journey to Jerusalem. Armed with the letter from King Artaxerxes, Ezra gathered a group of exiles, prayed for God's help, assigned responsibilities to some of the returnees, made the trip, and upon his arrival immediately went to work.

journey
Ezra 7:7–10

letter
Ezra 7:11–26

The Second Main Wave Returns

the big picture

Ezra 8:1-20

This is a list of the family heads who accompanied Ezra on his journey from Babylon to Jerusalem. It includes a list of family heads who were priests (vv. 1–2), family heads who were descendants of royalty (vv. 2b–3a), and a count of the common people under each family head (vv. 3b–14). When the group assembled it was discovered that there were no Levites present so Ezra recruited some (vv. 15–17), and thirty-eight men plus two hundred and twenty servants responded (vv. 18–20).

Babylon was full of faithful Jews in 458 BC, but most were prospering under good King Artaxerxes and many seemed fairly comfortable. It had been more than 125 years since their nation had been destroyed. Most had never seen Holy Jerusalem or the beautiful Temple of God. Their prosperity, comfort, and unfamiliarity with their ancestral homeland and the hardships that lay ahead probably explains why the number of returnees was so small and why the number of priestly families was just two: one headed by Phinehas and another headed by Ithamar. The list identifies approximately 1,773 adult males who returned. Nothing is said about women and children, but the entire group may have numbered 5,000 to 10,000 people in total.

Some commentators question the accuracy of this list because some of the names in this second wave of returnees are the same as those in the list of first-wave returnees. But these are names of families and not names of individuals. Some members of these families returned in the first wave and then were joined by other relatives about eighty years later. The Bible clearly states that this is a list of those who returned during the reign of King Artaxerxes and the other is a list of those who returned during the reign of King Cyrus. It is important to keep in mind that God keeps lists of faithful people in his heavenly books.

Prayer Is Better Than an Army

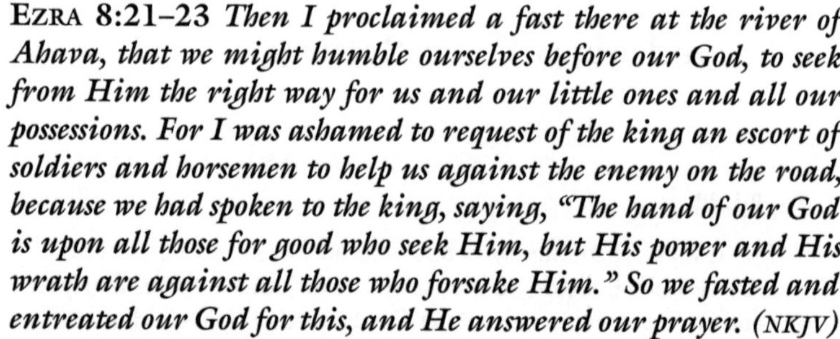
Ezra 8:21–23 ***Then I proclaimed a fast there at the river of Ahava, that we might humble ourselves before our God, to seek from Him the right way for us and our little ones and all our possessions. For I was ashamed to request of the king an escort of soldiers and horsemen to help us against the enemy on the road, because we had spoken to the king, saying, "The hand of our God is upon all those for good who seek Him, but His power and His wrath are against all those who forsake Him." So we fasted and entreated our God for this, and He answered our prayer.*** *(NKJV)*

list
Ezra 2:1–62

Artaxerxes
Ezra 8:1

Cyrus
Ezra 1:1–11

Ahava Canal
Ezra 8:15

silver and gold
Ezra 7:15–16

asked
Ezra 7:6

arrived
Ezra 7:8–9

fast
to go without eating

humble
acknowledge their dependence upon God

Ezra assembled the small group at the Ahava Canal, but his heart was troubled. This would be a dangerous trip through hostile territory with lots of vulnerable women and children, and a fortune in silver and gold. So he asked the exiles to **fast**, **humble** themselves, and pray. And he was specific about what he wanted: a safe and successful journey for the exiles, their children, and their possessions.

He could have asked King Artaxerxes for a military escort, and the implication is that he would have received it. But he refused to do this because it would have clearly contradicted his statement to the king that God is with those who trust him and against those who abandon him. He wanted the king to see his steadfast faith in God. So the Jews went without food, acknowledged their dependence upon God, prayed for protection, and their prayers were answered. They arrived safely in Jerusalem four months later.

consecrated
dedicated entirely to God

what others say

Max Lucado

Do you want to know how to deepen your prayer life? Pray. Don't prepare to pray. Just pray. Don't read about prayer. Just pray. Don't attend a lecture on prayer or engage in a discussion about prayer. Just pray.[1]

Mark D. Roberts/Lloyd J. Ogilvie

When we consider the dangers the returning exiles were facing on this journey, Ezra's simple trust in God's protection is a bit unsettling. He and his companions would be sitting ducks, easy prey for marauding bandits. Hundreds if not thousands of children could be slaughtered. Yet Ezra's commitment to live consistent with what he confessed commends a daring course—a course that God honored.[2]

Holy People Bearing Holy Gifts

the big picture

Ezra 8:24–30

Ezra selected twelve priests and twelve Levites, and carefully divided the silver, gold, and precious articles among them (vv. 24–27). He reminded these twenty-four men that they, as well as the treasures they received, were consecrated to God; and he asked them to guard the treasures carefully until they could be checked in at Jerusalem (vv. 28–30).

Since this great treasure was given to God for his house in Jerusalem, Ezra quickly selected twenty-four men, twelve priests, and twelve Levites to take charge of it. He carefully portioned out almost 25 tons of silver, almost 4 tons of silver articles, almost 4 tons of gold, and 22 other extremely valuable items. He reminded the priests and Levites that this treasure was **consecrated** to the Lord, and because they were handling consecrated things, these men were considered consecrated too. He asked them to carefully safeguard the treasure and reminded them that everything would be inventoried in the presence of witnesses at the Temple in Jerusalem. They accepted this responsibility.

first
Ezra 7:9

Ahava
Ezra 8:15

silver
Ezra 8:25–30

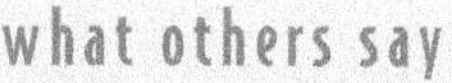

H. G. M. Williamson

Holiness is a characteristic of God himself and hence by extension of anyone or anything dedicated to him. This was especially true of priests (Exod. 29:1; 39:30; Lev. 21:6), Levites (Num. 3:12–13) and of the Tabernacle and its equipment (Exod. 29:36; 30:29; 40:9, etc.), of which the vessels mentioned in these verses would have been regarded as a continuation.[3]

With God's Help We Made It

EZRA 8:31 ***Then we departed from the river of Ahava on the twelfth day of the first month, to go to Jerusalem. And the hand of our God was upon us, and He delivered us from the hand of the enemy and from ambush along the road. (NKJV)***

Ezra left Babylon on the first day of the first month (Nisan/March–April, 458 BC). He traveled to the Ahava River where he assembled with the group and camped out for three days. During this three-day period he discovered that he didn't have any Levites in the group, so he seemingly took eight more days to round up some. The group pulled up stakes and departed from that location on the twelfth day of the month and arrived in Jerusalem on the first day of the fifth month (July–August, 458 BC). God was good to the group. They traveled about nine hundred miles in four months (about seven and one-half miles per day), and God protected them all along the way.

Walking nine hundred miles with women and children, while moving several tons of silver and gold, in that climate was not easy. God truly helped these people, and they had much to rejoice about when they finally arrived at Jerusalem.

A Special Delivery

EZRA 8:32–34 ***So we came to Jerusalem, and stayed there three days. Now on the fourth day the silver and the gold and the articles were weighed in the house of our God by the hand of Meremoth the son of Uriah the priest, and with him was Eleazar the son of Phinehas; with them were the Levites, Jozabad the son of Jeshua and Noadiah the son of Binnui, with the number and weight of everything. All the weight was written down at that time. (NKJV)***

After this long hard trip the exhausted group needed a break. They rested and relaxed three days before doing anything else. The following day they went to the Temple and met with two priests, Meremoth and Eleazar, and two Levites, Jozabad and Noadiah. They delivered their treasure, inventoried it, and picked up a written receipt.

It's important for Christians to notice how careful Ezra was to fully account for God's money. Most church treasurers and many church members want accurate, well-documented records. The church is harshly criticized when funds are mishandled, and the government sometimes checks church records. God expects us to be good stewards. Gifts to God are holy. Does your congregation treat them that way?

Religion and Politics

EZRA 8:35–36 ***The children of those who had been carried away captive, who had come from the captivity, offered burnt offerings to the God of Israel: twelve bulls for all Israel, ninety-six rams, seventy-seven lambs, and twelve male goats as a sin offering. All this was a burnt offering to the LORD. And they delivered the king's orders to the king's satraps and the governors in the region beyond the River. So they gave support to the people and the house of God.*** *(NKJV)*

After delivering their gifts to the priests and Levites, the former exiles went to the Temple altar to worship. This was the first opportunity they had to offer sacrifices in their own homeland. Their first offering was a burnt offering of twelve bulls, one for each of the twelve tribes of Israel. This was followed by a burnt offering of ninety-six rams and seventy-seven lambs for thanksgiving. And then they offered twelve goats for a sin offering, again probably one for each of the twelve tribes of Israel, but it was also for cleansing because they were defiled from being in a foreign land.

altar
Ezra 3:1–3

Trans-Euphrates
Ezra 7:25–26

When the sacrifices were over, Ezra and his associates delivered copies of the king's orders to the political leaders of the **Trans-Euphrates** province. Since these were the orders of the king, and disobedience was punishable by death, the political leaders readily complied. They gave Ezra their full cooperation and did all they could to help the Jews with their work at the Temple.

Trans-Euphrates
area west of the Euphrates River

what others say

H. A. Ironside

The burnt offering was not brought because things had been going wrong; it was the expression of the offerer's worship. He brought it to God as an evidence of the gratitude of his heart because of what God was to him and had done for him, and all went up to Jehovah as a sweet savor.[4]

Bible Dictionary

Animal sacrifices [sin offerings), also called guilt offerings, were presented for unintentional or intentional sins for which there was no possible restitution (Lev. 4:5–13, 6:24–30), and were supposed to be accompanied by repentance to receive divine forgiveness (Nu. 15:30).[5]

Chapter Wrap-Up

- The chapter begins with a list of priests, royalty, family heads, and those who joined them on the trip. Ezra discovered that there were no Levites, so he recruited 38 men and they brought along 220 Temple servants.
- Ezra assembled the group at the Ahava Canal. He didn't want to ask for a military escort, so they fasted, humbled themselves, and prayed for God's protection.
- Ezra selected twenty-four men and asked them to take possession of the treasure until it could be delivered and accounted for at the Temple.
- The group arrived safely at Jerusalem, rested three days, and then delivered the treasure to the Temple.
- The group worshiped at the Temple by sacrificing many animals for thanksgiving offerings and for sin offerings. Then they delivered the king's orders to the political leaders in the area.

Study Questions

1. With regard to those who initially decided to return with Ezra, what three groups of people did they come from? What group was absent?

2. Why didn't Ezra want to ask the king for an escort? What did he do to ensure a safe trip for the returnees?

3. What did Ezra do to ensure that none of the treasure disappeared before it was delivered in Jerusalem?

4. Ezra called the twelve priests and Levites holy. What made them holy?

5. What four things did the returnees do when they arrived at Jerusalem?

Ezra 9
Ezra's Prayer

Chapter Highlights:
- A Terrible Thing
- We Have Sinned
- God Is Good
- We Didn't Listen
- We Need Mercy

Let's Get Started

Ezra was thrilled with his commission to lead a group of exiles back to Jerusalem and to teach the Word of God. This good man was obedient and he got off to a great start. But four months after his arrival, he was confronted with a serious problem that shocked him. Some of the Jews had lost their moral compass, and he was responsible for dealing with it.

months
Ezra 7:9

Canaanites
Deuteronomy 7:1–4

Jebusites
Exodus 34:11–16

separated
remaining faithful to God's teachings

Lonely Men

EZRA 9:1 ***When these things were done, the leaders came to me, saying, "The people of Israel and the priests and the Levites have not separated themselves from the peoples of the lands, with respect to the abominations of the Canaanites, the Hittites, the Perizzites, the Jebusites, the Ammonites, the Moabites, the Egyptians, and the Amorites.*** *(NKJV)*

After completing the tasks in the preceding chapter, a delegation of Jewish leaders at Jerusalem gave Ezra a report of widespread sin among the Jews. Even the priests and Levites were involved. Instead of being the **separated** people God called them to be, some had intermarried with the Canaanites, Hittites, Perizzites, Jebusites, Ammonites, Moabites, Egyptians, and Amorites. And they were involved in their wicked ways.

what others say

Knute Larson and Kathy Dahlen

Before Israel entered the promised land, God instructed them not to intermarry with the Canaanites whose land they were about to occupy. The reason was purely religious, not racial (Jews had married non-Jews before without divine judgment—Moses and Joseph to name two). The emphasis was on the "detestable practices" of the surrounding peoples, specifically their idol worship: "Do not intermarry with them . . . For they will turn your sons away from following me to serve other gods" (Deut. 7:3–4).[1]

Part of the problem may have been that most of the exiles who returned to Israel in the first main wave were men. These men wanted families, but there weren't enough Jewish women to go around. We can sympathize with them, but sinning was not the right answer to this situation. God always provides a way out of every temptation. Instead of sinning, they probably should have recruited more women to leave Babylon.

God did not absolutely refuse to allow Jewish men to take foreign wives. When the foreign women turned from their old religion and accepted him as their God, he accepted them. Ruth was a foreigner who married a Jew and became an ancestor of King David.

They're All Doing It

EZRA 9:2 ***For they have taken some of their daughters as wives for themselves and their sons, so that the holy seed is mixed with the peoples of those lands. Indeed, the hand of the leaders and rulers has been foremost in this trespass.*** *(NKJV)*

The concerned leaders who reported to Ezra believed these mixed marriages were threatening the purity of the **holy people**. The problem was far more serious than a few ordinary people doing forbidden things. Some of those most deeply involved in detestable practices were the religious and political leaders who should have been setting a good example for others.

Tim LaHaye

The Bible is a living Book written by a loving God to His children and it is "profitable" (practical). In it He provides basic principles, guidance, and inspiration on how to live. It was written to people, and because human nature hasn't changed in the years since its writing, it has a message for God's people today.[2]

temptation
1 Corinthians 10:13

God
2 Timothy 3:16

unbelievers
1 Corinthians 7:14

holy people
the Jews

In the New Testament, believers are told not to marry unbelievers. The believer who marries an unbeliever usually finds it more difficult to attend church regularly, raise the children for God, abstain from watching immoral television programs, and conduct other aspects of their lives in ways that are pleasing to God. Also, it is likely that if the religious and political leaders of a nation do not set a good example, the ordinary citizens will not be likely to live holy lives.

A Temper Tantrum

tore
Genesis 37:29–34

appearance
2 Samuel 14:25–26

> EZRA 9:3 *So when I heard this thing, I tore my garment and my robe, and plucked out some of the hair of my head and beard, and sat down astonished.* (NKJV)

Disobedience and separation from God are the reasons God sent the Jews into captivity in the first place. Now after he had graciously allowed them to return home, they were going back to their same old wicked ways. This is why Ezra reacted the way he did. He tore his inner and outer garments to show deep distress and mourning. He pulled out some of his hair and beard to mar his appearance and demonstrate moral outrage and pain. Then he sat down in stunned silence, perhaps contemplating what God might do.

Concern Among the Faithful

> EZRA 9:4 *Then everyone who trembled at the words of the God of Israel assembled to me, because of the transgression of those who had been carried away captive, and I sat astonished until the evening sacrifice.* (NKJV)

Ezra's open expression of disappointment produced an immediate response from those who took the Word of God seriously. They had great respect for God, so they gathered around Ezra to give him their support. But Ezra was so astonished he refused to move until about 3:00 p.m.

Tolerance and inclusiveness are widespread teachings in the church today as theologians and preachers urge God's people to be broad-minded about premarital sex, adultery, divorce, abortion, and homosexuality. When religious leaders depart from the clear teachings of the Word of God, the faithful should support those who stand firm.

The Way It Is

the big picture

Ezra 9:5–15

Ezra began to pray and confess the sins of Israel's people (vv. 5–7a). He acknowledged that the sins of their ancestors led to the Assyrian and Babylonian captivity (v. 7b). He credited Israel's return to the grace of God (vv. 8–9). He confessed Israel was ignoring God's prohibition against intermarriage (vv. 10–14). He acknowledged God's righteousness and Israel's guilt (v. 15).

confess
1 John 1:9

people
2 Chronicles 7:14

Ezra included himself with Israel as he humbly prayed about "our iniquities" (9:6 NKJV). He used the opportunity to confess shame and disgrace for the entire nation and acknowledged the seriousness of the matter by saying Israel's guilt was piled up to heaven. He noted that Israel's past sins were the reason why God allowed the chosen people to suffer affliction in foreign lands. And the grace of God is why he kept his covenants, the people survived, and the nation was granted a second chance. Ezra confessed that the nation was ignoring what God's Word says about intermarriage. He acknowledged that God had always treated the Jews better than they deserved, that God is righteous and has to punish sin, that all Israel was guilty, and that the entire nation was at the mercy of God.

what others say

Charles R. Swindoll

Doing the will of God is rarely easy and uncomplicated. Instead, it is often difficult and convoluted. Or, back to my preferred term, it is *mysterious*. Because we don't know where He is taking us, we must bend our wills to His—and most of us are not all that excited about bending. We'd much prefer resisting. That's why the Christian life is often such a struggle. I don't mean that it's a constant marathon of misery. It's just a struggle between our will and His will.[3]

Chapter Wrap-Up

- Some of the leaders told Ezra that there was a serious problem with intermarriage between the exiles and non-Jews in the area. This problem involved the common people as well as the religious and political leaders and sparked a demonstration of grief in Ezra, who tore his clothes, pulled hair from his head and chin, sat stunned for a while, and then prayed.
- Ezra's prayer expressed shame, disgrace, and guilt. And Ezra acknowledged that sin is why the people's ancestors went into captivity.
- Ezra's prayer acknowledged it was the grace of God that preserved a remnant, protected them in captivity, caused the king to act kindly toward them, and caused the Temple to be rebuilt.
- Ezra's prayer confessed that the people had not listened to the Word of God given through the prophets. God's spokesmen had warned that God was giving the Jews a land occupied by wicked people and told them not to intermarry because doing so would lead to their corruption.
- Ezra acknowledged God's goodness, confessed the righteousness of God, and admitted that Israel could not survive in the presence of God without his mercy.

Study Questions

1. How widespread was the disobedience to God in Israel?
2. Why was God against intermarriage?
3. How did Ezra react to the report of disobedience, and how did those who respected the Word of God react?
4. How did Ezra connect this sin to Israel's past sin?
5. How did Ezra think God had treated the exiles?

Ezra 10
Changed Lives

Chapter Highlights:
- The Proposed Solution
- The Proclamation
- The Priest Speaks
- The Positive Response
- The People Affected

Let's Get Started

Chapter 9 left off with Ezra humbly praying to the Lord God of Israel. His immediate personal demonstration of grief and his prayer of confession at the hour of sacrifice attracted a very large crowd. This chapter reveals what happened.

Lord
Ezra 9:5–15

knees
Ezra 9:5

words of God
Ezra 9:4

Where Did All These People Come From?

EZRA 10:1 ***Now while Ezra was praying, and while he was confessing, weeping, and bowing down before the house of God, a very large assembly of men, women, and children gathered to him from Israel; for the people wept very bitterly.*** *(NKJV)*

While the stunned Ezra was praying, confessing, crying, and dropping to his knees in front of the Temple, a large crowd of Jews who respected the words of God gathered around him. This crowd included men, women, and children. They could hear Ezra's emotional prayer. A deep sense of conviction came over them. They understood the seriousness of what some had done and they began to weep bitterly.

what others say

G. Ernest Thomas

When prayer seems difficult, and we are tempted to give up, we should recall that Jesus himself, Paul, and other New Testament leaders remind us that prayer requires strenuous effort, and often includes periods of discouragement. It is reported that Jesus "told them a parable, to the effect that they ought always to pray and not lose heart" (Luke 18:1). Many who heard him knew what it meant—that prayer was indeed difficult. They must have felt less lonely in their prayer life because of his words.[1]

Elamites
Ezra 2:7; 8:7

covenant
Joshua 24:1–28; Jeremiah 34:15

knees
Ezra 9:5

Elamites
descendants of Elam

There's Hope

EZRA 10:2 ***And Shechaniah the son of Jehiel, one of the sons of Elam, spoke up and said to Ezra, "We have trespassed against our God, and have taken pagan wives from the peoples of the land; yet now there is hope in Israel in spite of this.*** (NKJV)

One of the **Elamites**, a man named Shechaniah, acted as spokesman for the people and admitted that the Jewish men had disobeyed God by marrying Gentile women. But he did not believe the situation was hopeless.

I Have a Plan

EZRA 10:3 ***Now therefore, let us make a covenant with our God to put away all these wives and those who have been born to them, according to the advice of my master and of those who tremble at the commandment of our God; and let it be done according to the law.*** (NKJV)

Shechaniah admitted that some of the Jewish men had broken the covenant the nation had made with God. He probably reasoned that because these marriages had been forbidden by God, they were invalid in God's eyes. So, on behalf of the faithful Jewish men, he suggested that the unfaithful Jews should give up their foreign wives and children. He said that this was the will of God and that this should be done to bring the nation in compliance with the Law of Moses.

Sending these foreign wives away seems harsh, but Shechaniah was reacting to the terrible thought that the wayward nation was in grave danger because God might decide to destroy it again. Sending their children away would deeply hurt the transgressing fathers, but this recognized that the children needed their mothers' loving care. The children would not be separated from their mothers.

It's Your Responsibility

EZRA 10:4 ***Arise, for this matter is your responsibility. We also are with you. Be of good courage, and do it."*** (NKJV)

Looking to Ezra for leadership, Shecaniah reminded Ezra that he was in charge. Ezra had been on his knees praying when Shecaniah urged him to get up, to be of good courage, and to act. Shechaniah added that Ezra would have the support of the faithful Jews.

oath
a solemn pledge or vow

fast
go without food and water

Take a Stand

Ezra 10:5 ***Then Ezra arose, and made the leaders of the priests, the Levites, and all Israel swear an oath that they would do according to this word. So they swore an oath.*** *(NKJV)*

Ezra stood up. He knew this would be difficult and wanted to be sure no one would change their mind, so he required the priests, Levites, and all the people to swear that they would do what Shechaniah had suggested. Everyone took the **oath**. Since this oath involved a covenant with God, they probably invoked his approval for those who obeyed and his punishment for those who failed.

Fast Time

Ezra 10:6 ***Then Ezra rose up from before the house of God, and went into the chamber of Jehohanan the son of Eliashib; and when he came there, he ate no bread and drank no water, for he mourned because of the guilt of those from the captivity.*** *(NKJV)*

Ezra left the crowd that gathered in front of the Temple and entered the Temple storeroom where the priestly garments were kept. He had just been involved in public prayer, confession, and grief, and now he wanted to spend some private time with God. He knew that God hates sin and he wanted to privately **fast** and pray.

what others say

The Pulpit Commentary

Strict fasts of this kind had been observed by Moses twice (Exodus 34:28, and Deuteronomy 9:18), and by the Ninevites (Jonah 3:7), but they were very uncommon. Usually it was considered enough to abstain from eating (1 Samuel 1:7; 20:34; 2 Samuel 3:35). Sometimes the person who fasted merely abstained from "meat and wine, and *pleasant* bread" (Daniel 3:3). Ezra's great earnestness appears in the severity of his fast, which (it is to be remembered) was not for his own sins, but for those of his brethren.[2]

king
Ezra 7:26

rain
Deuteronomy 11:10–17

proclamation
command or edict

Holy City
another name for Jerusalem

An Offer You Can't Refuse

EZRA 10:7–8 *And they issued a proclamation throughout Judah and Jerusalem to all the descendants of the captivity, that they must gather at Jerusalem, and that whoever would not come within three days, according to the instructions of the leaders and elders, all his property would be confiscated, and he himself would be separated from the assembly of those from the captivity. (NKJV)*

After Ezra finished fasting and praying, he and the leaders wasted no time. They immediately issued a **proclamation** that was published or announced throughout the region of Judah and Jerusalem. Ezra was sent there by King Artaxerxes and he had the authority to do this. All of the exiles were required to assemble in the **Holy City** within three days. The penalty for failure to show up was loss of property and expulsion from the community of exiles.

This was no doubt one of the most difficult tasks these returnees had to undertake. But sin grieves God. Knowing that sin cannot be ignored, these faithful leaders concluded that they had to put a stop to it by dissolving these forbidden marriages.

Three Days Later

EZRA 10:9 *So all the men of Judah and Benjamin gathered at Jerusalem within three days. It was the ninth month, on the twentieth of the month; and all the people sat in the open square of the house of God, trembling because of this matter and because of heavy rain. (NKJV)*

The twentieth day of the ninth month is the twentieth day of Chisleu (November/December 458 BC). On this day everyone obeyed the proclamation and all the men gathered in Jerusalem. It was a big crowd and they sat down in the large open square in front of the Temple. It was a very difficult day and the men were trembling for two reasons: first, dissolving these mixed marriages was very stressful, and second, these men were sitting outside in the chilling winter rain.

Two Things You Need to Do

EZRA 10:10–11 ***Then Ezra the priest stood up and said to them, "You have transgressed and have taken pagan wives, adding to the guilt of Israel. Now therefore, make confession to the LORD God of your fathers, and do His will; separate yourselves from the peoples of the land, and from the pagan wives."*** *(NKJV)*

Ezra stood before those who were sitting in the cold rain. His first words summarized the problem in a twofold way: first, some of the men had been unfaithful by intermarrying with non-Jews, and second, they had added to Israel's guilt. He was reminding his listeners that Israel's ancestors went into captivity because they had been unfaithful to God, and he was telling them they were doing the same thing. These people weren't doing any better than their ancestors had done and their failure was adding to the overall guilt of the nation.

Ezra finished his remarks by urging these men to do two things:

- Confess their sins.
- Do the will of God.

What was the will of God? Ezra believed God wanted these men to separate themselves from the non-Jews around them and from their foreign wives.

what others say

Knute Larson and Kathy Dahlen

This decision stands in marked contrast to the teachings of the New Testament. Jesus clearly prohibited divorce except in instances of immorality (Matthew 5:32); Paul, within the framework of certain concessions, instructed Christians to refrain from divorce, even if married to an unbeliever (1 Corinthians 7:12–17). However, to Ezra and the other leaders, the survival of the Jewish faith and community seemed at risk. Drastic measures were needed to purify the community from a growing corruption.[3]

Not in This Weather

EZRA 10:12–14 ***Then all the assembly answered and said with a loud voice, "Yes! As you have said, so we must do. But there are many people; it is the season for heavy rain, and we are not able to stand outside. Nor is this the work of one or two days, for there***

family heads
head of a family clan or division

are many of us who have transgressed in this matter. Please, let the leaders of our entire assembly stand; and let all those in our cities who have taken pagan wives come at appointed times, together with the elders and judges of their cities, until the fierce wrath of our God is turned away from us in this matter." (NKJV)

All of those who had assembled agreed with what Ezra said. He was right, they had sinned, and they needed to separate themselves. But there was a problem and a request. The problem revolved around the large number of people there, the inclement weather, the lack of indoor facilities, and the need to proceed carefully. It involved getting out of the rain and allowing a little time to carry this out.

The request was for the **family heads** to act as representatives for their affected family members before the community leaders, for the family heads to set up an appointment for each individual they represented, and for each individual to appear with his representative to have his case heard on a separate basis before the community leaders. This seemed to be a practical way to proceed, and it would also please God.

Count on Us

EZRA 10:15 *Only Jonathan the son of Asahel and Jahaziah the son of Tikvah opposed this, and Meshullam and Shabbethai the Levite gave them support.* (NKJV)

Considering the serious consequences of this proposal, it's not surprising that some of the men opposed it, but it is surprising that the dissenters were so few in number. There were only four: Jonathan, Jahaziah, Meshullam, and Shabbethai.

We Did It

EZRA 10:16–17 *Then the descendants of the captivity did so. And Ezra the priest, with certain heads of the fathers' households, were set apart by the fathers' households, each of them by name; and they sat down on the first day of the tenth month to examine the matter. By the first day of the first month they finished questioning all the men who had taken pagan wives.* (NKJV)

Everyone followed the suggestion. Ezra selected a representative from each family division and prepared a list of the ones he believed should serve. The community leaders came together and met with the family representatives on the first day of the tenth month, Tebeth (December/January 458 BC), and the group completed their work three months later on the first day of the first month, Nisan (March/April 457 BC).

list
Ezra 2:1–61

priests
Ezra 10:18–22

Levites
Ezra 10:23

singers and gatekeepers
Ezra 10:24

Israelites
Ezra 10:25–43

Kay Arthur, David Lawson, and Bob Vereen

> Had the fathers forgotten to teach their sons and daughters the Word of God? Is that why Ezra was dispatched by God—because of such a time as this? Ezra, a man of the Word of God, arrived on the scene of moral decay, and immediately the conviction of sin fell upon the people. No one summoned the people—they came. Weeping, they confessed their sin openly, repented, and put it away. Yes, it was costly. Yes, it was painful. But it was necessary.[4]

Did You Know They're Getting a Divorce?

the big picture

Ezra 10:18–44

> This is a list of priests, Levites, singers, gatekeepers and Israeli men who intermarried and then divorced their wives. Some of these men were married to foreign wives who bore them children.

Ezra ended his historical record with a list of those who got a divorce. Seventeen were priests, ten were Levites, one was a singer, three were gatekeepers, and the remainder were ordinary Israelites citizens. They represented less than 1 percent of the Jews living in the area at this time, but the sad part of the story is that approximately 113 men were required to get a divorce.

what others say

Max Lucado

> True repentance involves turning away from sin, getting rid of the things in your life that relate to that sin, and getting a new heart and a new spirit. It implies that you are walking in one direction, then you make a U-turn and start walking in the opposite direction. The Israelites in Ezra are an excellent

example of this. They had disobeyed God by marrying non-Jewish women, and they repented by separating themselves from them. They didn't just tell God they knew they were wrong, they demonstrated their change of heart through their actions.[5]

Chapter Wrap-Up

- Ezra was praying and confessing when he was joined by a large crowd of Jews. A spokesman for the group acknowledged Israel's unfaithfulness and recommended a covenant with God to send away the foreign wives and children.
- Ezra put the group under oath, fasted, prayed, and then issued a proclamation for all the exiles to gather in Jerusalem within three days or lose their property and their rights in the assembly of exiles.
- The people gathered in Jerusalem and sat in the rain while Ezra reminded them that some were guilty of intermarriage, and urged them to confess and separate themselves.
- The people agreed to follow Ezra's recommendation, but they wanted the family heads to act on their behalf, and they wanted to appear with community leaders at a later date to address the problem.
- Intermarriage affected more than one hundred couples, including priests, Levites, singers, gatekeepers, and others. Some of these couples had children.

Study Questions

1. Who proposed the solution to Israel's problem and what was the proposal?
2. What was done to inform the people of the proposed solution? What was the penalty for those who refused to obey?
3. When the Jews assembled in Jerusalem, what did Ezra tell them to do? Did all of them do it?
4. Why didn't the Jews take care of the problem the first time they assembled in Jerusalem?
5. In the list of names, what groups were guilty? Was anyone other than the adults affected?

Part Two
THE BOOK OF NEHEMIAH

Introduction—Nehemiah 1–6 The Third Wave Returns

The books of Ezra and Nehemiah were one book until Jerome published the Latin Vulgate. He divided it into two books called First Ezra and Second Ezra but the name of Second Ezra was changed to Nehemiah not long after that.

Nehemiah is the principal character in the book of Nehemiah, and most authorities think he recorded these words around 425–420 BC. He was the **cupbearer** in the palace of King Artaxerxes of Persia. His book is similar to the book of Ezra in that it contains several historical lists, decrees, and documents. However, it is different because it covers events during the silent years of Ezra. Most of these events occurred between 445 and 430 BC (see chart "Persian Kings" on page 38).

cupbearer
Nehemiah 1:11

Cyrus
Ezra 1:2–11

letter
Ezra 7:6–26

wall
Nehemiah 2:7–8

cupbearer
the one who tasted and served what the king drank

what others say

Charles R. Swindoll

> Nehemiah's dedication and dependence on God teach us that, no matter what we do, we labor under the sovereign hand of our Lord. God provides us with a passion to participate in His work, and gives us the strength and resources to perform it. When we take on with passion and dedication the tasks He has given us, we get the satisfaction of a job well done, and God gets the glory.[1]

Let's Get Started

The first wave of returnees, led by Zerubbabel, went home when King Cyrus issued a decree for the Jews to go back and rebuild the Temple. The second wave of returnees, led by Ezra, went home when King Artaxerxes gave a letter to Ezra granting him permission to go back and teach the Law of Moses. The third wave, led by Nehemiah, returned when King Artaxerxes gave Nehemiah a letter granting him permission to rebuild the wall and gates of Jerusalem.

Nehemiah 1
Nehemiah's Prayer

Chapter Highlights:
- Tell Me About It
- It's Not Good
- A Burdened and Praying Heart

Let's Get Started

The book of Ezra deals with the long struggle to rebuild the Temple and the decision of the Jews to obey the Law of Moses. But another very important thing was needed to reestablish the nation. This was the Holy City. So Nehemiah describes the valiant effort to rebuild Jerusalem.

Hanani
Nehemiah 7:2

walls
2 Kings 25:8–12

Tell Me About It

NEHEMIAH **1:1–2** ***The words of Nehemiah the son of Hachaliah. It came to pass in the month of Chislev, in the twentieth year, as I was in Shushan the citadel, that Hanani one of my brethren came with men from Judah; and I asked them concerning the Jews who had escaped, who had survived the captivity, and concerning Jerusalem.*** *(NKJV)*

Chislev
the ninth month, our November/ December

twentieth year
twentieth year of the reign of King Artaxerxes or 445 BC

citadel
palace

Susa
the capital of Persia, also called Shushan

Some commentators say that the book of Nehemiah was written by Ezra, but the book begins with the author saying these are Nehemiah's words. He reveals that it was the month of **Chislev** (also called Kieslev and Chisleu) in the **twentieth year**, and he was in the **citadel** of **Susa**. His brother, Hanani and some other men from Judah visited him, and he asked them about the returnees and the city of Jerusalem (see chart "Hebrew and Gregorian Calendars" on page 24).

It's Not Good

NEHEMIAH **1:3** ***And they said to me, "The survivors who are left from the captivity in the province are there in great distress and reproach. The wall of Jerusalem is also broken down, and its gates are burned with fire."*** *(NKJV)*

Hanani and his friends told Nehemiah that the exiles who returned were having a very difficult time. When King Nebuchadnezzar destroyed Jerusalem he broke down the walls and burned the gates to

Jerusalem
Nehemiah 1:1–3

this man
King Artaxerxes

the Holy City. It was defenseless and the Jews were being persecuted and ridiculed.

A Burdened and Praying Heart

the big picture

Nehemiah 1:4-11

When Nehemiah heard this he cried, fasted, and prayed for several days (v. 4). He asked God to hear his prayer, and he confessed his sins and the sins of Israel (vv. 5–7). He asked God to remember his instructions to Israel and to help him with the king (vv. 8–11).

When Nehemiah heard about the perilous condition of his brave people and the city of Jerusalem, he grieved deeply, and fasted and prayed day and night for an unknown but extended period of time. First, he humbly and reverently addressed the merciful God, who keeps his covenants with the faithful. Second, he asked our loving God to both hear and listen. Third, he drew near to God by confessing his own sins and those of his family. Fourth, he confessed the blatant sins of all Israel. Fifth, he acknowledged that God had justly scattered the unfaithful Jews. Sixth, he reminded God of his gracious promise to restore Israel if the people repented. Seventh, he reminded God that he had redeemed Israel. Eighth, he asked God to hear his prayer and those of God's servants. And finally, he asked God to give him favor in the presence of **this man**.

what others say

Oral Roberts

When Nehemiah heard about the broken-down walls of Jerusalem and the city lying waste, it grieved him tremendously. This was the city of his fathers. He was so burdened over the reproach the situation was bringing on God's people that he wept, fasted, and prayed to the extent he became almost physically ill.[1]

The Holy Bible

The rebuilding of the walls around Jerusalem and the revival among the people had roots in the unchanging and unwavering laws of God. The truth of God's Word and the righteousness of his Law are the same yesterday, today, and tomorrow.[2]

John Wesley said, "Some have exalted religious fasting beyond all Scripture and reason; and others have utterly disregarded it." Some people fast and brag about it. Those who do are fasting for the wrong reason, and obviously they are not nearly as spiritual as they want others to think. Fasting should be a private matter between God and the participant. It should never be used to call attention to oneself. But fasting is important because, when done for the right reason, it enhances the participant's relationship with God, rids the participant's body of undesirable impurities, and enables the participant to wage a spiritual war with Satan and his demons.

fasting
Matthew 6:16–18

Chapter Wrap-Up

- Nehemiah's brother and others visited him at Susa and told him that the Jews were being persecuted and that the walls and gates of the city had been reduced to rubble.
- The heartbroken Nehemiah fasted and prayed for days. He prayed for the God of heaven to hear him; confessed his and Israel's sins; acknowledged the justice of God; reminded God that Israel was his chosen people and he had redeemed them; and asked God to grant him favor with King Artaxerxes.

Study Questions

1. Where was Nehemiah when he learned about the situation in Jerusalem? What was that situation and how did he find out?
2. What did Nehemiah do when he heard about the situation in Jerusalem? How long did this go on?
3. What do we learn about Israel's sin and God's attitude toward it from Nehemiah's confession?
4. What did Nehemiah ask God to do? What was Nehemiah's title?

Nehemiah 2
An Answer to Prayer

Chapter Highlights:
- Nehemiah's Request
- The King's Answer
- Unhappy Enemies
- Nehemiah's Inspection
- Toil and Trouble

Let's Get Started

This chapter teaches that Nehemiah's prayer for favor with King Artaxerxes was answered. Nehemiah asked the king for permission to rebuild Jerusalem and his request was granted. But removing the old rubble, rebuilding the walls, replacing the burned-out gates, and dealing with Israel's determined enemies was a **herculean** task. It was only accomplished because Nehemiah believed he was doing God's will and he absolutely refused to let anything deter him. He never questioned God's power and always, regardless of the circumstances, moved ahead with the building project.

favor
Nehemiah 1:11

Gabriel
Daniel 9:21–27

cupbearer
Nehemiah 1:11

herculean
very difficult

Messiah
Jesus

Nisan
our March/April

I Didn't Have a Smiley Face

> NEHEMIAH 2:1 ***And it came to pass in the month of Nisan, in the twentieth year of King Artaxerxes, when wine was before him, that I took the wine and gave it to the king. Now I had never been sad in his presence before.*** *(NKJV)*

This is a very important date in Bible prophecy. The angel Gabriel told Daniel a decree would be issued to restore and rebuild Jerusalem. Gabriel's revelation and the date of this decree are used to determine when the **Messiah** would appear the first time. This was the month of **Nisan** during the twentieth year of King Artaxerxes. Many excellent prophetic writers say this was March 14, 445 BC, a few well-known prophetic scholars say it was March 5, 444 BC, and there are other opinions. Whatever the date is, Gabriel said the Messiah would appear 483 years (483 years x 360 days/year = 173,880 days) from this date.

On Nisan 1 in the twentieth year of Artaxerxes, one of the king's servants took some wine to the king. The king's cupbearer was Nehemiah. It was his job to taste the king's wine to ensure the flavor was good, to ensure it was safe to drink, and, if so, to serve it to the thirsty king. Nehemiah was usually in a good mood when he did

favor
Nehemiah 1:11

city of his ancestors
Jerusalem

this, but this particular day was a painful one for him and he was showing signs of sadness.

Triumphal Entry of Jesus
(On Palm Sunday Five Days Before Passover)

If the 20th Year of Artaxerxes Was . . .	The Triumphal of Jesus Would Be . . .
March 14, 445 BC	April 6, AD 32
March 5, 444 BC	March 30, AD 33

What's Wrong?

NEHEMIAH 2:2–3 *Therefore the king said to me, "Why is your face sad, since you are not sick? This is nothing but sorrow of heart." So I became dreadfully afraid, and said to the king, "May the king live forever! Why should my face not be sad, when the city, the place of my fathers' tombs, lies waste, and its gates are burned with fire?" (NKJV)*

King Artaxerxes asked normally happy Nehemiah why he looked so sad. He recognized that Nehemiah was not sick, and he wisely deduced that something else was wrong. Nehemiah knew his answer to this question could cost him his life, so he was understandably nervous. But he had asked God to give him favor with the king, and he humbly came forward with the desires of his heart. He addressed the king with a common compliment and went on to tell him that he was grieving because the **city of his ancestors** was in ruins and the gates to the city had been burned. King Nebuchadnezzar had done this when he had invaded Jerusalem for the third and final time. He had been so angry with the rebellious Jews that he had leveled the city, knocked down the wall, and burned the Temple. He had turned the whole area into a wilderness of briers and thorns. He had leveled it into a place for oxen and sheep to roam (Isaiah 7:25).

I Want a Job Change

NEHEMIAH 2:4–5 *Then the king said to me, "What do you request?" So I prayed to the God of heaven. And I said to the king, "If it pleases the king, and if your servant has found favor in your sight, I ask that you send me to Judah, to the city of my fathers' tombs, that I may rebuild it." (NKJV)*

After Nehemiah told the king why he was so sad, the king responded with an inquiry about what Nehemiah wanted him to do. Nehemiah knew this was a touchy situation so he quickly offered a silent prayer before he answered the king. Then, with God's help, he wisely framed his answer in a way that showed respect for the king's authority: he wanted to rebuild the city in Judah where his **fathers** were buried. He was appealing to the king's sympathy.

fathers
ancestors

petitions
prayers

what others say

G. Ernest Thomas

Our minds struggle with the mystery of how divine providence is broad enough to answer the **petitions** of millions of men and women for guidance in the midst of life's perplexities. Yet the experience of Christians in the first century has been repeated in every age. Seeking men have always found direction for their lives through earnest prayer.[1]

It is not a sin to be sad. Jesus was saddened and crying when:

- Lazarus died and his sisters were grieving.
- He looked over Jerusalem and pondered its future because the Jews did not recognize him.
- He prayed in the Garden of Gethsemane before being abandoned by God on the cross.

Sadness over the death of a loved one or over sin is okay. In this case, Nehemiah's sadness was used of God to obtain a decree to rebuild Jerusalem. And it's no accident or coincidence that it happened exactly 173,880 days before Messiah, the Prince, made his triumphal entry as a newborn baby.

You Can Have a Leave of Absence

NEHEMIAH 2:6 *Then the king said to me (the queen also sitting beside him), "How long will your journey be? And when will you return?" So it pleased the king to send me; and I set him a time.* (NKJV)

Nehemiah does not say why the queen's presence is significant and any assumption about this would be mere speculation. But this verse does note that the queen was sitting next to the king, and he wanted

twelve years
Nehemiah 5:14

citadel
the fortress that protected the Temple

residence
the governor's palace

Nehemiah to tell him how long this trip would take and when he would return to his job at the palace. Although Nehemiah surely answered the king, he did not record his answer here. Later he writes that he spent twelve years in Judah. And later still, he writes that he went back for a second time. At any rate, the king was pleased with Nehemiah's answer and granted him permission to go, but it was Nehemiah who set the timing.

what others say

Max Lucado

Nehemiah exchanged the royal robe for coveralls and got to work. The project took twelve years and was uphill all the way. He was accused of everything from allowing faulty construction to being power-hungry. In spite of grumpy workers and lurking enemies, he made it. With the wall built and the enemy silent, the people rejoiced and Nehemiah went back to Persia.[2]

Some Won't Like It

NEHEMIAH 2:7–10 ***Furthermore I said to the king, "If it pleases the king, let letters be given to me for the governors of the region beyond the River, that they must permit me to pass through till I come to Judah, and a letter to Asaph the keeper of the king's forest, that he must give me timber to make beams for the gates of the citadel which pertains to the temple, for the city wall, and for the house that I will occupy." And the king granted them to me according to the good hand of my God upon me. Then I went to the governors in the region beyond the River, and gave them the king's letters. Now the king had sent captains of the army and horsemen with me. When Sanballat the Horonite and Tobiah the Ammonite official heard of it, they were deeply disturbed that a man had come to seek the well-being of the children of Israel.*** *(NKJV)*

Nehemiah knew there would be serious opposition to what he was doing and someone might try to harm him as he crossed hostile territory on this dangerous journey to Jerusalem. He asked the king for letters to the governors along the way. These letters would command them to provide him with safe conduct. He also asked the king for a letter to the manager of the king's forest in the area to provide him with lumber for three things: for the gates of the **citadel** by the

Temple, for the city wall, and for his **residence**. His requests were granted and he credited God with helping him find favor with the king. He delivered his letters as he traveled toward Jerusalem and he was accompanied by troops in the Persian army. When he arrived at Jerusalem and word spread about his mission to help the Jews rebuild the city, two powerful enemies of Israel, Sanballat and Tobiah, were very upset.

Nehemiah fasted and prayed. His prayer was answered and he credited God with helping him find favor with the king. He even believed God helped him obtain all the extra provisions he had asked for.

A Night Job

NEHEMIAH 2:11–13 ***So I came to Jerusalem and was there three days. Then I arose in the night, I and a few men with me; I told no one what my God had put in my heart to do at Jerusalem; nor was there any animal with me, except the one on which I rode. And I went out by night through the Valley Gate to the Serpent Well and the Refuse Gate, and viewed the walls of Jerusalem which were broken down and its gates which were burned with fire.*** *(NKJV)*

Nehemiah arrived in Jerusalem and remained there for three days, probably resting up from the long hard trip. Then he took a few good men and toured the broken-down wall under the cover of darkness. He did not tell these men or anyone else what God wanted him to do, and the only animal he took was the one he rode on. He started his personal inspection at the **Valley Gate**, moved counter-clockwise toward the **Serpent Well**, and then on toward the **Refuse Gate**.

favor
Nehemiah 1:11

Valley Gate
a gate overlooking the Valley of Hinnom (Gehenna)

Serpent Well
a spring or well unknown to modern scholars

Refuse Gate
the gate through which the city garbage and rubbish was removed

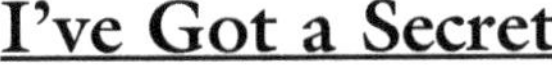

I've Got a Secret

NEHEMIAH 2:14–16 ***Then I went on to the Fountain Gate and to the King's Pool, but there was no room for the animal under me to pass. So I went up in the night by the valley, and viewed the wall; then I turned back and entered by the Valley Gate, and so returned. And the officials did not know where I had gone or what I had done; I had not yet told the Jews, the priests, the nobles, the officials, or the others who did the work.*** *(NKJV)*

Valley Gate
Nehemiah 2:13

Fountain Gate
A water fountain was near this gate.

King's Pool
the Pool of Siloam

Then Nehemiah traveled toward the **Fountain Gate** and the **King's Pool**, but at this point he encountered a large amount of debris, and the animal he was riding could go no farther. So instead of continuing on in the direction he had started, he turned and went through the Kidron Valley, inspecting what he could of the wall as he went along. Finally, he turned around and went back to his starting point at the Valley Gate. His plan remained a secret for now.

Help Wanted

NEHEMIAH 2:17–18 ***Then I said to them, "You see the distress that we are in, how Jerusalem lies waste, and its gates are burned with fire. Come and let us build the wall of Jerusalem, that we may no longer be a reproach." And I told them of the hand of my God which had been good upon me, and also of the king's words that he had spoken to me. So they said, "Let us rise up and build." Then they set their hands to this good work. (NKJV)***

Following his secret inspection of the wall, Nehemiah called many of the Jews together, reviewed some of the problems, and reminded them of the condition of the city, along with its broken-down wall and burned gates. He urged them to rebuild the wall of Jerusalem to restore the honor of God's people and get rid of the reproach of those around them. He also told them how God had blessed him and what King Artaxerxes had told him. This fired up the people and they started to work.

what others say

David C. Cook

In the books of Ezra and Nehemiah, the concept of "the hand of the Lord my God" (see Ezra 7:6, 28; 8:31) or "the gracious hand of my God" (see 7:9; 8:18, 22; Nehemiah 2:8, 18) explains the influencing force behind everything that happens. Emperors, nations, and the people of God are all tools in that gracious hand.[3]

Three Blind Men

NEHEMIAH 2:19–20 ***But when Sanballat the Horonite, Tobiah the Ammonite official, and Geshem the Arab heard of it, they laughed at us and despised us, and said, "What is this thing that*** *you are doing? Will you rebel against the king?" So I answered them, and said to them, "The God of heaven Himself will prosper us; therefore we His servants will arise and build, but you have no heritage or right or memorial in Jerusalem."* (NKJV)

rebellious
Ezra 4:12

Three of Israel's enemies, **Sanballat**, **Tobiah**, and **Geshem**, went to Jerusalem to mock and ridicule Nehemiah and those who were helping him. By this time everyone knew what the newly invigorated Jews were doing, but this misguided threesome pretended they didn't know. They even resurrected the old charge that the Jews were a rebellious people. Nehemiah responded by speaking of his faith in God. He informed this contemptible trio of hecklers that God was behind this project, the Jews would complete it, and he would not allow the non-Jews to have anything to do with Jerusalem.

Sanballat
probably the governor of Samaria

Tobiah
probably the governor of Ammon

Geshem
probably the chieftain of a group of Arab tribes

what others say

Charles R. Swindoll

Nehemiah knew that he and the people of Jerusalem were doing God's work, and he was not going to listen to anyone actively opposed to what he knew was right. And furthermore, he did not intend to associate with those who would seek to stop what was obviously of God. He was determined to allow no one but God to stop the work.[4]

No one likes to be ridiculed, and these unjustly scorned Jews were already a discouraged people. This pagan threesome knew ridicule had worked in the past, and they probably believed it would work again. They wanted Nehemiah and his helpers to throw up their hands and quit.

Chapter Wrap-Up

- When King Artaxerxes asked Nehemiah why he was so sad, Nehemiah said it was because Jerusalem was in ruins. Nehemiah then requested permission to go there to rebuild it.
- The king granted his request and gave him letters to obtain safe passage and permission to obtain lumber from the king's forest and a contingent of troops to protect him.
- Two men, Sanballat and Tobiah, were upset when they heard that Nehemiah was going to rebuild Jerusalem.
- Nehemiah took a few good men and made a night inspection of the broken-down walls and burned gates. There was so much rubble near the Fountain Gate and King's Pool that he had to turn around and return to his starting point.
- Nehemiah gathered the Jews, reminded them of the situation, pointed out that he had the help of God and the king, and got them to agree to begin rebuilding the city. Sanballat and Tobiah gained the help of Geshem and the three began to mock and ridicule the Jews.

Study Questions

1. In chapter 1 Nehemiah prayed that God would grant him favor with the king. Does chapter 2 indicate he believed God would give it?

2. Why was Nehemiah sad in the king's presence? Do you think the way he referred to Jerusalem was playing on the king's sympathies?

3. What did Nehemiah want the king to do to help him? What did the king do?

4. What do you think is the reason why he was so confident the walls would be rebuilt?

5. What are the indicators that opposition to this project is mounting?

Nehemiah 3
Construction Begins Again

Chapter Highlights:
- The Right Stuff
- An Enormous Project
- The Men of Tekoa

Let's Get Started

This chapter is primarily a list of those who had a zeal for God and rebuilt or repaired the wall of Jerusalem, its four towers and ten gates. About forty different work crews are mentioned, and they worked in a counter-clockwise direction on about forty-five sections of the wall. Interestingly, one group that did not work on the wall is also mentioned.

The Right Stuff

the big picture

Nehemiah 3:1–32

Those who worked on the wall included the high priest and his fellow priests (v. 1), the men of Jericho (v. 2), the sons of Hassenaah (v. 3), Meremoth, Meshullam son of Berechiah, and Zadok (v. 4), the men of Tekoa except their nobles (v. 5), Jehoiada and Meshullam son of Besodeiah (v. 6), men from Gibeon and Mizpah (v. 7), Uzziel and Hananiah the perfume-maker (v. 8), Rephaiah (v. 9), Jedaiah and Hattush (v. 10), Malchijah and Hashub (v. 11), Shallum (v. 12), Hanun of Zanoah (v. 13), Malchijah (v. 14), Nehemiah son of Azbuk (v. 16), the Levites and Hashabiah (v. 17), Bavai (v. 18), Ezer (v. 19), Baruch (v. 20), Meremoth (v. 21), priests in the area (v. 22), Benjamin, Hasshub, and Azariah (v. 23), Binnui (v. 24), Palal (v. 25), Pedaiah (v. 25), the temple servants (v. 25), the men of Tekoa (v. 27), more priests (v. 29), Zadok and Shemaiah (v. 29), Hananiah son of Shelemiah, Hanun son of Zalaph, and Meshullam (v. 30), Malchijah (v. 31), the goldsmiths and merchants (v. 32).

This was an enormous project. It involved building four towers (vv. 1, 11, 27) and ten gates (vv. 1, 3, 6, 13, 14, 15, 26, 28, 29, 31). Those who worked on it came from a wide variety of places that included Jericho, Tekoa, Jerusalem, Zanoah, Beth Haccerem, Mizpah, and Keilah (vv. 2, 5, 13, 14, 15, 17). They came from differing professions, such as, priests, Levites, goldsmiths, and perfume-makers (vv. 1, 8, 17). The work crew included both men and women (v. 12).

works
Revelation 2:2

nobles
Nehemiah 3:5

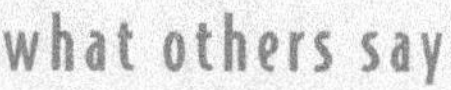

David Hocking

> Are we doing the work of the Lord and are we finishing the work that God gives us to do? Won't it be sweet to stand before the Lord and hear Him say, "Well done, thou good and faithful servant. Enter thou into the joy of the Lord"?[1]

something to ponder

Jesus often said, "I know your works," and here it's recorded that the men of Tekoa worked on the wall, "but their nobles did not put their shoulders to the work of their Lord" (Nehemiah 3:5 NKJV). There are always people who refuse to do God's work, and he knows who they are. Christians should not want it to be permanently recorded in God's books that they wouldn't do his work.

Chapter Wrap-Up

- Nehemiah enlisted the help of many different types of people. He divided them into work crews and appointed each crew to work on a different section of the wall. Some crews worked on more than one section, and some sections contained gates and towers.

Study Questions

1. What indications do we have that the Jews were unified as a people?
2. Did each group repair just one section of the wall?

Nehemiah 4
External Opposition

Chapter Highlights:
- Ridicule and Prayer
- Plots and Prayer
- Threats, Fear, and Divine Help
- Work and Weapons

Let's Get Started

Israel's enemies have already tried to stop the work on the wall by mocking and ridiculing the Jews, but their verbal abuse did not have the impact they were hoping for. This chapter begins with another attempt to use evil speaking to stop the process. When this verbal intimidation failed a second time, the situation grew more serious. Many Jews were afraid and discouraged, but Nehemiah was in touch with God and he knew exactly how to deal with it.

mocking and ridiculing
Nehemiah 2:19

feeble
not strong enough to do the job

He Was More Than Angry

NEHEMIAH **4:1–3** ***But it so happened, when Sanballat heard that we were rebuilding the wall, that he was furious and very indignant, and mocked the Jews. And he spoke before his brethren and the army of Samaria, and said, "What are these feeble Jews doing? Will they fortify themselves? Will they offer sacrifices? Will they complete it in a day? Will they revive the stones from the heaps of rubbish—stones that are burned?" Now Tobiah the Ammonite was beside him, and he said, "Whatever they build, if even a fox goes up on it, he will break down their stone wall."*** *(NKJV)*

Sanballat was furious, outwardly mean, and even cruel when he heard the Jews were rebuilding the wall. He returned to his old failed tactic of verbal harassment to try to stop it. He wanted others to join him, so he ridiculed the Jews in public in front of his associates and some of his puppet troops. He accused the Jews of being too **feeble** to undertake such an impossible task. By asking if the Jews would restore the wall, he was inferring that they would not be able to do it. By asking if they would offer sacrifices, he was suggesting that there was something wrong with that and it should not be done. By asking if they would finish in a day, he was suggesting that it would take too long and they would quit before they had finished. By asking if they could bring the stones back to life from those

love
Matthew 5:44

heaps of rubble, he was suggesting that they didn't have adequate building materials. Tobiah suggested that even a small animal could knock down any flimsy wall that these misguided people could build.

Prayer Changes Things

> **Nehemiah 4:4–6** ***Hear, O our God, for we are despised; turn their reproach on their own heads, and give them as plunder to a land of captivity! Do not cover their iniquity, and do not let their sin be blotted out from before You; for they have provoked You to anger before the builders. So we built the wall, and the entire wall was joined together up to half its height, for the people had a mind to work.*** *(NKJV)*

Nehemiah responded to this barrage of criticism with a salvo of prayer. His conversation with God is unusual because he asked God to let Israel's enemies reap what they were sowing. He even asked God to not forgive and not forget their sins and to thwart what they were doing. Then he quit praying, got up, and went back to work.

The ridicule did not work. Instead, it stimulated Nehemiah and his helpers to work even harder. They had a compelling reason to get the job done, so they worked as hard as they could until the wall was completed to half of its planned height.

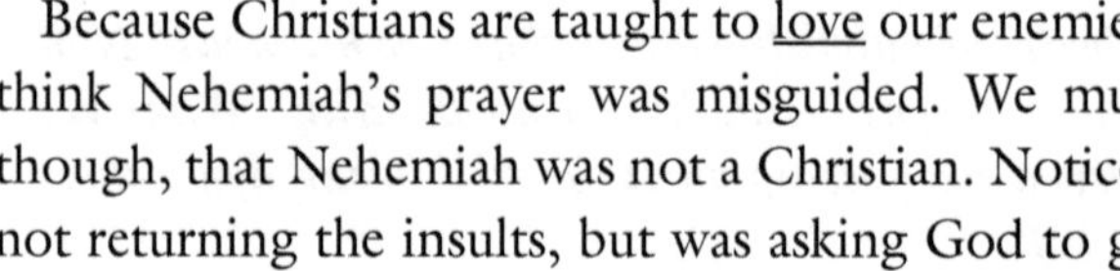

Because Christians are taught to love our enemies, some of us may think Nehemiah's prayer was misguided. We must keep in mind, though, that Nehemiah was not a Christian. Notice, too, that he was not returning the insults, but was asking God to get involved.

Words Are Not Enough

> **Nehemiah 4:7–9** ***Now it happened, when Sanballat, Tobiah, the Arabs, the Ammonites, and the Ashdodites heard that the walls of Jerusalem were being restored and the gaps were beginning to be closed, that they became very angry, and all of them conspired together to come and attack Jerusalem and create confusion. Nevertheless we made our prayer to our God, and because of them we set a watch against them day and night.*** *(NKJV)*

Word that the Jews were making steady progress and the walls were being closed up infuriated Israel's enemies. They could tell it was going to take more than verbal abuse to stop this monumental project. In response, Israel's enemies united and conspired to attack Jerusalem. They didn't want to capture the city. They just wanted to stir up opposition, discredit the project, to give King Artaxerxes reports of turmoil, deceive him into thinking he had made a mistake when he authorized the project, and persuade him to revoke his permission for Nehemiah to rebuild the city. Nehemiah got word of what they were doing and responded in two ways: first, he prayed; and second, he took precautions and posted guards day and night.

King
Nehemiah 2:1–6

what others say

Robert Martin Walker

Prayer connects us with what God is already doing in our life. Through prayer we cooperate with God's loving actions on our behalf and on behalf of others. We need not use flowery phrases to persuade God to help us. Neither do we need to pile on huge amounts of words to convince God to hear our prayers.[1]

Discouraged and Afraid

NEHEMIAH 4:10–12 *Then Judah said, "The strength of the laborers is failing, and there is so much rubbish that we are not able to build the wall." And our adversaries said, "They will neither know nor see anything, till we come into their midst and kill them and cause the work to cease." So it was, when the Jews who dwelt near them came, that they told us ten times, "From whatever place you turn, they will be upon us."* (NKJV)

The unrelenting tactics of Israel's enemies did not go unnoticed. Apprehension and low morale prevailed among the Jews because rumors were circulating that their enemies were planning a surprise attack to kill them and put an end to this project once and for all. Also, the Jews who lived in the area just outside the wall were repeatedly coming in with reports of an imminent attack. Along with all this, the task of moving all the rubble from the old wall was overwhelming them.

what others say

Don Fields

"Sticks and stones may break my bones, but names will never hurt me" We usually hear children saying this. But when we

fear
Romans 8:15

want to oppose something because it is getting in our way, we adults have a slightly more sophisticated way of doing the same thing. The enemies of Israel started out at the "sticks and stones" level, but they were soon into slander, intimidation and threatening with weapons.[2]

Get Your Sword

NEHEMIAH 4:13–16 *Therefore I positioned men behind the lower parts of the wall, at the openings; and I set the people according to their families, with their swords, their spears, and their bows. And I looked, and arose and said to the nobles, to the leaders, and to the rest of the people, "Do not be afraid of them. Remember the Lord, great and awesome, and fight for your brethren, your sons, your daughters, your wives, and your houses." And it happened, when our enemies heard that it was known to us, and that God had brought their plot to nothing, that all of us returned to the wall, everyone to his work. So it was, from that time on, that half of my servants worked at construction, while the other half held the spears, the shields, the bows, and wore armor; and the leaders were behind all the house of Judah. (NKJV)*

Nehemiah took the death threats seriously and responded with countermeasures. He examined the wall and determined where he thought the most likely points of attack were. He identified the lowest points in the vulnerable places. He brought each worker's family inside the wall so he wouldn't have to worry about what was happening to his wife and children. He posted half his men as guards near these families and made sure they were all well armed. He gathered the other half of the men together to encourage them to continue the work without fear while recognizing the power of God and the need to defend their families and homes. This discouraged Israel's enemies and they withdrew. When the threat was over, the morale of the Jews soared and they were able to turn their focus back to their work.

what others say

David Hocking

The next time you get discouraged and feel like you can't cope with anything more, life seems too tragic to face, then *Remember the Lord.* The Bible says *"God has not given us a spirit of fear, but of power and of love and of a sound mind."*

mind." When you have your mind focused on the Lord, it doesn't matter what is happening around you, you can have peace and stability.[3]

Be Prepared

NEHEMIAH 4:17–20 ***Those who built on the wall, and those who carried burdens, loaded themselves so that with one hand they worked at construction, and with the other held a weapon. Every one of the builders had his sword girded at his side as he built. And the one who sounded the trumpet was beside me. Then I said to the nobles, the rulers, and the rest of the people, "The work is great and extensive, and we are separated far from one another on the wall. Wherever you hear the sound of the trumpet, rally to us there. Our God will fight for us."*** *(NKJV)*

Nehemiah decided that he wouldn't take any chances. From that day on he took measures to protect his people. He spread them out around the wall. Half worked while the other half were armed and ready to fight. The military leaders were posted behind the workers so they would be in position to defend them. Those who carried building supplies worked with one hand and carried a weapon in the other so they would be ready to fight on a moment's notice. The builders needed both hands to do their work, so they strapped their weapons to their side. Nehemiah stood watch with a trumpeter at his side so he could sound an alarm if there were a surprise attack. He told everyone they were expected to move to battle if the alarm was sounded. He also reminded the people that God would be on their side to encourage them.

what others say

Jack W. Hayford with Joseph Snider

Nehemiah's direction and equipping of the Jerusalemites for resistance and victory displays timeless principles: (a) The enemy is real, not imaginary; (b) the battle is crucial; defeat or victory is at stake; (c) victory is certain when God's people draw on His resources.[4]

They Needed a Bath

NEHEMIAH 4:21–23 *So we labored in the work, and half of the men held the spears from daybreak until the stars appeared. At the same time I also said to the people, "Let each man and his servant stay at night in Jerusalem, that they may be our guard by night and a working party by day." So neither I, my brethren, my servants, nor the men of the guard who followed me took off our clothes, except that everyone took them off for washing. (NKJV)*

The work continued with half the people armed and half the people working from the first rays of the sun until the stars were visible at night. Those who came from outside the city were asked to spend the night at the work site rather than going home, so they would be available as night guards and not lose valuable work time. Nehemiah excluded no one, including himself. Everyone kept their clothes on day and night and even kept their weapons with them when they went for a drink of water.

Chapter Wrap-Up

- When Israel's enemies heard that the wall was going up, they were very angry. They used ridicule and insults as means to stop the project, but Nehemiah prayed and the work continued.
- When the work continued Israel's enemies became more angry and desperate. They plotted to attack the Jews and use this unrest to try to persuade King Artaxerxes to stop the work, but Nehemiah prayed again and the work continued.
- The hard work was making the Jews tired, and the increasing threat of attack was making them afraid. Nehemiah's response was to post guards, encourage the people, remind them God was on their side, and urge them to fight. The result was that the Jews returned to work.
- At this point, half the Jews worked and half remained armed. A trumpeter was appointed to sound an alarm in the event of attack. People worked long hours, spent the night at the work site, and wore their clothes day and night.

Study Questions

1. What tactics did Israel's enemies use to stop the work?
2. How much of the wall was completed when Israel's enemies plotted to fight against the Jews? What was the first thing the Jews did to counteract this attack?
3. What were some of the things Nehemiah did to protect his workers?
4. In addition to the ridicule and threats, what other things discouraged the Jews and made them afraid?
5. Why did the Jews need a trumpeter? Who was going to fight for them?

Nehemiah 5 Internal Problems

Chapter Highlights:
- Complaints About the Rich
- Stop It
- The Rich Agree
- Nehemiah Sets the Example

Let's Get Started

Chapter 4 documents some of the external problems caused by Israel's enemies. That was just a partial report. More is revealed in chapter 6. But here in chapter 5, Nehemiah turned to the internal problems. He discussed how some of the rich and powerful Jews were mistreating those who had very little.

enemies
Nehemiah 4:11–12

night
Nehemiah 4:22

what others say

J. Vernon McGee

Now we see opposition coming from within. This is where the Devil strikes his greatest blow. In the history of the church we have seen that when the Devil could not destroy the church by persecution, the next thing he did was to join it! The devil had already caused discouragement among the Jews, and now he goes a step farther and causes conflict.[1]

The Bills Keep Coming

NEHEMIAH 5:1–5 *And there was a great outcry of the people and their wives against their Jewish brethren. For there were those who said, "We, our sons, and our daughters are many; therefore let us get grain, that we may eat and live." There were also some who said, "We have mortgaged our lands and vineyards and houses, that we might buy grain because of the famine." There were also those who said, "We have borrowed money for the king's tax on our lands and vineyards. Yet now our flesh is as the flesh of our brethren, our children as their children; and indeed we are forcing our sons and our daughters to be slaves, and some of our daughters have been brought into slavery. It is not in our power to redeem them, for other men have our lands and vineyards." (NKJV)*

The threat by Israel's enemies to attack and kill the Jews caused Nehemiah to ask the Jews to stay inside the city at night. But not being able to go home for several weeks caused a great hardship on many of the workers. Some of the people owed money, or had very little food stored up, and were stationed at the wall where they were not gathering their crops, caring for their animals, or earning money in other ways. A famine was also causing problems. Some poor Jews who had large families complained that family members would die if they didn't provide food for them. Others complained that they now had to mortgage their land, crops, and homes to buy food. They were even borrowing money to pay the king's taxes. They loved their children and believed their children were as valuable as those of the rich Jews, but their children were being sold into slavery and the workers had no remedy for their poverty. The hunger, poverty, high taxes, high interest, and even greed in some cases sparked an outcry for help.

what others say

Charles R. Swindoll

Opposition wasn't limited to the outside. Inside the walls, strife threatened to divide the Jewish community. In order to survive, many Jews had to borrow money from their fellow countrymen. Those loaning the money were apparently charging excessive interests, making it necessary for the borrowers to sell their homes and businesses, even sell their sons and daughters into slavery.[2]

It Made Me Mad

NEHEMIAH 5:6–11 ***And I became very angry when I heard their outcry and these words. After serious thought, I rebuked the nobles and rulers, and said to them, "Each of you is exacting usury from his brother." So I called a great assembly against them. And I said to them, "According to our ability we have redeemed our Jewish brethren who were sold to the nations. Now indeed, will you even sell your brethren? Or should they be sold to us?" Then they were silenced and found nothing to say. Then I said, "What you are doing is not good. Should you not walk in the fear of our God because of the reproach of the nations, our enemies? I also, with my brethren and my servants, am lending them money and grain. Please, let us stop this usury! Restore now to them, even this day, their lands, their vineyards, their olive groves, and their houses, also a hundredth of the money and the grain, the new wine and the oil, that you have charged them." (NKJV)***

Nehemiah was more than a little angry when he heard these terrible charges, but he decided to wait and think things through before he responded. After a period of serious reflection, he approached the wealthy Jews and accused them of exacting **usury** and doing harm to their fellow countrymen. His strong face-to-face rebuke of their evil conduct must have fell on deaf ears because they didn't do anything differently. In response to their inaction, he assembled a great number of Jews to confront them publicly. He noted that many Jews had bought some of their countrymen out of slavery, but now the rich had caused them to be sold back into slavery again. He accused these rich men of selling fellow Jews into slavery because they knew other Jews would buy them back. Apparently, these wealthy men knew this charge was true because they sat speechless. Not satisfied with their silence, Nehemiah asked them why they didn't respect God and try to avoid the **reproach** of the Gentiles. He informed the rich that many Jews were lending money and food to the poor without selling them into slavery for lack of repayment. He told the rich Jews to stop charging excessive interest, to return the property they had seized, and to refund the interest they had charged.

interest
Exodus 22:25; Leviticus 25:36–37

money changers
Matthew 21:12–13

anger
Mark 3:1–5

usury
excessive interest

reproach
ridicule

Some think it is a sin to get angry, but that is not what the Scriptures teach. Jesus got angry with the Temple money changers. He accused them of turning the house of prayer into a den of robbers. He displayed anger with those Jews who accused him of doing wrong when he healed a man on the Sabbath. Even today, God sometimes inspires his people to be angry about injustice or actions by people who claim to serve him but are actually doing things that dishonor him and thwart his plans. This anger is what sometimes inspires God's people to take steps to reverse injustice or deter evil.

You Win

NEHEMIAH 5:12–13 ***So they said, "We will restore it, and will require nothing from them; we will do as you say." Then I called the priests, and required an oath from them that they would do according to this promise. Then I shook out the fold of my garment and said, "So may God shake out each man from his house, and from his property, who does not perform this promise. Even thus may he be shaken out and emptied." And all the assembly said, "Amen!" and praised the LORD. Then the people did according to this promise.*** *(NKJV)*

interest
Deuteronomy 23:19–20

folds
the equivalent of our pockets

Nehemiah prevailed. The rich Jews agreed to return the money and property. They also agreed to not charge interest and to not make other future demands of the needy Jews. But Nehemiah did not take their word for this. While he had these moneylenders there, he summoned the priests and required the wealthy to take an oath to keep their promises. Nehemiah was still skeptical, however, so he shook out the **folds** of his robe to symbolize what he wanted God to do to them if they broke their word. He symbolically called upon God to not number them among his people and to empty their pockets if they went back on their promises. The entire assembly confirmed this by saying, "Amen." Everyone praised God and the wealthy kept their promises.

Nehemiah's Government

Nehemiah 5:14–19 ***Moreover, from the time that I was appointed to be their governor in the land of Judah, from the twentieth year until the thirty-second year of King Artaxerxes, twelve years, neither I nor my brothers ate the governor's provisions. But the former governors who were before me laid burdens on the people, and took from them bread and wine, besides forty shekels of silver. Yes, even their servants bore rule over the people, but I did not do so, because of the fear of God. Indeed, I also continued the work on this wall, and we did not buy any land. All my servants were gathered there for the work. And at my table were one hundred and fifty Jews and rulers, besides those who came to us from the nations around us. Now that which was prepared daily was one ox and six choice sheep. Also fowl were prepared for me, and once every ten days an abundance of all kinds of wine. Yet in spite of this I did not demand the governor's provisions, because the bondage was heavy on this people. Remember me, my God, for good, according to all that I have done for this people.*** *(NKJV)*

Having revealed the internal problems among the Jews, Nehemiah stated that it was in the twentieth year of the king's reign that Artaxerxes appointed him governor of Judah. This was a position he held for twelve years. As governor, Nehemiah was entitled to food, wages from taxes, an expense account, and other benefits. But because he was mindful of the hardship of his people, he chose not to accept the entitlements. Along with this, even though large payments were required by those who had ruled before him,

Nehemiah's respect for God and compassion for his people motivated Nehemiah to refuse to pay them or those who had assisted them during their rule. Nehemiah and his men were committed to rebuilding the wall but not to acquiring the possessions of others. Out of his own pocket he regularly fed those who served his government and also paid for the entertainment of many guests from other areas. This required a significant amount of food every day, but Nehemiah personally contributed to the effort rather than exploiting it.

give account
Romans 14:12

seen
Matthew 6:1

"Each of us shall give account of himself to God" (NKJV). Some people do good works for personal gain, some do good works to be seen of men, and others do good works to honor God. Love for God and compassion for his people should be what motivates us to do good works.

Chapter Wrap-Up

- Internal problems over money almost stopped the work on the wall. Famine forced some Jews to mortgage their farms, crops, and houses to obtain money for food. Taxes collected for King Artaxerxes also caused a burden, and excessive interest charged by affluent Jews forced some impoverished people to sell their children into slavery.
- After thinking this over, an angry Nehemiah accused the affluent Jews of charging usury. He assembled a large number of Jews together and accused the affluent Jews of selling their countrymen into slavery. He said the affluent Jews were wrong and should respect God, stop charging usury, return the seized property, and return the interest they had collected.
- The affluent Jews agreed to return the seized property and the interest they had charged. Nehemiah required them to take an oath before the priests. He emptied his pockets and called on God to empty theirs and shake them out of his kingdom if they broke their oath. Everyone agreed, and the affluent Jews kept their promises.
- Nehemiah became governor and served for twelve years. He tried to help the Jews by not taking his food and money allotments. He devoted himself to rebuilding the wall and did not try to financially profit from the endeavor. He was moved by his desire for God's favor and his compassion for people in need.

Study Questions

1. Identify three internal problems that threatened to stop the work on the wall.
2. Who was causing these internal problems and for what reason?
3. What did Nehemiah tell the affluent Jews to do? Did they agree to do it?
4. In your opinion, why did Nehemiah require the affluent Jews to take an oath after they had already agreed to do what he had asked? Who administered the oath?
5. How long did Nehemiah rule? What were some of the things he did to help his people?

Nehemiah 6
Construction Completed

Chapter Highlights:
- Deceit
- False Accusations
- Intimidation
- Construction Completed
- Betrayal

Let's Get Started

In chapter 4, Nehemiah wrote about external opposition and in chapter 5, he wrote about internal problems. It would seem that all the opposition and problems within the new community had been dealt with, but this was not so. Chapter 6 shows that the external opposition was relentless. In fact, it turned personal for Nehemiah when Israel's enemies decided to focus their attention on him. They refused to accept failure and seemed to believe they could still stop God's work by killing, embarrassing, or shaming Nehemiah.

what others say

Irving L. Jensen

Scorn and military conspiracy were the two strategies of the enemy in chapter 4. Now the strategy was trickery with intent to murder Nehemiah. As you study these verses, observe especially Nehemiah's alertness to the enemies' devices and his complete trust in God.[1]

A Dangerous Invitation

NEHEMIAH 6:1–5 ***Now it happened when Sanballat, Tobiah, Geshem the Arab, and the rest of our enemies heard that I had rebuilt the wall, and that there were no breaks left in it (though at that time I had not hung the doors in the gates), that Sanballat and Geshem sent to me, saying, "Come, let us meet together among the villages in the plain of Ono." But they thought to do me harm. So I sent messengers to them, saying, "I am doing a great work, so that I cannot come down. Why should the work cease while I leave it and go down to you?" But they sent me this message four times, and I answered them in the same manner. Then Sanballat sent his servant to me as before, the fifth time, with an open letter in his hand.*** *(NKJV)*

When Israel's enemies learned that the wall was near completion (everything had been rebuilt except the gates), they invited

Geshem
Nehemiah 2:19

plain of Ono
an area about 25 miles northwest of Jerusalem

spiritual warfare
evil instigated by Satan

Geshem
an Arab leader

Nehemiah to meet with them in one of the villages on the **plain of Ono**. Nehemiah sensed that this was a scheme to distract him, stop the work, lure him out of the city, and perhaps physically harm him. Installing the gates probably could have gone on without him, but he sent messengers with the excuse that his work was too important for him to leave. His enemies wouldn't take no for an answer, so they repeated the same desperate invitation four times. Nehemiah responded to them in the same polite way each time. The fifth time Sanballat sent one of his assistants to Nehemiah with the same invitation, but this time he included an unsealed letter. Leaving the letter unsealed means that it wasn't a private message. Sanballat was actually counting on a gossip reading it and spreading the word about what it said.

what others say

Jack W. Hayford

These verses set forth the craftiness of satanic forces in their attempt to derail God's purpose and plan by attacking the leader. When engaged in **spiritual warfare**, we should recognize that man is not the enemy. Nehemiah recognized this fact and chose not to become embroiled in the battle with flesh and blood.[2]

A Poison-Pen Letter

NEHEMIAH 6:6–9 ***In it was written: It is reported among the nations, and Geshem says, that you and the Jews plan to rebel; therefore, according to these rumors, you are rebuilding the wall, that you may be their king. And you have also appointed prophets to proclaim concerning you at Jerusalem, saying, "There is a king in Judah!" Now these matters will be reported to the king. So come, therefore, and let us consult together. Then I sent to him, saying, "No such things as you say are being done, but you invent them in your own heart." For they all were trying to make us afraid, saying, "Their hands will be weakened in the work, and it will not be done." Now therefore, O God, strengthen my hands.*** *(NKJV)*

Sanballat's unsealed letter charged that people were saying Israel was rebuilding the wall around Jerusalem because the Jews were planning to revolt against King Artaxerxes. It stated that **Geshem** had checked out these reports and confirmed that they were true. It also said there were reports that Nehemiah was planning to make himself the new king of Israel and that he had selected some prophets to proclaim him as their king. Sanballat also tried to intimidate Nehemiah by suggesting that King Artaxerxes would hear these reports and be very angry. He invited Nehemiah to meet with him again. Nehemiah replied that the charges were false and Sanballat was imagining things. He believed Sanballat hoped to weaken the Jews with a scare tactic and cause them to slow or stop the work. Nehemiah prayed that God would strengthen the Jews instead.

rebellious
Ezra 4:12–24

what others say

W. Herschel Ford

> Before prayer we can do little—after prayer we can do much. Much effort without prayer often results in failure—the same effort with prayer may result in great success. We are living in a busy age, are always in a hurry, and are cumbered with much serving. Does it help to take time to pray? Yes, indeed. Many great things happen when God's people call upon Him.[3]

The charge that Jerusalem was a rebellious and wicked city was an old charge. It had been used to successfully stop the work on the wall once before. It is not surprising that Israel's enemies tried it again. They were grasping for an easy tactic they thought would hinder the work. Nehemiah realized that they were trying to weaken him, so he prayed that God would strengthen him.

Get Him to Sin

Nehemiah 6:10–14 ***Afterward I came to the house of Shemaiah the son of Delaiah, the son of Mehetabel, who was a secret informer; and he said, "Let us meet together in the house of God, within the temple, and let us close the doors of the temple, for they are coming to kill you; indeed, at night they will come to kill you." And I said, "Should such a man as I flee? And who is there such as I who would go into the temple to save his life? I will not go in!" Then I perceived that God had not sent him at all, but that he pronounced this prophecy against me because Tobiah and Sanballat had hired him. For this reason he was hired, that I should be afraid and act that way and sin, so that they might have cause for an evil report, that they might***

prophesied
predicted

discerned
recognized or perceived

hireling
paid by them

Noadiah
a prophetess, female prophet

reproach me. My God, remember Tobiah and Sanballat, according to these their works, and the prophetess Noadiah and the rest of the prophets who would have made me afraid. *(NKJV)*

On one occasion Nehemiah visited a priest named Shemaiah in his house. Shemaiah pretended to be Nehemiah's friend and **prophesied** that the two should meet at the Temple and lock themselves inside because men were plotting to find Nehemiah at night to kill him. Nehemiah **discerned** that Shemaiah was a false prophet because he did not believe God would want him to be afraid or to run from his enemies. He also knew that it was a violation of the Law for him, a non-priest, to lock himself inside the Temple. He deduced that Shemaiah was a **hireling** of Tobiah and Sanballat, and that this was a crafty plot to make him sin so he would lose credibility with the Jews. He prayed that God would not forget the opposition of Tobiah, Sanballat, **Noadiah**, and others.

what others say

Kay Arthur, David Lawson, and Bob Vereen

Shemaiah was one of the priests, and for whatever reason he was shut up at home. When Nehemiah came to visit him, Shemaiah said that Nehemiah's life was in danger. The solution Shemaiah presented to Nehemiah was for them to hide themselves within the temple. As a layman, Nehemiah was not allowed in the temple.[4]

W. Herschel Ford

Prayer helps us to overcome temptation . . . The Bible gives us a guarantee of overcoming power. "There hath no temptation taken you but such as is common to man: but God is faithful, who will not suffer you to be tempted above that ye are able; but will with the temptation also make a way to escape, that ye may be able to bear it" (1 Corinthians 10:13).[5]

Many people in the church today either prophesy over people or think being prophesied over is exciting and intriguing. In the case of Shemaiah and Ezra, a priest was prophesying over one of God's laymen. This priest, however, was a false prophet with an evil agenda. Not everyone who claims to be a prophet is a spokesperson for God. The Bible speaks of false prophets in sheep's clothing who inwardly are like ravenous wolves, and also of an end-time False Prophet who will be satanically inspired. The lesson to be learned is that one must be cautious in this area.

God Wins

NEHEMIAH 6:15–16 ***So the wall was finished on the twenty-fifth day of Elul, in fifty-two days. And it happened, when all our enemies heard of it, and all the nations around us saw these things, that they were very disheartened in their own eyes; for they perceived that this work was done by our God.*** (NKJV)

God's plan was not thwarted; his enemies did not stop the fulfillment of the work that he had set in motion. The massive wall was completed in just fifty-two days, on the twenty-fifth day of **Elul**. Word of this remarkable feat demoralized Israel's enemies because they realized that this great project could not have been finished so quickly without divine help. They were also afraid and lacking in confidence because they now knew that their opposition to this project was really in opposition to God's will.

Arah
Ezra 2:5; Nehemiah 7:10

Meshullam
Nehemiah 3:4

Berechiah
Nehemiah 3:4, 30

Elul
our August/September

breaches
openings or gaps

what others say

John Danielson

Critics have claimed fifty-two days were not enough time to do God's work. They overlook the fact that Nehemiah had thousands of zealous workers on the job. They repaired the **breaches**—they joined sections of wall left standing. Their spiritual motivation was that God was with them.[6]

Misguided Jews

NEHEMIAH 6:17–19 ***Also in those days the nobles of Judah sent many letters to Tobiah, and the letters of Tobiah came to them. For many in Judah were pledged to him, because he was the son-in-law of Shechaniah the son of Arah, and his son Jehohanan had married the daughter of Meshullam the son of Berechiah. Also they reported his good deeds before me, and reported my words to him. Tobiah sent letters to frighten me.*** (NKJV)

This chapter concludes with another example of the opposition Nehemiah faced. During the time when the wall was still being rebuilt, some Jewish leaders were corresponding with Tobiah. They had agreed to provide him with information about the construction of the wall because they were related to him by marriage through Shechaniah, son of Arah, and his son Jehohanan, who married the daughter of Meshullam, a descendant of Berechiah. These in-laws were trying to foster good relations between Tobiah and Nehemiah, but there was no reconciliation because Tobiah was using the information to try to intimidate Nehemiah into stopping the work.

Chapter Wrap-Up

- When Israel's enemies learned that the wall was complete except for the gates, they tried to lure Nehemiah to the Plain of Ono. Because Nehemiah knew they wanted to harm him, he made excuses and refused to go. Those who were trying to lure him out of Jerusalem repeated their invitation four times and then on the fifth occasion Sanballat sent Nehemiah an unsealed letter.
- Sanballat's letter was a design to spread a false rumor that the Jews were planning to rebel, Nehemiah was planning to be crowned king, and Nehemiah had named prophets to proclaim him as king. Sanballat said he wanted to talk to Nehemiah because the king would hear this rumor, but Nehemiah denied the rumor and accused Sanballat of imagining things. He believed this was a scare tactic to slow or stop the work. He prayed for God to strengthen the workers.
- At his own house Shemaiah prophesied that Nehemiah should meet him in the Temple to hide from those who wanted to kill him. Nehemiah believed it was wrong for a man who trusted God to run. He also believed that it was a sin for a layman to defile the Temple by entering it. Nehemiah concluded that Shemaiah was a false prophet who was paid by Israel's enemies to discredit him. Nehemiah prayed that God would remember what his enemies had done.
- When the wall was completed in just fifty-two days, Israel's enemies became afraid because they realized that Israel's God had helped his people.
- One continuing problem was the fact that some Jews working on the wall were related by marriage to Tobiah. They gave him regular reports on their progress. They did this because they had promised him they would do so and they believed he would settle his differences with Nehemiah. Instead of making peace with Nehemiah, he used the information to intimidate him.

Study Questions

1. What invitation did Sanballat and Geshem give to Nehemiah? Did he accept? Why?

2. What was the rumor in Sanballat's letter? Was it true? How did Nehemiah respond?

3. What did Tobiah and Sanballat hire Shemaiah to do? What made Nehemiah think Shemaiah was a false prophet?

4. How long did it take to rebuild the wall? What did Israel's enemies think was the reason why the wall was completed so fast? What effect did this belief have on them?

5. How was Tobiah getting progress reports on the wall construction? What was he doing with the information?

Introduction—Nehemiah 7–13 God's Word Takes Hold

The wall around Jerusalem was finished in record time, but Nehemiah knew that his job was not over. He was not ready to go back to Babylon. He still needed to take precautions against a surprise attack, and the time he had spent in Jerusalem revealed that the people knew very little about the precious Word of God. Knowing this, Nehemiah appointed leaders to protect the city and began to teach the Law of Moses. The power of the Word started influencing their hearts, and the newly enlightened people started changing their ways. Even greater progress was in store for the new nation.

finished
Nehemiah 6:15

Nehemiah 7
The Third Census

Chapter Highlights:
- Security and City Dwellers Wanted
- Check the Census
- Guarding the Gate
- Proving the Genealogy

Let's Get Started

This chapter opens with a reminder that the wall construction around Jerusalem was complete. It goes on to document several steps that were taken to protect the Holy City from Israel's enemies in the future. The wall provided badly needed protection, but Israel was still surrounded by determined enemies and it would be a mistake to become careless. Nehemiah wanted the city to remain, grow, and prosper.

wall
Nehemiah 6:15

gates
Nehemiah 3:1–32

gatekeepers
Ezra 2:42

singers
Ezra 2:41

Levites
Ezra 2:40

Hanani
Nehemiah 1:2

God-fearing
one who respects God

Security and City Dwellers Wanted

the big picture

Nehemiah 7:1–73

Following the completion of the wall and gates, Nehemiah appointed gatekeepers, singers, and Levites to guard the gates (v. 1). He put two men in charge of Jerusalem's security, instructed them on when the gates should be open, and told them to appoint guards (vv. 2–3). Then because the population of Jerusalem was so small, he used the list of exiles compiled by Ezra to identify a group of Jews who could qualify to live in the city (vv. 4–73).

After the wall and gates were completed, Nehemiah turned his attention to the security and population of the city. The Temple gatekeepers, singers, and Levites were appointed to guard the gates. Nehemiah's brother Hanani, known for his bravery and faithfulness, and Hananiah, known as the **God-fearing** commander of the palace guard, were appointed to take command of the guards. Nehemiah instructed them to keep the massive gates closed and barred until the morning sun was high in the sky. He also told them to station some of the residents of Jerusalem along strategic places on the wall and to have others who lived near the wall to use their homes for defensive purposes. Because there was a lot of open space inside the city and not many homes, Nehemiah assembled the Jews to compile a list

list
Ezra 7:6–73

of people to build houses and live in Jerusalem. He used the list of Exiles compiled by Ezra to identify those who could prove their genealogy. Those who could not trace their ancestry were not allowed to build in Jerusalem. He said, "God put it into my heart" (Nehemiah 7:5 NKJV) to do this. He was purposely establishing Jerusalem as a city committed to Jehovah.

what others say

Warren W. Wiersbe

A city is much more than walls, gates, and houses; a city is people. In the first half of this book, the people existed for the walls; but now the walls must exist for the people. It was time to organize the community so that the citizens could enjoy the quality of life God wanted them to have. God had great things in store for Jerusalem, for one day His Son would walk the city streets, teach in the temple, and die outside the city walls.[1]

Knute Larson and Kathy Dahlen

Many people start reading the Bible, but then stop when they come upon similar records of names or family descendants. They seem boring. We often want to skip ahead to the action. But these lists are important. They demonstrate that God not only watches history but that he guards his people and protects his community . . . He knows what we do, even "in secret," out of the spotlight of world attention away from the crowd.[2]

Minor differences exist between the list of exiles found in Ezra chapter 2 and the list that appears in this chapter. Critics say these differences are errors in the Bible. Believers say these differences can be explained and there are no errors. Whatever the explanation, one should remember that the Scriptures are inspired by God and he does not make errors.

Chapter Wrap-Up

- Walls and gates were not enough to protect the city from Israel's enemies, so Nehemiah appointed the gatekeepers, singers, and Levites to serve as guards. He designated Hanani and Hananiah to command them and to be responsible for the security of the city. He made arrangements to keep the gates closed and barred, except for during the brightest part of the day. He also had guards posted at certain places on the wall and stationed residents on the wall near their own homes.
- Because Nehemiah believed the city would be more secure if more people lived inside the walls, he assembled the Jews and used Ezra's census to recruit people to relocate there. Those who could not prove their genealogy were not allowed to do this.

Study Questions

1. What three groups of people did Nehemiah appoint to guard the gates to the city? Did he name to command these three groups? What special instructions did he give about the gates?
2. What were the qualifications of Hanani and Hananiah?
3. Other than the guards at the gates, what security arrangements did Nehemiah make to protect the city?
4. Why did Nehemiah want more Jews to move to Jerusalem? What did he use to determine who could relocate there? What did they have to prove?

Nehemiah 8
Ezra Reads the Law

Chapter Highlights:
- **Reading the Law**
- **The Law Explained**
- **The People's Response**
- **The Feast of Booths**

Let's Get Started

The first great event in the reestablishment of Israel came when Cyrus issued the decree to let the Jews return to the land. The second great event came when a group of returnees rebuilt the Temple. The third great event came when the wall around Jerusalem was completed. This chapter is about a fourth great event: a return to the Law of Moses. This was the beginning of another revival led by Ezra the scribe and priest.

go to

Cyrus
Ezra 1:2–4

Temple
Ezra 3:7–13; 6:13–18

wall
Nehemiah 6:15–16

scribe
Ezra 7:6, 11, 21

Water Gate
Nehemiah 3:26

Ezra
Ezra 7:8

book
scroll

Law
all the rules God gave to Moses

Moses
a great Jewish leader

All the People

NEHEMIAH **8:1** ***Now all the people gathered together as one man in the open square that was in front of the Water Gate; and they told Ezra the scribe to bring the Book of the Law of Moses, which the LORD had commanded Israel.*** (NKJV)

The Jews gathered with one purpose in the square in front of the Water Gate. Nothing is said about how many assembled. Nehemiah was more interested in the fact that they came together in one accord than in how many were there. This is the first time Nehemiah mentioned Ezra the priest, scribe, and teacher. He was present, and those in charge urged him to bring out the **book** containing the **Law** that God gave to **Moses**. Another important point to be noted here is that these people felt a need to hear the Scriptures.

"All the people" is a phrase that appears over and over again in this chapter. The word "people" appears thirteen times in the first twelve verses. Nehemiah is conveying the idea that the people were united in what they were doing.

A Good Way to Start the Year

NEHEMIAH **8:2** ***So Ezra the priest brought the Law before the assembly of men and women and all who could hear with understanding on the first day of the seventh month.*** (NKJV)

trumpets
Leviticus 23:23–24

altar
Ezra 3:2–3

Tishri
our September/October

Pentateuch
the first five books of the Old Testament

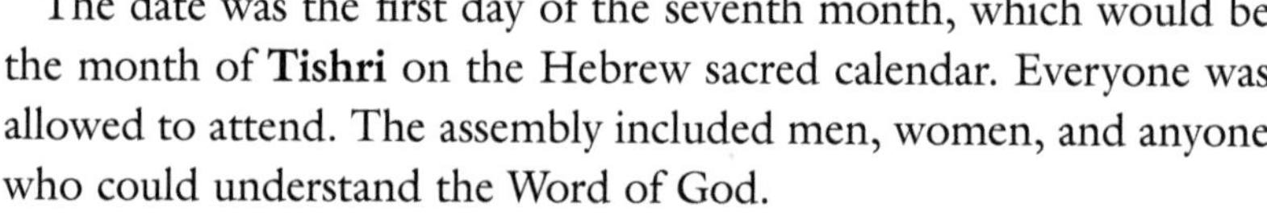

The date was the first day of the seventh month, which would be the month of **Tishri** on the Hebrew sacred calendar. Everyone was allowed to attend. The assembly included men, women, and anyone who could understand the Word of God.

> what others say
>
> **Emmaus Bible School**
>
> From the human standpoint the Bible was written by not less than thirty-six authors over a period of about sixteen hundred years. But the important thing to remember is that these men wrote under the direct control of God. God guided them in writing the very words. This is what we mean by inspiration . . . Thus the Bible is the Word of God.[1]

The first day of the seventh month on the Hebrew sacred calendar is called Rosh Hashanah. It was the Jewish New Year on the Hebrew civil calendar. Some call it the "Feast of Trumpets" because God told the Jews to remember it with the blowing of trumpets. This was also a very special occasion because it was the anniversary of the day the first exiles built the altar (see "The Jewish Feasts" chart on page 27).

A Long Service

NEHEMIAH 8:3 ***Then he read from it in the open square that was in front of the Water Gate from morning until midday, before the men and women and those who could understand; and the ears of all the people were attentive to the Book of the Law. (NKJV)***

Ezra faced the people in the square near the Water Gate and read aloud from the scroll containing the writings of Moses. He started reading at daybreak (about sunrise) and read until noon, a period of approximately six hours. He may have read as much as one-fourth of the **Pentateuch** as the people listened carefully.

> what others say
>
> **Tim LaHaye**
>
> Daily Bible reading is to your spiritual life what daily eating is to your physical life. We are all familiar with the necessity of regular mealtimes. If we skip meals or rush them, their primary

values are lost. Just as the body needs a regular feeding time to maintain its energy level, so the spiritual man must regularly be fed the Word of God.[2]

Jerusalem
Ezra 7:6–8

KJV
the King James Version of the Bible

What's That?

NEHEMIAH 8:4 ***So Ezra the scribe stood on a platform of wood which they had made for the purpose; and beside him, at his right hand, stood Mattithiah, Shema, Anaiah, Urijah, Hilkiah, and Maaseiah; and at his left hand Pedaiah, Mishael, Malchijah, Hashum, Hashbadana, Zechariah, and Meshullam.*** *(NKJV)*

The Jews built a high wooden platform or stage for this special service, and Ezra stood upon that so he could be easily seen and heard by the assembly. The platform was large enough for thirteen other men to stand there with Ezra, six on his right and seven on his left.

The **KJV** says Ezra stood upon a "pulpit of wood." Some commentators think the idea of a pulpit of wood originated with the Babylonians, but this is the first known reference of one being used. Ezra may have brought the idea with him when he moved from Babylon to Jerusalem.

Respect for the Word of God

NEHEMIAH 8:5 ***And Ezra opened the book in the sight of all the people, for he was standing above all the people; and when he opened it, all the people stood up.*** *(NKJV)*

Ezra unrolled the sacred scroll in front of the assembly. Everyone could see what he was doing because he was elevated on the platform. In ancient times a servant would stand out of respect and honor for his master while his master was speaking to him. As Ezra unrolled the scroll all the people reverently rose on their feet to honor God and hear what he had to say. There's little doubt that those on the stage with Ezra also rose to their feet.

what others say

Emmaus Bible School

It is not enough to say that the Bible *contains* the Word of God. This might imply that parts of it are inspired and parts are not. *Every part of the Bible is inspired.* "All Scripture is given by inspiration of God."[3]

Today, not all, but many congregations of Christians follow this same practice of standing on their feet while the Word of God is read. It is something Christians do to show respect for the Scriptures, which are **God-breathed**. Christians usually stand for a few minutes. These Jews stood for about six hours.

They Worshiped God

God-breathed
2 Timothy 3:16–17

hands
Psalms 28:2; 63:4; 119:48; 134:2; 1 Timothy 2:8

God-breathed
inspired by God

Amen
"It is so," or "So be it."

Scriptural
taught in the

NEHEMIAH **8:6** ***And Ezra blessed the LORD, the great God. Then all the people answered, "Amen, Amen!" while lifting up their hands. And they bowed their heads and worshiped the LORD with their faces to the ground.*** (NKJV)

In a Jewish service the people pronounce a blessing before the Scriptures are read. This service began in this traditional way when Ezra opened by praising God. The Lord had proven his greatness by having the exiles released and causing many to return, and by causing the altar, Temple, and wall to be rebuilt in the midst of ongoing opposition. All the people worshiped by raising their hands in praise to God and bowing their heads in humility. They eagerly signaled their agreement with what Ezra said by emphatically adding a double "**Amen.**"

what others say

Matthew Henry

Let us learn to address ourselves to the services of religion with solemn stops and pauses, and not to go about them rashly; let us consider what we are doing when we take God's book into our hands, and open it, and so also when we bow our knees in prayer; and what we do let us do deliberately.[4]

Lifting one's hands to worship and praise God is very common and meaningful in several denominations of the church, but it is rarely done in some denominations and congregations for a variety of reasons. Nevertheless, the practice is **scriptural**.

Teacher's Aides

NEHEMIAH **8:7–8** ***Also Jeshua, Bani, Sherebiah, Jamin, Akkub, Shabbethai, Hodijah, Maaseiah, Kelita, Azariah, Jozabad, Hanan, Pelaiah, and the Levites, helped the people to***

understand the Law; and the people stood in their place. So they read distinctly from the book, in the Law of God; and they gave the sense, and helped them to understand the reading. *(NKJV)*

Teaching and interpreting the Scriptures was the traditional responsibility of the Levites. And all of these people had spent most of their lives in Babylon, so they might have had trouble with some of the Hebrew or with what it meant. So Ezra stationed Levites in the congregation to interpret and explain what he read and said. He read a small portion of the Law, and thirteen Levites circulated among the standing people to explain what they did not understand. Ezra was making sure the people knew what the Word of God says.

what others say

Charles R. Swindoll

When you study the Bible, always pay close attention to the words. Never miss the significant ones. Pull out your dictionary; trace the meaning of key words. Talk the words through; think the words through. Compare that word with another word and another place in Scripture where a similar word is used so that you will begin to see the meaning of the passage.[5]

In a worship service God wants the Scriptures to be read and respected, but he also wants them to be understood. This is why he had people there to explain them. Pastors who want to honor God will speak from the Word and take deliberate steps to help the people hear the Word and understand it. Religious education is good, but religious education that doesn't make the Word easier to understand is of little value.

Don't Cry

NEHEMIAH 8:9 ***And Nehemiah, who was the governor, Ezra the priest and scribe, and the Levites who taught the people said to all the people, "This day is holy to the LORD your God; do not mourn nor weep." For all the people wept, when they heard the words of the Law.*** *(NKJV)*

Some critics contend that Ezra and Nehemiah were not contemporaries, but this verse refutes that. The Word of God is quick and powerful. The Jews listened carefully and began to cry when it was read and explained to them. Then Nehemiah, Ezra, and the Levite teachers reminded them that this was a holy day, the first day of the **seventh month**, and it was a time to rejoice, not a time to cry. This shows that the people were not weeping for joy because of their opportunity to hear the Scriptures or because the words were sweet and wonderful. Instead, they were mourning on an occasion that was meant to be a joyous celebration.

These people had come out of captivity and some had learned very little about the Word of God. Hearing the Word of God and having it explained to them was something that **convicted** them of their sin. They responded by weeping over their failures and the failures of their ancestors.

Share and Rejoice

NEHEMIAH 8:10 ***Then he said to them, "Go your way, eat the fat, drink the sweet, and send portions to those for whom nothing is prepared; for this day is holy to our LORD. Do not sorrow, for the joy of the LORD is your strength."*** *(NKJV)*

Nehemiah urged the Jews to go home and celebrate by enjoying the food and drinks that had been prepared for this occasion. It is wrong for some to feast while others go hungry. He added that some did not have anything, so he encouraged those who had plenty to share what they had with those who had nothing. He reminded the Jews that this was a **sacred** day, and he wanted them to know that **rejoicing** in the Lord would give them strength.

first day
Nehemiah 8:2

seventh month
Tishri (our September/October)

convicted
convinced them of their transgressions

sacred
belonging to, or set apart for, God

rejoicing
showing joy, cheer, or delight

what others say

Warren W. Wiersbe

It is as wrong to mourn when God has forgiven us as it is to rejoice when sin has conquered us. The sinner has no reason for rejoicing and the child of God has no reason for mourning (Matthew 9:9–17). Yes, as God's children we carry burdens and know what it is to weep (Nehemiah 2:1–2); but we also experience power that transforms sorrow into joy.[6]

I Heard an Echo

NEHEMIAH 8:11–12 ***So the Levites quieted all the people, saying, "Be still, for the day is holy; do not be grieved." And all the***

***people went their way to eat and drink, to send portions and rejoice greatly, because they understood the words that were declared to them.* (NKJV)**

The Levites echoed Nehemiah's instructions. They calmed the weeping people, reminded them that this was a sacred day, and urged them not to weep. The people departed to have their meal, share their food, and celebrate. Why did they celebrate? *Because they now understood the words that had been made known to them.* They had started out weeping over their sins, but had left rejoicing over what the Scriptures said.

booths
Leviticus 23:33–43

feast
Ezra 3:4

booths
small temporary shelters

feast
Here it refers to the Feast of Tabernacles.

The Next Day

NEHEMIAH 8:13–15 *Now on the second day the heads of the fathers' houses of all the people, with the priests and Levites, were gathered to Ezra the scribe, in order to understand the words of the Law. And they found written in the Law, which the LORD had commanded by Moses, that the children of Israel should dwell in booths during the feast of the seventh month, and that they should announce and proclaim in all their cities and in Jerusalem, saying, "Go out to the mountain, and bring olive branches, branches of oil trees, myrtle branches, palm branches, and branches of leafy trees, to make booths, as it is written."* (NKJV)

After most of the Jews had departed, the family heads, priests, and Levites gathered around Ezra for more study of the Scriptures. He concentrated on the Scriptures that God gave to Moses that told the Israelites to live in **booths** during the **feast** of the seventh month. They learned that they should notify all the Jews in Jerusalem and the surrounding towns to go into the nearby hills and gather branches from olive, myrtle, palm, and shade trees for the purpose of making booths. Nehemiah didn't say in this passage whether they followed through by making the announcement, but the next verse indicates that they did.

what others say

Clarence H. Wagner Jr.

The holiday commemorates the desert wanderings of the Children of Israel, when they came out of Egypt on their way to the Promised Land. Even though they were wandering

eighth day
Leviticus 23:36;
Numbers 29:35

offerings
Numbers 29:12–40

because of their own disobedience, God was with them and divinely protected them and provided for their needs. For the celebration of Sukkot, the Israelites were commanded to build tabernacles or booths and actually live in them for a week each year, so they could remember God's presence and His faithfulness as a protector and provider.[7]

Richard Booker

The Feast of Tabernacles also had a forward look. The shelter was loosely constructed so that the Hebrews could see through its roof into heaven. This would remind them that they were pilgrims passing through this life and that God had an even greater rest for them in the future when He would come and live among them permanently.[8]

A Great Celebration

NEHEMIAH 8:16–18 ***Then the people went out and brought them and made themselves booths, each one on the roof of his house, or in their courtyards or the courts of the house of God, and in the open square of the Water Gate and in the open square of the Gate of Ephraim. So the whole assembly of those who had returned from the captivity made booths and sat under the booths; for since the days of Joshua the son of Nun until that day the children of Israel had not done so. And there was very great gladness. Also day by day, from the first day until the last day, he read from the Book of the Law of God. And they kept the feast seven days; and on the eighth day there was a sacred assembly, according to the prescribed manner.*** *(NKJV)*

The people did as the family heads, priests, and Levites suggested. They gathered branches and built booths on the flat roofs of their houses, in the courts of their yards, at the Temple, and in two of the city squares. All the exiles built and lived in small booths. The celebration was more joyful than any celebration since the days of Joshua. Ezra read the Word of God to the people every day, and they celebrated the Feast of Tabernacles for seven days. On the eighth day, in connection with a closing ceremony, they assembled and gave offerings according to the established custom of their ancestors.

what others say

Zola Levitt

The Lord will establish His Tabernacle in Jerusalem (Ezekiel 37:26–27), and all the world will come every year to appear before the King and worship Him. How fitting a conclusion to each festival year in the schedule of the feasts![9]

G. Ernest Thomas

Daily reading of the Bible, and frequent periods for the study of God's Word, is one of the essential disciplines of the spiritual life. The Bible is the record of God's relationship with man, and of man's growing understanding of God's nature. Seekers for Christian truth have always studied the Bible as the most dependable means to learn about God. They have found insight as well concerning the demands of faith upon their personal lives and upon their society.[10]

Chapter Wrap-Up

- All the Jews gathered with one accord near the Water Gate in Jerusalem and asked Ezra to bring out the scroll Moses had written. On the first day of the seventh month, Ezra read to the people for about six hours. He stood on a platform with thirteen officials, and all the people stood in front of him. Ezra praised God, and the people raised their hands, said "Amen," bowed down with their faces to the ground, and worshiped God.
- Thirteen Levites circulated through the crowd while reading from scrolls and explaining the Scriptures so that all the people could understand.
- When the people heard the Word of God, they began to weep. Then when Nehemiah, Ezra, and the Levites told them this was a sacred day and urged them not to cry but to instead celebrate and share the food, their mourning was turned to joy.
- The next day the family heads, priests, Levites, and Ezra gathered to read the Law of Moses. They found that God had instructed the Jews to gather branches and make booths to live in during the Feast of Tabernacles. When the people obeyed God's instruction to do this, they rejoiced like never before. This lasted for seven days, and Ezra read the Law each day. The people assembled on the eighth day and offered sacrifices.

Study Questions

1. Why is the Book of the Law of Moses so important to Israel? What did Ezra do with it on the first day of the seventh month? Who was present?

2. How did the people respond when Ezra read the Book of the Law? How did they respond when he praised the Lord?

3. What did the Jews do for those who didn't understand what was read to them and for those who didn't have anything to eat?

4. After the Book of the Law was read, what were the people doing that Nehemiah and the Levites then told them not to do? What did they tell them to do instead and why?

5. What did the Jews build, who told them to build them, what was their purpose, and what did they commemorate?

Nehemiah 9
Confession, Praise, and Prayer

Chapter Highlights:
- Let's Meet Again
- Me First
- Study, Confession, and Worship
- Call to Prayer

Let's Get Started

When Ezra read from the Book of the Law of Moses, the people praised and worshiped God. Hearing and understanding what God said touched them deeply and they began to weep and grieve over their sins. This was the beginning of another **revival** among the former exiles.

read
Nehemiah 8:1–3

worshiped
Nehemiah 8:5–6

weep
Nehemiah 8:9–11

exiles
Ezra 10:1–17

Feast of Tabernacles
Leviticus 23:33–44

food
Nehemiah 8:10

mourning
Genesis 37:25–36

grieving
Nehemiah 8:11

dust
1 Samuel 4:12

Let's Meet Again

NEHEMIAH 9:1 ***Now on the twenty-fourth day of this month the children of Israel were assembled with fasting, in sackcloth, and with dust on their heads.*** (NKJV)

In chapter 8, the Jews celebrated the weeklong Feast of Tabernacles, which fell between the fifteenth and the twenty-second of **Tishri**. Then, two days after that, on the twenty-fourth of Tishri, they gathered together in Jerusalem once again. Now, instead of enjoying much food and drink like they had done during the Feast of Tabernacles, they now dedicated themselves to **fasting**. Instead of rejoicing like they had done during the Feast of Tabernacles, they performed acts of **contrition**: putting on sackcloth, going into mourning, grieving over their sins, and throwing dust on their head.

revival
renewed zeal to obey God

Tishri
our September/October

fasting
the act of denying oneself something such as food or drink to show humility

contrition
sorrow and repentance

what others say

Martha Bergen

Sackcloth was a garment of dark, coarsely woven goat or camel hair. It was generally worn as a sign of mourning and grief and, thus, characterized somber occasions. Its rough texture served as a means toward chastisement among the penitent.[1]

Sometimes the Jews would sit on the ground and sprinkle handfuls of dust and dirt over their head and body. This signified different things:

separated
Ezra 6:21

- It is a symbol of the grave and death, *for dust you are and to dust you will return.*
- It is a symbol that sin makes people dirty and of low estate.
- It is a symbol that sinners are as worthless as powdered dirt.

separated
abandoned

pagan
a person who does not worship the true God

confessed
acknowledged

Me First

NEHEMIAH 9:2 ***Then those of Israelite lineage separated themselves from all foreigners; and they stood and confessed their sins and the iniquities of their fathers.*** *(NKJV)*

This was a meeting of those Jews who had **separated** themselves from the **pagan** practices of the non-Jews. They were willing to live by God's standards. It was easier to do that if they assembled with like-minded believers. They stood and **confessed** all their sins. They also confessed the sins that had been committed by their wayward ancestors.

Although confession is sometimes connected to salvation in the Bible (Matthew 10:32), it is more often connected with the forgiveness of sins (1 John 1:9). The core meaning of the word is "to say the same thing." This simply means that people are to say the same thing that is in their heart and the same thing that God says about their sins. A person isn't to say one thing but mean something else, because God knows what is in a person's heart. Also, a person is to agree with what God says about their sin, because what God says about it is what is truth. Confession, then, is a combination of honesty with oneself and with God, and agreement with what God says about the sin.

what others say

Max Lucado

We will never be cleansed until we confess we are dirty. We will never be pure until we admit we are filthy. And we will never be able to wash the feet of those who have hurt us until we allow Jesus, the one we have hurt, to wash ours.[2]

Study, Confession and Worship

NEHEMIAH 9:3 ***And they stood up in their place and read from the Book of the Law of the LORD their God for one-fourth of the day; and for another fourth they confessed and worshiped the LORD their God.*** *(NKJV)*

The Levites and the people stood where they were and read from the scroll that contained the words God had given to Moses. They spent one-fourth of a day reading (three hours) and another fourth of a day in confession and worship.

Levites
Nehemiah 8:7–8

Moses
Nehemiah 8:1

Standing while the Scriptures are read is a practice in many churches today. It is a way of recognizing the authority behind the Scriptures and showing respect for God. It is an act of showing agreement with the Scriptures, which are an expression of his mind, heart, and will. It is an outward expression that shows that they love the Word of God. When God's people let the Word of God change them, they are expressing a desire to know God more and know more about him.

Expressions of worshiping God may be done alone or when part of a group of other worshipers. Separating oneself from all distractions enhances one's focus on God, but there are times when it is important to gather with others to worship God in singing together, praying as a group or one at a time, reading Scriptures aloud, and other forms of expressing heartfelt love and dedication to God.

The word "worship" comes from the same root word as the English word "worth." It means to declare God's worth, greatness, and glory. It stems from an understanding of who God is. It often involves the reading of Scripture, praying, and singing. For worship to be meaningful it must also be expressed through a lifestyle of righteousness and service. A life that expresses worship of God is one that honors him and is a living demonstration of what the Word of God says.

what others say

Grant R. Jeffrey

> The early Christians, Jewish scribes, and generations of Christian believers shared an unshakable conviction that the Scriptures contain the infallible, inspired, and authoritative words of God. The Bible itself claims that "All scripture is given by inspiration of God, and is profitable for doctrine, for reproof, for correction, for instruction in righteousness" (2 Timothy 3:16 NKJV).[3]

Observe the events:

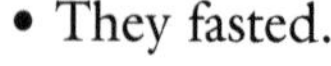

- They fasted.
- They wore sackcloth.
- They put dust on their heads.
- They confessed their sins.
- They confessed the sins of their ancestors.
- They spent three hours reading from the Word of God.
- They spent three hours confessing their sins and worshiping God.
- They praised God.
- They prayed.

A Call to Prayer

> NEHEMIAH 9:4–5 ***Then Jeshua, Bani, Kadmiel, Shebaniah, Bunni, Sherebiah, Bani, and Chenani stood on the stairs of the Levites and cried out with a loud voice to the LORD their God. And the Levites, Jeshua, Kadmiel, Bani, Hashabniah, Sherebiah, Hodijah, Shebaniah, and Pethahiah, said: "Stand up and bless the LORD your God forever and ever! Blessed be Your glorious name, which is exalted above all blessing and praise!" (NKJV)***

It was the duty of the Levites to lead the worship services. On this occasion eight Levites stood on the stairs of the platform, and it seems that at least three others were standing somewhere near them. These Levites urged the Jews to stand and join them in praise of the eternal God.

Many people are squeamish about praising God. They worry about what others might think. Praising God involves humbling ourselves, submitting to him, and doing things his way. It involves recognizing who he is: his love, goodness, mercy, grace, protection, deliverance, and his many wonderful actions and attributes. In public settings, praising God may be expressed with music, singing, clapping, lifting of hands, prayer, acts of being of service to others, and more. Is expressing adoration to God in public embarrassing, or does it come naturally because one's focus has been on worshiping

platform
Nehemiah 8:4

God all day long in other settings? Or, on the other hand, could it be that worshiping alone at home seems awkward because no one else is there to impress? Because God inhabits the praise of his people, worshiping him in a heartfelt way may lead people to become very aware of his presence and be so strengthened and emboldened in their faith that depression and anxiety become things of the past for them. When this happens to just one individual, it is called personal revival. When it happens to a larger group of people, it is sometimes simply called a revival.

created
Genesis 1:1–31

Abraham
Genesis 12:1–9

what others say

Bible Dictionary

[Praise is) to say good things about and to give honor to God (Psalm 9:1; Proverbs 27:2). God's people are expected to praise God and live a worthy life (Philippians 1:9–11; Ephesians 1:11–14).[4]

The Longest Prayer

the big picture

Nehemiah 9:6–38

The people praised God and acknowledged that he is the Creator (v. 6). They recalled his dealings with Abraham, the Exodus, and his dealings with the Jews at Mount Sinai (vv. 7–15). They acknowledged the rebellion of the Jews and God's patience with them in the wilderness (vv. 16–21). They credited God for their conquest of the Promised Land and for giving them deliverers when their enemies were oppressing them (vv. 22–28). They credited God for sending prophets to call for repentance and acknowledged that the prophets were ignored (vv. 29–31). They asked God to understand that their suffering had been great and admitted that God's punishments were just because their kings, leaders, priests, and ancestors were all guilty (vv. 32–35). They told God they were in great distress, that they were making a commitment to him, and that they were putting it in writing (vv. 36–38).

This is the longest prayer in the Bible. It begins by honoring the glorious name of God; acknowledges that there is only one God, the One who created and gives life to everything. It also recalls that he is the One who moved Abraham to the Promised Land, found him

covenant
Genesis 15:18–21

Egypt
Exodus 1:1–22

Sinai
Exodus 19:1–20:17

territory
Joshua 12:1–24

seals
their signatures or stamps used to make agreements legally binding

faithful, made a covenant with him, promised him the land of Israel, and kept his promise. The prayer notes that God saw the suffering of the Jews in Egypt at the Red Sea, that he performed miracles to help them, and that he led them to safety. It recalls that God met the Jews at Mount Sinai; gave them just laws, regulations, and decrees through Moses; and fed them, gave them drink, and told them to go in to possess the land. It admits that their ancestors rebelled against God, forgot what he did for them, returned to their old sins despite his forgiveness, grace, compassion, and constant provision for them in the wilderness. It recalls the amount of territory God gave their ancestors, how God multiplied their ancestors, how God helped their ancestors conquer their enemies, and the abundance of good things God gave to their ancestors. The prayer again recalls the rebellion of their ancestors: that they killed God's prophets, that they blasphemed God, that they were defeated because God turned them over to their enemies, and that their defeat caused them to cry out to God. It also recalls that this cycle of rebellion and relief was repeated over many years, and that repentance always brought God's help. It called upon God to notice the seriousness of their current suffering and pointed out that they were repenting and making a new commitment to serve him. It also noted that they were putting their commitment in writing, and the Levites and priests were authenticating it by affixing their **seals**.

what others say

Don Fields

Revival and renewal are always preceded by contrition and remorse for our sins. Israel is at the end of itself, and the Lord is the only one who can deliver them, so they are returning to him. We too must be humbled, broken and serious to be recipients of God's renewal.[5]

E. M. Bounds

What the Church needs today is not more machinery or better, not new organizations or more and novel methods, but men whom the Holy Ghost can use—men of prayer, men mighty in prayer. The Holy Ghost does not flow through methods but through men. He does not come on machinery, but on men. He does not anoint plans, but men—men of prayer.[6]

Chapter Wrap-Up

- Two days after the Feast of Tabernacles the former exiles gathered to grieve over their sins. They confessed their sins and those of their ancestors. They spent about three hours reading the Law of Moses and about three hours worshiping God. Then there was a call to prayer.
- The people began to pray by praising God and acknowledging him as the only God, the Creator and Giver of life. Then they recalled major events in their history from the time of Abraham to their present time. They recalled the constant failures of their ancestors and proclaimed God's constant justice, righteousness, love, mercy, patience, and compassion in his dealings with them. They pointed out their present suffering and then concluded their prayer by promising to do better than their ancestors had done. They put their oath in writing and affixed it with a seal.

Study Questions

1. Name six things the Jews did before they prayed.
2. How much time was spent reading the Word of God and how much time was spent in confession and worship before the longest prayer was prayed? What did the Levites urge the people to do before the prayer?
3. What does the prayer say about Creation?
4. What did God promise to give Abraham's descendants? What did he give to Moses and the people at Mount Sinai?
5. What cycle did Israel's ancestors fall into? How did God response? Did this give Ezra reason to hope?

Nehemiah 10
A Commitment to Keep

Chapter Highlights:
- **Signed and Sealed**
- **The Agreement**
- **Where Do I Put My Name?**
- **Agree to Do**

Let's Get Started

This chapter spells out the terms of the binding agreement mentioned in chapter 9. It also provides a list of eighty-four leaders, Levites, priests, and others who put their seals on it. Applying their seals to it signified their firm intention to keep it. The Law of Moses warned them to not make oaths they didn't intend to keep. Not keeping an oath would result in the judgment of God. Surprisingly, Ezra's name is not on the list.

governor
Nehemiah 5:14

Oaths were very common in Old Testament times, but Jesus told his followers not to make binding oaths (not to swear that they would keep their word). Christians should consider their words binding even if they did not swear that they would keep them. God knows what every individual says. He expects his followers to tell the truth, obey him, and keep their promises. He expects their motivation for obedience to him to be from a heart full of love for him rather than from fear of judgment.

Where Do I Put My Name?

the big picture

Nehemiah 10:1–27

The agreement was signed by Nehemiah the governor (v. 1a), twenty-two priests (vv. 1b–8), seventeen Levites (vv. 9–13), and forty-four others (vv. 14–27).

Nehemiah's was the first signature and corresponding seal on the list of those making a written commitment to God. He was now the governor of the area. Of the twenty-two priests mentioned, fifteen are family names and seven are the names of individual priests. The same is true of the list of Levites: some are family names and some are individual names. The forty-four others are mostly leaders.

This Is What We Agree to Do

separated
Ezra 6:21;
Nehemiah 9:2

understand
Nehemiah 8:7–12

Sabbath
Exodus 20:8–10

seventh
Exodus 23:10–12

debts
Deuteronomy 15:1–2

pay
Exodus 30:11–16

wood
Leviticus 6:12–13

firstfruits
Deuteronomy 26:1–15

firstfruit
the first part of the harvest, first offspring of the animals

tithe
the tenth part of one's income

the big picture

Nehemiah 10:28–39

The remainder of the Jews joined their leaders in the covenant. They committed to follow the Law of Moses and all the commandments of God. They promised not to allow their children to intermarry with foreigners, to keep the Sabbaths, to pay the temple taxes, to provide wood for the Temple, and to give all the firstfruit and tithe offerings.

All those Jews who had separated from foreigners and who could understand joined their leaders in the covenant. They took an oath to obey the Law of Moses and asked for a curse to come upon them if they failed to keep their promise. To keep their religion pure, they promised to forbid intermarriage between their children and foreigners. As a way of remembering the Sabbath and keeping it holy, they promised to not do business on the Sabbath, and they extended it to the holy days. As a part of this, they promised to let the land rest every seventh year and to cancel the debts of those who owed them on those seventh years. To keep the traditions of their ancestors, they promised to pay a Temple tax. To keep the Law of Moses, they promised to provide wood for the burnt offerings at the Temple, give **firstfruit tithe** offerings at the Temple, and provide whatever was needed for the operation of the Temple.

what others say

Charles Stanley

We need to see the big picture, God's big picture. He is not concerned about the money you owe someone or your apologizing to someone for something you may not remember. But He is concerned about your obedience to the initial prompting of His Spirit. He is concerned about how long it takes you to obey Him once you know the truth.[1]

Chapter Wrap-Up

- Nehemiah, twenty-two priests, seventeen Levites, and forty-four family heads signed the covenant that the exiles made with God.
- The remainder of the exiles who separated themselves from foreigners and understood what they were signing joined their leaders by binding themselves with an oath to follow the Law and obey God. They agreed to prevent intermarriage between their children and foreigners, keep the Sabbath, and pay Temple taxes. They also agreed to contribute wood, firstfruit offerings, tithes, and the other needs of the house of God.

Study Questions

1. Why do you think the exiles signed the agreement?
2. In addition to their signatures, name two other ways the exiles bound themselves to keeping the covenant.
3. What would the exiles forbid their children to do?
4. What would the exiles do every seventh year?
5. How did the exiles determine when a family would take wood to the Temple for the burnt offerings?

Nehemiah 11
The People Are Registered

Chapter Highlights:
- People Wanted
- Jerusalem's New Residents
- Their Hometown
- What Town?

Let's Get Started

This chapter begins with an explanation of what Nehemiah did to increase the population of the holy city. He secured a commitment for ten percent of the people to move there. He made a list of those who relocated and a list of other cities and towns where other exiles lived. Nehemiah knew that a nation needs a capital. He wanted Jerusalem to be that capital. He knew it needed people. He wanted Jerusalem to have more people than any other Jewish city, enough people to defend it on every side from all of its determined enemies, and he wanted it to be developed and improved. In a sense, he developed a plan and worked to make the city what God wanted it to be. After all, since God had put his name on the Holy City, it would not be good to let it remain small or almost uninhabited.

lots
Numbers 26:55–56;
1 Chronicles 24:5

Get the Moving Van

NEHEMIAH 11:1–2 ***Now the leaders of the people dwelt at Jerusalem; the rest of the people cast lots to bring one out of ten to dwell in Jerusalem, the holy city, and nine-tenths were to dwell in other cities. And the people blessed all the men who willingly offered themselves to dwell at Jerusalem.*** *(NKJV)*

All the leaders settled in Jerusalem. This was probably because the Temple was there and this was going to be the seat of their government and religion. Most of the common people lived in the surrounding towns and country, probably because many of them were farmers and ranchers and because their ancestors had lived in those places. As a result of this situation, Nehemiah had to look to the ordinary citizens when he wanted more people to live in Jerusalem. He did this by casting lots to select the 10 percent of the people who would relocate to Jerusalem. The Jews believed that how the lot fell was not coincidence, but was God making the decision. Casting lots for this was a means of determining which people God wanted to live in Jerusalem. It seems reasonable to assume that God and

Nehemiah didn't split families. People selected by casting lots probably moved their entire families. Their friends, neighbors, and relatives surely commended them for making this sacrifice of uprooting their families and relocating yet another time. It is very likely that some didn't want to move even though it was considered a godly and patriotic thing to do. Because the Jews viewed this as a way of determining God's will, those selected moved to the city even if they had been hoping someone else would be selected.

It was not unusual for the Jews to cast lots during Old Testament times. They did this to determine God's will on questions of importance. The Law of Moses permitted this practice. The casting of lots was used during New Testament times as well. In fact, Peter and those who gathered with him on the Day of Pentecost cast lots to determine who would be the new disciple to replace Judas Iscariot. This process of selection pointed to a man named Matthias, but most scholars believe this was a mistake because all the evidence indicates that God's true choice was Paul—not Matthias. The old way of determining God's will was passing away and the new was soon to come when the Holy Spirit would descend and the Church Age would begin. Rather than casting lots, Christians today normally depend on guidance from the Scriptures and from the Holy Spirit that dwells in them and leads them with a still, small voice or varying levels of peace or unsettling conviction about a matter.

Those Who Sold Their Property and Moved

the big picture

Nehemiah 11:3–24

Those who moved to Jerusalem included leaders from other towns (vv. 3–4a); descendants of Judah and Benjamin (vv. 4b–9); priests (vv. 10–14), Levites (vv. 15–18), and singers and gatekeepers (vv. 19–24).

The first category of people who moved to Jerusalem were leaders who had been living and working among those people who were dwelling in towns and villages outside the city. These Israelites, priests, Levites, Temple servants, and descendants of Solomon's servants had made the determination to be close to the people they served. The second category of people included 468 families who were descendants of **Judah**, the third included 928 families who were descendants of **Benjamin**, the fourth included 284 priests, and the fifth included 172 Levites and gatekeepers.

Judah
Nehemiah 11:4–6

Benjamin
Nehemiah 11:7–8

Judah
one of the twelve sons of Jacob

Benjamin
one of the twelve sons of Jacob

The Levites were originally dispersed throughout the country, but their main office and supervisor were in Jerusalem. The singers received special financial support from King Artaxerxes. He sent them money because he wanted the Jews to pray for him and his family—many people today would cite separation of church and state as grounds to oppose this kind of arrangement. Ever-watchful gatekeepers who provided excellent security at all the entrances to the city were also among those who now dwelled there.

what others say

Charles R. Swindoll

They pulled up their domestic roots, left their lovely homes, started over from scratch, submitted themselves to a government they hadn't elected, and lived in a city policed by a group of people they didn't know. Although they seemed to be insignificant, they were very important because they became the new inhabitants of the city.[1]

The Preacher's Outline & Sermon Bible

Seeing the names of these leaders who tackled the massive problems is a strong reminder that godly leaders are needed to establish and strengthen any city or society. Without strong leadership, no people can thrive, not for long. A people's economy, culture, society, government, and judicial system suffer enormously without strong leadership. Godly leaders are desperately needed within every community, city, state, and nation of this world.[2]

What Town Do You Live In?

the big picture

Nehemiah 11:25-36

These verses provide a list of places where the exiles settled. Not many are listed, and the Scriptures mention that many struggled with poverty, squatters and the challenges of starting all over.

Concerning the towns and villages around Jerusalem, seventeen are mentioned that were located in the territory of Judah and fifteen are mentioned that were in the territory of Benjamin. It is believed that some of these towns and villages were strictly Jewish settlements, but others were probably only partially Jewish. Because the Levites were teachers and expounders of the Law and not landowners, some of them were shifted to Benjamin because there was a disproportionate number of them in some towns and cities but not enough in others. They were relocated to provide for the religious needs of the people.

what others say

Jack W. Hayford with Joseph Snider

Many of the place names listed in these verses had impressive histories. Micmash was where Saul and Jonathan fought the Philistines (1 Samuel 14). Aija was the Ai Joshua had difficulty conquering because of Achan's sin (Joshua 7–8). Bethel was where Jacob's ladder reached to the heavens (Genesis 28:10–22). Anathoth was the birthplace of Jeremiah (Jeremiah 1:1). Ramah was the city of Samuel (1 Samuel 7:17).[3]

Chapter Wrap-Up

- To increase the population of Jerusalem, Nehemiah had the common people cast lots to select the 10 percent of the people who would relocate. He also found others who would move voluntarily.
- Nehemiah made a list of the descendants from the tribes of Judah and Benjamin, and named the priests, Levites, and gatekeepers who would also be relocating.
- Nehemiah's list included the names of the towns and villages from where the people were moving.

Study Questions

1. How did the people determine who would live in Jerusalem? What portion of the population did they want to relocate?
2. Most of the common people were from what two tribes of Israel?
3. Other than the descendants of Judah and Benjamin, what other groups of people moved to Jerusalem?

Nehemiah 12
Registration and Dedication

Chapter Highlights:
- Days of Zerubbabel
- Six Generations of High Priests
- The Days of Joiakim
- Dedication Wall
- Tithes and Offerings

Let's Get Started

This chapter begins with several lists and concludes with information about the dedication of the wall. It is important to notice that the lists are from different time periods. One list is of the priests and Levites in the days of Zerubbabel and Jeshua. Another is a list of priests who lived one generation later in the days of Joiakim. Sandwiched in between these two lists is a list of high priests, starting with Jeshua and spanning the next six generations. This is followed by a list of other family heads and details about the wall dedication service.

Zerubbabel
Ezra 2:1–63

Jeshua
Ezra 2:2

Lots of Religious Leaders

the big picture

Nehemiah 12:1–11

This is a list of twenty-two priests (vv. 1–7) and eight Levites (vv. 8–9) who returned with Zerubbabel and Jeshua. Starting with Jeshua the names of six generations of high priests are listed (vv. 10–11).

It is important to remember that a priest, Levite, or high priest was born into the position rather than being ordained into it. The list of priests and Levites includes the names of those exiles who were priests and Levites when Zerubbabel and Jeshua returned. Jeshua was the high priest at that time. His is the first name on a list of six generations of high priests that extended over a period of about two hundred years. This information has been important to Jews in every generation since then. Even today many Jews carefully trace their genealogies to prove their Jewish ancestry and heritage.

Iddo
Ezra 5:1

One Generation Later

the big picture

Nehemiah 12:12–21

This is a list of the heads of twenty priestly families that lived in the days of Joiakim the high priest.

Jeshua was the high priest in Zerubbabel's day. He was succeeded by his son Joiakim. Other heads of the priestly families are listed in these verses. One of them was named Iddo. He was an ancestor of the prophet Zechariah, whose writings appear later in this book. This establishes the fact that Zechariah descended from a family of priests.

Others

the big picture

Nehemiah 12:22–26

This is a list of three Levites who were family heads in the days of Eliashib (v. 22), three Levites who were family heads in the days of Eliashib's son Johanan (vv. 23–24), and six gatekeepers who served in the days of Joiakim (vv. 25–26).

These lists are of little importance to the average Christian, but they demonstrate that God records the names and deeds of people. Six important Levite families and six important gatekeepers in Old Testament times are identified here. Many of these names appear on other lists of distinguished Jews. "The book of the chronicles" that the writer refers to (12:23 NKJV) is not 1 and 2 Chronicles in the Bible. It would appear that the returnees were developing and maintaining an archive of historical records by this time. Most authorities believe these were kept in special rooms at the Temple. The Jews definitely had scrolls with genealogical records on them, scrolls with the records of the kings of Israel, and scrolls with the records of the kings of Judah. Many historical facts found in the Bible come from those scrolls.

Prepare to Celebrate

NEHEMIAH 12:27–30 *Now at the dedication of the wall of Jerusalem they sought out the Levites in all their places, to bring*

them to Jerusalem to celebrate the dedication with gladness, both with thanksgivings and singing, with cymbals and stringed instruments and harps. And the sons of the singers gathered together from the countryside around Jerusalem, from the villages of the Netophathites, from the house of Gilgal, and from the fields of Geba and Azmaveth; for the singers had built themselves villages all around Jerusalem. Then the priests and Levites purified themselves, and purified the people, the gates, and the wall. *(NKJV)*

purified
Numbers 19:1–13; 2 Chronicles 29:1–36

purified
made themselves ceremonially clean

It is likely that shortly after the completion of the wall—some say the time period was about three months—Nehemiah brought the Levites, musicians, and singers together for a day of celebration and dedication of the wall around Jerusalem. He planned a joyful ceremony with lots of singing and music. The priests and Levites **purified** themselves first, however, and then purified other exiles. The gates and the wall of the city were then purified as well.

Purification was a practice the Jews started at God's direction in the wilderness. All those who carried the Tabernacle, the Ark of the Covenant, the altar, the Temple vessels, the candlesticks, and anything that had to do with worship had to be ritually purified. Even those who erected and those who took down the Tabernacle had to be purified. This stemmed from the idea that God is holy, morally pure, and without sin; and therefore, all who worship him and everything that has to do with worship of him must be purified. Those who served in any way offered sacrifices to have their sins forgiven. In some cases they were required to take a ritual bath and dress in clean clothes. Only then could they approach their awesome God, in purity and holiness, as a forgiven person. With these conditions being met, he would not have to turn away from them because of sin and could gladly accept their worship.

what others say

Charles R. Swindoll

We're not told exactly what was meant by "purification," but it no doubt had to do with personal cleansing through a sin offering. In order to carry on the celebration of the wall, their hearts had to be pure. We too need to remember that to minister to other people, our hearts must be clean before God. Holiness precedes happiness.[1]

clergy
people such as priests and preachers who have qualified to do religious work

laity
people who are not clergy

It's a Parade

the big picture

Nehemiah 12:31–39

For the ceremony, Nehemiah separated out two large choirs to start at the southwest corner of the wall and march around the top. One choir was composed of a group of leaders, priests, musicians, and singers led by Ezra. This choir marched to the right toward the Dung Gate, the Fountain Gate, and the Water Gate on the east (vv. 31–37). Nehemiah followed the other choir to the left. This group passed several gates and towers on that side of the city and arrived at the Gate of the Guard where the wall stopped (vv. 38–40).

To dedicate the nine-foot-wide wall, Nehemiah assembled two large choirs of **clergy** and **laity** to march around the top of it. Ezra led one choir to the right. He was followed by half the leaders, priests with trumpets, and Levites and laypeople with musical instruments. Nehemiah sent the other choir to the left. Nehemiah and the remainder of the leaders, priests, Levites, and other people followed. The two groups circled the wall and met by the Gate of the Guard near the Temple area. There was at least one section of wall that they could not march on. When they came to that section, they quickly exited and returned on sets of steps so they could rejoin the joyful parade.

what others say

Preacher's Outline & Sermon Bible

Having the people walk along the top of the wall caused them to focus on the results of their labor. Realizing that they had accomplished such a massive project would stir them to continue the rebuilding of Jerusalem. Since they had accomplished so much in just 52 days, they would be confident they could achieve any task, even the rebuilding of the city and nation. But there was also another benefit of marching across the top of the wall. The enemy nations surrounding Jerusalem would have had spies observing the festive occasion. Seeing such a joyful experience and the strength of the wall would make the enemy think twice before attacking.[2]

Joy Down in My Heart

the big picture

Nehemiah 12:40-43

The two choirs gave thanks to God and entered the Temple with Nehemiah, half the officials, the priests with their trumpets, and some of the Levites. The choirs sang, the people offered many sacrifices, and everyone rejoiced including the women and children. The sound could be heard for a great distance.

Jezrahiah
Nehemiah 12:42

offered
Ezra 6:16–18

agreement
Nehemiah 9:38

After coming to a stop near the Gate of the Guard, the two groups prayed. Then most of the people entered the Temple. The choirs sang under the direction of Jezrahiah. The priests and Levites offered many sacrifices to thank God for his goodness. There was universal joy as entire families came together with all the men, women, and children giving praise to God. It is clear that the words "joy" and "rejoiced" are not to be overlooked: these words appear five times in verse 43. Their rejoicing was so great that it could be heard far away. This great morale booster preceded the difficult work that would be done in the years to come.

A Promise to Keep

the big picture

Nehemiah 12:44-47

On the same day, men were appointed to supervise the storerooms where the contributions, firstfruit offerings, and tithes were kept. The people agreed to give the amounts required by the Law of Moses because they were pleased with the way the religious leaders, singers, and gatekeepers followed the Word of God. The people gave all that was required for the upkeep of the Levites. And the Levites gave all that was required for the upkeep of the priests.

The people had made a binding agreement with God, put it in writing, and signed it. They had promised not to neglect the house of God. Now, on the same day they held their dedication service, they appointed men to take charge of the tithes and offerings they planned to give for this purpose. They were committed, and they readily agreed to give what the Law of Moses required for the support of the priests and Levites. They wanted to do this despite hav-

Solomon
2 Chronicles
8:12–15

ing to also pay high taxes to the Persian government. They paid this gladly because they were proud to have the priests, Levites, singers, and gatekeepers following the Word of God as was given to them through King David and his son Solomon. They joyfully contributed all that they were supposed to give for the upkeep of the Levites. The Levites shared with the priests according to what the Word of God prescribed. To facilitate this, men were appointed to collect and administer the offerings. This portion of Scripture describes the day as having a parade, sacrifices, singing, blowing of trumpets, playing on stringed instruments, rejoicing, giving, and attending to God's business. The next chapter reveals that they read Scripture from the Book of Moses.

what others say

Charles Stanley

Prayer, giving, and fasting are private acts of worship, and therefore should be done privately. We should do them out of love for God, not because we crave the world's praise. If we do these things for the praise of the world, then that is all the blessing we will receive.[3]

Chapter Wrap-Up

- This chapter begins with a list of priests and Levites who returned from Babylon during the days of Zerubbabel and Jeshua, and a list of six high priests beginning with Jeshua.
- Nehemiah included a list of heads of priestly families who lived during the days of Joiakim.
- Next is a list of Levites during the days of Eliashib, Levites during the days of Johanan, and gatekeepers during the days of Joiakim.
- Nehemiah scheduled a dedication service. The priests and Levites purified themselves, the people, the gates, and the wall. Two large processions paraded around the top of the wall, stopped, prayed, entered the Temple, sang, offered sacrifices, and rejoiced.
- Men were appointed to manage the storehouses, and the people agreed to give tithes and offerings as required by the Law. They gladly supported the Levites because they were pleased that their religious leaders, singers, and gatekeepers were observing the Law. The Levites also gave their proper share to the priests.

Study Questions

1. What is significant about the list of priests and Levites found in the first eleven verses of this chapter?
2. Who was in charge of the songs of thanksgiving in the days of Jeshua?
3. Who was Hananiah?
4. What evidence does this chapter provide to show that God permitted the use of musical instruments in worship services during Old Testament times?
5. What guideline did the Jews go by when deciding how much to give?

Nehemiah 13
Reformation Begins

Chapter Highlights:
- Mixed Marriages
- Desecrated the Temple
- Stopped Tithing
- Profaned the Sabbath
- Much Prayer

Let's Get Started

When Nehemiah asked King Artaxerxes for permission to go to rebuild Jerusalem, Nehemiah set a time for his eventual return to Babylon. This chapter reveals that Nehemiah kept his word. He did, in fact, return to Babylon and to King Artaxerxes for an unspecified period of time (perhaps a few years). The people strayed from their commitment to God while he was back in Babylon and away from Jerusalem. Nehemiah was granted permission to return. Upon his return, he was compelled once again to deal with mixed marriages, **desecration** of the Temple, a lack of tithing, and **profaning** of the Sabbath. Nehemiah fixed himself in sincere prayer, for some very tough decisions were before him.

set a time
Nehemiah 2:1–6

Babylon
Nehemiah 13:6

desecration
showing disrespect for or defiling something

profaning
showing irreverence or disregard for something

what others say

Don Fields

Sometimes we emphasize loving people and not endangering our relationships with them over challenging them to get right with the Lord. When we think like this, we have accepted the world's values and not kingdom values! If relationship with God is the most important thing in the world, then to help people get back into right relationship with God is the best thing we can do for them. When we don't do this, what we are really saying is that we are more concerned about what that person thinks than what God thinks.[1]

It Was News to Us

NEHEMIAH 13:1–3 ***On that day they read from the Book of Moses in the hearing of the people, and in it was found written that no Ammonite or Moabite should ever come into the assembly of God, because they had not met the children of Israel with bread and water, but hired Balaam against them to curse them. However, our God turned the curse into a blessing. So it was, when they had heard the Law, that they separated all the mixed multitude from Israel.*** *(NKJV)*

Moabites Deuteronomy 23:3–6

separated Ezra 9:1–15

foreign Ezra 10:1–44

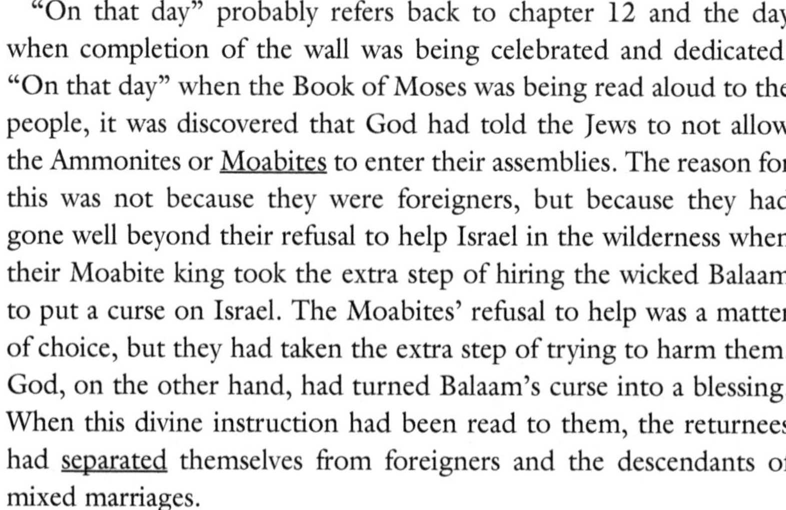

"On that day" probably refers back to chapter 12 and the day when completion of the wall was being celebrated and dedicated. "On that day" when the Book of Moses was being read aloud to the people, it was discovered that God had told the Jews to not allow the Ammonites or Moabites to enter their assemblies. The reason for this was not because they were foreigners, but because they had gone well beyond their refusal to help Israel in the wilderness when their Moabite king took the extra step of hiring the wicked Balaam to put a curse on Israel. The Moabites' refusal to help was a matter of choice, but they had taken the extra step of trying to harm them. God, on the other hand, had turned Balaam's curse into a blessing. When this divine instruction had been read to them, the returnees had separated themselves from foreigners and the descendants of mixed marriages.

This is not to say that foreigners could not convert to Judaism and made welcome. In fact, this was indeed possible. Ruth is an example of a Moabite who did just that. She was very popular with the people and even became an ancestor of Jesus. However, foreigners who did not convert were excluded.

There were very few copies of the Book of Moses anywhere, and it was next to impossible for any ordinary Jew to possess one. For this reason, most Jews would have had little knowledge of what was written in this book. They relied on the reading of the Scriptures in public, which became a normal practice.

Get This Stuff Out of Here

NEHEMIAH 13:4–9 ***Now before this, Eliashib the priest, having authority over the storerooms of the house of our God, was allied with Tobiah. And he had prepared for him a large room, where previously they had stored the grain offerings, the frankincense, the articles, the tithes of grain, the new wine and oil, which were commanded to be given to the Levites and singers and gatekeepers, and the offerings for the priests. But during all this I was not in Jerusalem, for in the thirty-second year of Artaxerxes king of Babylon I had returned to the king. Then after certain days I obtained leave from the king, and I came to Jerusalem and discovered the evil that Eliashib had done for Tobiah, in preparing a room for him in the courts of the house of God. And it grieved me bitterly; therefore I threw all the household goods***

of Tobiah out of the room. Then I commanded them to cleanse the rooms; and I brought back into them the articles of the house of God, with the grain offering and the frankincense. (NKJV)

"Before this" means before the events of this day. Before the Jews learned that they were suppose to exclude foreigners from their assemblies, a priest named Eliashib was put in charge of the Temple storerooms. Eliashib had close ties to an Ammonite named Tobiah. This Jewish priest foolishly allowed his non-Jewish friend Tobiah (some think they were related by marriage) to use one of the large storerooms that had been built for storage of grain offerings, incense, Temple articles, and tithes of wine and oil. He let a man who worshiped a foreign god take charge of a room at the Temple that was supposed to be storage for gifts to God.

Eliashib knew Nehemiah wouldn't approve of this, but he approved the arrangement while Nehemiah was out of the country. After twelve years in Israel, from the twentieth to the thirty-second year of King Artaxerxes' reign, Nehemiah had gone back to Babylon for an unspecified period of time once his leave of absence was up. Now, returning to Jerusalem with the king's permission, he learned about this violation of God's Law. Nehemiah reacted decisively and with great emotion by throwing Tobiah's possessions out the door. Then, he commanded that not only this storeroom, but all the storerooms be purified. Following that, he put the Temple equipment, grain offerings, and incense back in the rooms. Some are critical of Nehemiah for reacting this way, but Jesus acted similarly when he drove the money changers out of the Temple. God's house is not a storeroom for pagans, or a place of business for infidels. It is a house of prayer.

what others say

Mark D. Roberts/Lloyd J. Ogilvie

> This reveals two discouraging factors. For one, it indicates that the required offerings were not being given for the support of the Temple ministry, hence the empty storeroom. For another, Tobiah was a gentile, an Ammonite (2:19), who should not have been allowed in the sacred areas of the Temple. Tobiah's presence in the storeroom designated for holy implements caused the room to be desecrated. And it is perplexing that this compromise of the Temple's holiness and integrity did not appear to matter to Eliashib or to his fellow priests.[2]

neglect
Nehemiah 10:39

writing
Nehemiah 9:38

what others say

Charles R. Swindoll

People who envision these saints of the Old Testament with halos, untarnished robes, and well-polished sandals have missed the whole point of the narrative. Nehemiah went into the rooms and began to throw all of Tobiah's gear out into the streets. It was a spring house-cleaning.[3]

These Rooms Should Be Full

NEHEMIAH 13:10–14 ***I also realized that the portions for the Levites had not been given them; for each of the Levites and the singers who did the work had gone back to his field. So I contended with the rulers, and said, "Why is the house of God forsaken?" And I gathered them together and set them in their place. Then all Judah brought the tithe of the grain and the new wine and the oil to the storehouse. And I appointed as treasurers over the storehouse Shelemiah the priest and Zadok the scribe, and of the Levites, Pedaiah; and next to them was Hanan the son of Zaccur, the son of Mattaniah; for they were considered faithful, and their task was to distribute to their brethren. Remember me, O my God, concerning this, and do not wipe out my good deeds that I have done for the house of my God, and for its services!*** *(NKJV)*

After he threw Tobiah's possessions out, it didn't take long for Nehemiah to put the equipment, grain offerings, and incense back into the storerooms. He knew something was wrong and soon learned that the Levites and singers were not being properly supported. Because they had not been able to survive on what they were receiving from the people, they had been forced to leave the Temple and work in the fields.

The people had agreed to not neglect the house of God, and they had even put their oath in writing. After learning that the oath was not being fulfilled, Nehemiah called a meeting of the Israeli officials. He chastised them and asked them to explain why they were not keeping their written promise to God. He then called the Levites and singers together and ordered them to return to their duties at the Temple.

Nehemiah's actions brought a response from the people. It seems that they had stopped delivering their tithes to the storerooms when they believed the proper procedures were not being followed. Now that Nehemiah had put things in order, however, the people brought their tithes of grain, wine, and oil to the storerooms again. Nehemiah also took steps to see that this problem wasn't repeated. He put four men he could trust in charge of the storerooms and assigned them responsibility for distributing the grain, wine, and oil.

what others say

Max Lucado

It helps to remember that what we think of as our financial resources don't really belong to us. Everything that we have is loaned to us by God, and he gives it to us to use in ways that please him.[4]

Warren W. Wiersbe

When God's people start to decline spiritually, one of the first places it shows up is in their giving . . . The believer who is happy in the Lord and walking in His will has a generous heart and wants to share with others. Giving is both the "thermostat" and the "thermometer" of the Christian life: It measures our spiritual "temperature" and also helps set it at the right level.[5]

Tempting God

NEHEMIAH 13:15–18 *In those days I saw people in Judah treading wine presses on the Sabbath, and bringing in sheaves, and loading donkeys with wine, grapes, figs, and all kinds of burdens, which they brought into Jerusalem on the Sabbath day. And I warned them about the day on which they were selling provisions. Men of Tyre dwelt there also, who brought in fish and all kinds of goods, and sold them on the Sabbath to the children of Judah, and in Jerusalem. Then I contended with the nobles of Judah, and said to them, "What evil thing is this that you do, by which you profane the Sabbath day? Did not your fathers do thus, and did not our God bring all this disaster on us and on this city? Yet you bring added wrath on Israel by profaning the Sabbath." (NKJV)*

Another promise the Jews put in writing was that they would not buy merchandise or grain from the neighboring peoples on the Sabbath. But during his second trip back to Israel, Nehemiah looked

desecrating
abusing or showing contempt or disrespect for the things of God

around the outlying districts and saw Jewish men working on the Sabbath. He saw that they were treading the winepresses and loading grain, wine, grapes, figs, and other goods on their donkeys for transport to Jerusalem. He warned that this was wrong.

Nehemiah also saw non-Jews from Tyre who had settled in Jerusalem transporting fish and other merchandise into the Holy City to sell to careless Jewish customers on the Sabbath. He blamed this transgression on the Jewish leaders. He rebuked them for allowing it and accused them of **desecrating** the Sabbath. He reminded them that their ancestors had angered God by breaking his commandments and warned them that they were stirring up his anger by repeating this sin.

God created the Sabbath so his people could have a day of rest and worship. This is made possible by refraining from activities involved in earning money. As in days of old, our priorities are on display when we devote our day of rest and worship to earning money.

what others say

Mervin Breneman

Amos (8:5), Isaiah (58:13–14), and Jeremiah (17:19–27) warned the people against their laxity in keeping the day set apart for rest and worship. This Sabbath of rest and worship—one day of seven separated for God—is unknown in the ancient world outside of Israel. As part of the Ten Commandments (Exodus 20:8–11) it emphasizes the moral principle that all of our time belongs to God. This is symbolized by setting apart one day of each week.[6]

Let This Be Your Last Time

NEHEMIAH 13:19–22 ***So it was, at the gates of Jerusalem, as it began to be dark before the Sabbath, that I commanded the gates to be shut, and charged that they must not be opened till after the Sabbath. Then I posted some of my servants at the gates, so that no burdens would be brought in on the Sabbath day. Now the merchants and sellers of all kinds of wares lodged outside Jerusalem once or twice. Then I warned them, and said to them, "Why do you spend the night around the wall? If you do so again, I will lay hands on you!" From that time on they came no more on the Sabbath. And I commanded the Levites that they should cleanse themselves, and that they should go and guard the***

gates, to sanctify the Sabbath day. Remember me, O my God, concerning this also, and spare me according to the greatness of Your mercy! (NKJV)

Ashdod
a Philistine city

One thing Nehemiah did to combat buying and selling in Jerusalem on the Sabbath was to order that the gates to the city be shut at sunset on the evening before the Sabbath and to stay shut until the Sabbath was over. A second thing he did was to station his own guards at the gates on the Sabbath to prevent any merchandise from entering the city on that day. On one or two occasions, determined merchants showed up with their goods and set up shop just outside the city gates, probably to entice customers to come out and to catch travelers who were on their way into the city. When Nehemiah saw this he told them to not do it again and warned that he would arrest them if they disobeyed his order. When he saw that the sellers had heeded his warning and did not return, he withdrew his own guards and commanded the Levites to purify themselves and be the ones to guard the gates. He then prayed and asked God to remember him with mercy and love.

Separation Enforced

NEHEMIAH 13:23–28 ***In those days I also saw Jews who had married women of Ashdod, Ammon, and Moab. And half of their children spoke the language of Ashdod, and could not speak the language of Judah, but spoke according to the language of one or the other people. So I contended with them and cursed them, struck some of them and pulled out their hair, and made them swear by God, saying, "You shall not give your daughters as wives to their sons, nor take their daughters for your sons or yourselves. Did not Solomon king of Israel sin by these things? Yet among many nations there was no king like him, who was beloved of his God; and God made him king over all Israel. Nevertheless pagan women caused even him to sin. Should we then hear of your doing all this great evil, transgressing against our God by marrying pagan women?" And one of the sons of Joiada, the son of Eliashib the high priest, was a son-in-law of Sanballat the Horonite; therefore I drove him from me.*** (NKJV)

As Nehemiah traveled around the countryside, he encountered Jews who had married women from **Ashdod**, Ammon, and Moab.

Solomon
1 Kings 11:1–13

Sanballat
Nehemiah 2:10–20; 4:1–23; 6:1–14

The Jews had promised not to intermarry, but some did and now half their children spoke foreign languages and did not know how to speak Hebrew. Nehemiah reviled the unfaithful Jews, pronounced curses upon them, had some of them beaten, had the hair of some pulled out, and made them swear by God that if they permitted their children to intermarry, they would be inviting God to inflict them with the curses Nehemiah pronounced.

Nehemiah used King Solomon as an example of the dangers of intermarriage. God had allowedhim to become the king of Israel. God loved him. He was known for his great wisdom and was one of the greatest kings who ever lived. In spite of all this, he sinned against God as he succumbed to the evil influence of his foreign wives. Nehemiah used this example to frame his question as to whether these unfaithful Jews thought the nation should tolerate intermarriage in their time. Their implied answer is "definitely not."

The problem had already reached into the family of Eliashib the high priest. Eliashib's grandson had married Sanballat's daughter, who was a Horonite. This was so offensive to Nehemiah that he chased this wayward grandson of a high priest out of the country and forced him to live with foreigners.

Just a Little Talk with God

NEHEMIAH 13:29–31 ***Remember them, O my God, because they have defiled the priesthood and the covenant of the priesthood and the Levites. Thus I cleansed them of everything pagan. I also assigned duties to the priests and the Levites, each to his service, and to bringing the wood offering and the firstfruits at appointed times. Remember me, O my God, for good! (NKJV)***

This is the third time in this chapter that Nehemiah asked God to remember something. In this case, his concern was the priests who had married non-Jewish wives. He believed they had defiled the priesthood and broken the promise they had made to remain faithful to God. He believed that sin in the priesthood was one of the worst kinds of sin because it did so much damage to so many people and brought into question the work of all the priests. His request for God to remember them was probably a request for God to correct what they had done rather than a request for vengeance.

Then, Nehemiah performed an unknown ceremony of purification of the priests and Levites. He doesn't say what he did, but he does say he got rid of everything foreign. This could mean he removed all foreigners from positions of honor and responsibility among the priests and Levites, but it probably means he drove away the priests and Levites who would not give up their foreign wives and children.

foreign
Ezra 10:1–17

God of heaven
Nehemiah 1:4–11

After this, he restored the remaining priests and Levites to their proper positions of service. And knowing that they would need financial and other support, he arranged for people to provide wood for the burnt offerings at the Temple and start bringing in their first-fruit offerings again.

Finally, Nehemiah opened his book by praying to the God of heaven, and he closed it with a prayer to be remembered with favor. Most commentators would agree that God answered this request because Nehemiah's writings have become a permanent part of the Bible, and he is remembered with favor by Jew and Christian alike for his amazing contribution to the rebuilding of Jerusalem through his leadership and determination, faithfulness and prayers, and victory over criticism, slander, and compromise.

what others say

Mervin Breneman

Nehemiah reminds us that the tolerance of evil leads to spiritual stagnation, which leads to indifference on doctrinal matters; the final result is moral and spiritual degeneration.[7]

David Wilkerson

You may ask—what is the prayer that shakes hell? It comes from the faithful, diligent servant who sees his nation and church falling deeper into sin. This person falls on his knees, crying, "Lord, I don't want to be a part of what's going on. Let me be an example of your keeping power in the midst of this wicked age. It doesn't matter if no one else prays. I'm going to pray."[8]

Chapter Wrap-Up

- While the Book of Moses was being read to the Jews, they learned that God had forbidden them to include the Ammonites and Moabites in their assemblies because the ancestors of these foreigners had refused to help the Jews in the wilderness and had hired Balaam to curse them. When Nehemiah discovered that some of the Jews had intermarried with Gentiles, he rebuked them, asked God to curse them, beat some of them, pulled out the hair of some of them, pointed out Solomon's failure, and made them promise to not let their children do the same. He also drove away the grandson of the high priest for marrying a foreigner.
- The Temple was desecrated when Eliashib allowed a foreigner named Tobiah to store his household goods in the Temple storeroom. This happened while Nehemiah was out of the country, but he returned, discovered it, threw Tobiah's goods out, ordered the Temple rooms purified, and returned them to their original purpose.
- Because the Jews had stopped giving offerings, the Levites and singers left their posts to work in the fields. Nehemiah rebuked the Jewish officials for allowing this, returned the Levites and singers to their official duties, had the Jews resume their giving, and put trustworthy men in charge of handling and distributing the offerings.
- When Nehemiah saw Jews working and doing business on the Sabbath he warned them to stop. When he saw Gentiles selling to the Jews on the Sabbath he condemned the Jewish officials and reminded them that Sabbath violations had stirred God's wrath against Israel in the past. He had the city gates closed on the Sabbath and threatened some merchants who set up shop outside the wall. He ordered the Levites to purify themselves and guard the gates.
- Nehemiah prayed often. He wanted God to remember his deeds, his efforts to preserve true worship, and the deeds of the unfaithful priests and Levites.

Study Questions

1. What prompted the Jews to exclude the Ammonites and Moabites from their assemblies?
2. What mistake did Eliashib the priest make? Why did it take Nehemiah so long to find out about it and what did he do?
3. Why did the Levites go back to work in the fields? What steps did Nehemiah take to correct the situation?
4. Why did Nehemiah close the gates to the city on the Sabbath? Did it work?
5. What mistake did King Solomon make that was being repeated by the Jews? What did Nehemiah do to the high priest's grandson for doing this?

Part Three
THE BOOK OF HAGGAI

Introduction
The Book of Haggai

The book of Haggai contains two chapters with a total of thirty-eight verses. It is shorter than all other books in the Old Testament, except the book of Obadiah. The message is roughly 60 percent historical and 40 percent prophetic. We have divided the book of Haggai into the following four parts:

foundation
Ezra 3:10

Four Parts of Haggai

Year of Darius	Month/Day	Scripture
The call to rebuild the Temple	6/1	1:1–15
The call to behold God's glory	7/21	2:1–9
The call to stop sinning	9/24	2:10–19
The call to anticipate Messiah's return	9/24	2:20–23

Haggai is an obscure individual. Very little is known about him other than the fact that he probably went back to Israel with the first wave of returnees; he was a contemporary and coworker of Ezra, Zerubbabel, and Zechariah; and he was a prophet. Nevertheless, he is greatly revered by the Jews, who say he was a founding member of the "Great Synagogue" that later became known as the Sanhedrin. They buried him in a sepulcher reserved for priests because they believed he came from the tribe of Levi.

While he says very little about himself, he mentions several dates that reveal when these events took place. They occurred over a four-month period during the sixth through the ninth months of the second year of Darius. Most critics believe the year was 520 BC, and it's so clear that there is very little debate today about it.

The book of Ezra reveals that it wasn't long after the first wave of returnees arrived back in their homeland that they laid the foundation of the Temple. Since they were doing God's work, they believed God would make it easy for them to build a big beautiful Temple in a hurry. But it didn't happen that way. The social and economic conditions in Jerusalem were not good. The weather didn't help either. Food shortages were common. Materials were hard to get and of inferior quality. Workers stayed home to deal with their own needs.

standstill
Ezra 4:24

Haggai
Ezra 5:1; 6:14

The opposition from Israel's enemies was persistently great. The problems were overwhelming. As a result, this important project was soon brought to an abrupt standstill. The foundation was laid, but nothing else happened for about sixteen years. Then Haggai and Zechariah got involved. Both rightly understood that the Temple was indispensable to Israel's religious life. Both strongly urged the rebuilding of the Temple. Both played an important role in restarting the construction and both had the privilege of seeing the Temple completed in their lifetimes.

what others say

Master Reference Bible

The specific task of Haggai was to induce the Jews to resume their work on the temple which had been delayed for eighteen years. The first message was delivered in August 520. In less than a month work was resumed under the leadership of Zerubbabel and Joshua. The remaining messages were given before the end of that year.[1]

Haggai was very practical and down-to-earth. He firmly believed he was speaking "the Word of the Lord." He even said so several times. The Temple is God's house, a symbol of God's presence with his people, and Haggai's main desire was to see that it was rebuilt. He strongly rebuked the Jews for not doing that, but he was also quick to encourage them when they did get started. He alsorevealed several things about the future: the judgment of God, the kingdom of God, the messianic hope, a future Temple, and more. The big picture points to a glorious and wonderful future.

what others say

The Holy Bible

Haggai contains four appeals from the Lord, spoken to the people through the prophet. These appeals were all within the context of continuing to rebuild the Temple, which had been started many years earlier and never finished. Haggai has to appeal to the people and their leaders, which had both lost interest in the Temple.[2]

Haggai 1
The First Message

Chapter Highlights:
- Who Said What and When?
- God Wanted to Know
- Express Yourself
- I Wish it Would Rain
- I Worked!

Let's Get Started

It is just speculation, but most everyone assumes that Haggai was born in Babylon during the Captivity. He was one of the first prophets to prophesy after Cyrus issued his decree allowing the Jews to return home, and it seems likely that he returned to Jerusalem in the first wave of returnees that was led by Zerubbabel.

Cyrus
Ezra 1:2–4

Zerubbabel
Ezra 2:1–63

Elul
our August/September

Who Said What and When

HAGGAI 1:1 ***In the second year of King Darius, in the sixth month, on the first day of the month, the word of the LORD came by Haggai the prophet to Zerubbabel the son of Shealtiel, governor of Judah, and to Joshua the son of Jehozadak, the high priest, saying,*** *(NKJV)*

Haggai started prophesying in the second year of King Darius (see "Persian Kings," page 38). He even said it was the first day of the sixth month, which would be the month of **Elul** (see "Hebrew and Gregorian Calendars" chart, page 24). It was the custom of the Old Testament writers to link their writings to the kings of Israel and Judah, but when those kingdoms didn't exist, they linked them to the ruling Gentile kings. In the past the Jews regularly celebrated the appearance of the new moon on this date. The celebrations had always been held at the Temple, but there was no longer a Temple because Nebuchadnezzar had destroyed it. This may have been on Haggai's mind when God spoke to him. It is important to recognize that these are God's words, not Haggai's words. The words merely flowed through Haggai the prophet. They were specifically directed to Zerubbabel and the governor, and to Joshua, the high priest of Judah.

Many dates in the Bible are tied to a king of Israel or Judah. But the Northern Kingdom of Israel was destroyed by Assyria in 721 BC. Then, the Southern Kingdom of Judah was destroyed by

Times of the Gentiles
Luke 21:24

Times of the Gentiles
the period of Gentile domination of Israel

Babylon in 586 BC. History is now in a period of time referred to as the "**Times of the Gentiles,**" and some dates in the Bible are tied to Gentile kings. However, the Bible makes it clear that this will end because Israel will only be dominated by them. This domination will end finally with the second coming of Jesus.

It's Not What We Expected

HAGGAI 1:2 ***"Thus speaks the LORD of hosts, saying: 'This people says, "The time has not come, the time that the LORD's house should be built."'"*** *(NKJV)*

"The LORD of hosts" is a term that appears fourteen times in the book of Haggai. It is often used for the Leader of the armies of Israel, but sometimes refers to the Leader of the heavenly armies. It emphasizes God's power. He is the power behind Israel. He can do all things, overcome all opposition, and carry out his plans and purposes until everything he desires is done. This is definitely one of the main things Haggai wanted the discouraged Jews to understand: if God wanted the Temple to be rebuilt, nothing could stop it. His people may fail, but he will not. Nothing can thwart the accomplishment of his will.

After Cyrus issued his decree to let the Jews go, Zerubbabel led almost fifty thousand people back to Jerusalem. It seems that they expected to find old houses that were still occupiable. It appears that they expected to have peace and prosperity, the blessings of God, and a general ease. Instead, most of the old houses had been destroyed, the old population centers were deserted, and the land had been overcome with weeds and shrubs. Along with this, they found that openly hostile foreign squatters had settled on some of the land. There was much to do prior to rebuilding the Temple. Food needed to be found, land needed to be cleared, houses needed to be rebuilt, and squatters needed to be evacuated.

Times were harder than the returnees expected, so hard that they believed they had made a mistake in returning and should delay the rebuilding of the Temple.

As God begins to speak in this first message, it is important to note that the people—not God—have been saying that it is not time to rebuild the Temple. Notice that God said *the people* were saying it was not time to rebuild the Temple. It's obvious that they were using hard times as an excuse for not rebuilding the Temple.

Some people who face opposition today say, "It's just not God's will. The Lord is just not in it." The Jews gave up before they had even begun. God's people must not be dissuaded from doing God's work just because it doesn't happen to be convenient for them at the time.

Old Testament Names of God

Name	Meaning	Name	Meaning
Adonai	Lord, Master, Owner	Jehovah-nissi	God my banner, victory
Elohim	God, Greatness, Creator	Jehovah-rohi	God my shepherd, protects
El-Shaddai	God Almighty, Omnipotent	Jehovah-rophe	God heals
Jehovah	LORD, Am, Being, Living	Jehovah-shalom	God is my peace
Jehovah-jireh	God will provide	Jehovah-shammah	God is there, present
Jehovah-M'Kaddesh	God sanctifies, sets apart, cleanses	Jehovah-tsidkenu	God my righteousness

Something God Wanted to Know

HAGGAI 1:3–4 ***Then the word of the LORD came by Haggai the prophet, saying, "Is it time for you yourselves to dwell in your paneled houses, and this temple to lie in ruins?"*** *(NKJV)*

Notice this! Times were hard, but these people could afford to build paneled houses for themselves. Paneled houses were not cheap in those days. They were very expensive. God was doing more than asking a question. He was pointing out that the Jews were just making excuses when they said, "The time has not come, the time that the LORD's house should be built" (1:2 NKJV). No one questions the fact that the Jews needed good homes for their families. It was very important for their children to have a good place to sleep, but there is no such thing as a good excuse for not doing God's work. When people have their priorities in the right order, God's work comes first. In this case, work on the Temple had languished for sixteen years. It was obvious that it wasn't high on their list of priorities. Determined opposition played a big role in stopping construction, but the apathy and indifference of the Jews was a major contributor to the delay. They weren't saying they would never build it. They were simply saying, "Not now; let's do it later."

what others say

Chuck Missler

These are the right people, they are also in the right place, they are back in the homeland: the right people, at the right place, at the right time, and they also were pursuing the work of the Temple for the right reasons. But there is a problem. They didn't have their priorities right. They allowed their own personal cares to get in the way.[1]

This reversal of priorities may be seen today as well. Numerous people say they cannot afford to give to God even though they build expensive houses for themselves. They think they cannot afford to tithe, but they can afford nice furniture, new cars, good clothes, and expensive jewelry. They are too busy for God, but they are not too busy for many kinds of recreation or extended vacations to places around the world. They don't have the money or time to contribute to the purposes of God, but readily find a way to enhance their own lifestyles. The Jews didn't fool God then, and people today aren't fooling God either.

Think About It

Haggai 1:5–6 ***Now therefore, thus says the Lord of hosts: "Consider your ways! You have sown much, and bring in little; you eat, but do not have enough; you drink, but you are not filled with drink; you clothe yourselves, but no one is warm; and he who earns wages, earns wages to put into a bag with holes." (NKJV)***

God asked the people to consider what was happening. It's something he asked them to do five times in these 38 verses: in 1:5, 7; 2:15, and twice in 2:18 of the book of Haggai. He also wanted them to reflect on the fact that they were planting large crops, but their crops were not producing very much; they were eating and drinking, but they did not have enough; they were buying clothes, but their clothes weren't good enough; and they were working all the time, but they were constantly being reduced to poverty. He said it was almost like they had holes in their pockets.

Love and discipline are not opposites with God. This is a difficult concept for some to accept. God's people should support God's work. Those who withhold from him may really be withholding from themselves. He sometimes acts to thwart those who seek to enrich themselves at the expense of contributing to the fulfillment of his plans. In this case, he let the returnees suffer poor crops, famine, poverty, and unproductive hard work as means for chastening them and to make the point that they would not prosper without the blessings that come when people do things his way.

what others say

Stephen R. Miller

Not building the temple was not the problem; it was merely an external symptom. The problem was much deeper—an uncommitted life.[2]

Examine Yourself

HAGGAI 1:7–8 ***Thus says the LORD of hosts: "Consider your ways! Go up to the mountains and bring wood and build the temple, that I may take pleasure in it and be glorified," says the LORD. (NKJV)***

These two verses of Scripture reveal four things God told the Jews to do. First, the Jews had a conflict of interest because they were putting themselves before him and were putting their houses before his house. Because their priorities were wrong, God wanted them to reflect on the results of what they were doing. Their self-centeredness was an offense unto him, and he wanted to be their first priority. Second, God told them to go up into the mountains. He was saying, "Get up, get out of those nice houses, and go into the mountains. There are plenty of trees for you to cut." Third, God told them to not wait on others to bring the materials to them. They should go and gather the materials themselves. And fourth, he told them to get to work on the Temple and finish it.

He said if they did what he told them to do, two things would happen. First, their obedience would make him happy and pleased with his house. Second, he would be honored in it because the priests would make it a place of true worship.

good measure
Luke 6:38

In former times, the Temple was the most important place in Israel. God met the priests there. He was worshiped there. He revealed his will there. It was destroyed because the people broke that relationship. Now, God wanted to restore it right then and there.

Do You Want to Know Why?

> **HAGGAI 1:9** ***"You looked for much, but indeed it came to little; and when you brought it home, I blew it away. Why?" says the LORD of hosts. "Because of My house that is in ruins, while every one of you runs to his own house.*** *(NKJV)*

The Jews worked hard, but they were not prospering the way they expected. They looked for material things without doing spiritual things. They probably blamed their troubles on the ground conditions, enemies, or anything other than the fact that God was not blessing the fruit of their labor in the same way that he would if they had made him their first priority. In essence, they couldn't have the material blessings without first being a spiritual blessing.

The Jews were disappointed because God would not allow their materialism to interfere with their relationship with him. Crops and houses are important, but not nearly as important as God. He would no longer allow life without the Temple. Having the Temple was actually in their best interests. Putting off doing what we know God wants us to do not only offends God, but also harms us because God always has our best interests in mind when he requires something of us. He will often withdraw his hand of blessing to get our attention and cause us to recognize that having him be the first priority of our lives is the only way that we will be truly content. There is a connection between what Christians do for God and what he does for them. The people of God cannot bribe him to bless them, but he returns cheerful giving in good measure, pressed down, shaken together and running over.

It Sure Is Dry

> **HAGGAI 1:10** ***Therefore the heavens above you withhold the dew, and the earth withholds its fruit.*** *(NKJV)*

During Israel's dry season, it doesn't rain. The ground is often watered by an early morning dew. In Haggai's day God was holding back the dew. He was doing it as a divine judgment for their sin. The natural result of insufficient water is poor crops. It was a reminder to the returnees that they were dependent upon God. Even though they had built good houses for themselves, their dependence on God was unavoidable. Because their fields had been fallow for seventy years, the soil should have been rich. Good soil was not all that was needed, though. They also needed God to bless them with the sunshine and rain that cause seeds to sprout and plants to grow.

grain
barley, wheat, etc.

wine
vineyards, grapes, etc.

oil
olive trees

what others say

Mark J. Boda

The fundamental cause is that both "the heavens" and "the earth" are not cooperating with humanity to produce sustenance. The heavens are not providing the essential precipitation for life, nor is the earth providing the nutrients. The use of the "dew" is not surprising, especially considering the time of the year (August). The period between the "latter" (spring) and "early" (fall) rains is a time in which little to no rain falls in Israel. In a land almost exclusively reliant on water from precipitation, the presence of dew can mean the difference between life and death for vegetation.[3]

I Wish It Would Rain

HAGGAI 1:11 ***For I called for a drought on the land and the mountains, on the grain and the new wine and the oil, on whatever the ground brings forth, on men and livestock, and on all the labor of your hands." (NKJV)***

Drought gripped the land of Israel and God said it was his doing. It affected everything: the fields, the mountains, the **grain**, the **wine**, the **oil**, and everything that grows in the ground. It affected the men, the animals, and everything the people hoped to produce. Because they were withholding from God, he was withholding from them.

God still withholds his blessing and his protection today. For example, there are many reasons why natural disasters happen. In some cases disasters are caused by Satan. Wicked men cause famine and diseases by driving people out of desired areas and forcing too many to live in other areas. In other cases, people bring them on

disciplined
Hebrews 12:5–6

disciplined
punished

feared
respected

themselves by doing things like building in floodplains or on the sides of mountains. Accidents sometimes cause forest fires. The curse God placed on the creation as a result of Adam's sin cannot be overlooked. And finally, some people may be startled to learn that some natural disasters are caused by God. This is taught in both the Old and the New Testaments. There are times when he sends these things to give people an opportunity to repent and turn to him. Along with this, no matter what the cause of the disaster, each and every one can only happen if God allows it. Although it is hard to understand why God allows certain disasters to happen, we can find comfort in knowing that a loving God uses all things to reach out to us for our own good.

Is this true today? Are people their own worst enemy? Could some people be working in vain because they are failing to do God's work? He told the Jews he caused their problems and they had no one to blame but themselves. He **disciplined** them to get their attention and to show them the error of their ways.

It Worked!

> HAGGAI 1:12 ***Then Zerubbabel the son of Shealtiel, and Joshua the son of Jehozadak, the high priest, with all the remnant of the people, obeyed the voice of the LORD their God, and the words of Haggai the prophet, as the LORD their God had sent him; and the people feared the presence of the LORD.*** (NKJV)

Then Zerubbabel (the political leader), Joshua (the spiritual leader), and all the people did three things:

- They obeyed the voice of the Lord their God.
- They obeyed the words of this God-sent prophet.
- They **feared** the presence of God.

They accepted Haggai's message as being the word of God because they believed God had sent him to them. Prophets from God declared God's message or explained what God was doing. God also used them to tell the people what God planned to do in the future. It's important to realize that the people recognized Haggai as this kind of a man. The next chapter in his book reveals that he not only explained what was happening in his day, but he also recorded some amazing revelations about the future. These must be viewed as the words of God rather than the words of Haggai, but from God.

Comforting Words

> **Haggai 1:13** *Then Haggai, the Lord's messenger, spoke the Lord's message to the people, saying, "I am with you, says the Lord." (NKJV)*

This message was short and filled with assurance. The returnees decided to do God's work and he decided to be with them. "I am with you" was the same thing as telling the Jews, "You will be able to rebuild the Temple because I will help you." This reminds us of the words of Jesus when he said, "With God all things are possible" (Matthew 19:26 NKJV).

If God is with you, someone can throw you into a den of hungry lions and you will not be bitten. If God is with you, someone can throw you in a blazing furnace and you will not be burned. If God is with you, someone can throw you over the side of a ship, and a great fish can come along and swallow you, but you will not be hurt. If God is with you, someone can curse you, spit on you, beat you, put a crown of thorns on your head, hit you over the head, nail you to a cross, drive a spear through your side, and bury you in a tomb, but they cannot defeat you. If God is with you, nothing can separate you from his love. If God is with you, nothing can keep you from rebuilding the Temple.

go to

lions
Daniel 6:16–24

blazing
Daniel 3:15–27

ship
Jonah 1:3–2:10

cross
Matthew 27:31–50

love
Romans 8:38–39

This is an excellent example of God's forgiveness. He is motivated by love and could forgive Abraham for lying, Moses for killing, and David for committing adultery and murder. All the returnees needed to do was to repent and serve God. When they said they would do that, he forgave their selfishness and materialism. This provides us with a clue about how individuals, communities, and nations should respond today: turn from your sins and draw close to God.

They Rolled Up Their Sleeves

> **Haggai 1:14–15** *So the Lord stirred up the spirit of Zerubbabel the son of Shealtiel, governor of Judah, and the spirit of Joshua the son of Jehozadak, the high priest, and the spirit of all the remnant of the people; and they came and*

witnessing
telling others about the goodness of God

lukewarm
not passionate

worked on the house of the LORD of hosts, their God, on the twenty-fourth day of the sixth month, in the second year of King Darius. *(NKJV)*

The challenge to "consider your ways" and the knowledge that God was "with" the Jews encouraged Zerubbabel, Joshua, and all the people to the extent that they immediately started to work on the Temple. Haggai received his first message in the second year of Darius the king, in the sixth month, in the first day of the month. The people started the work on the Temple on the twenty-fourth day of the same year and month. In summation, it took the Jews only twenty-three days to go up to the mountains, cut trees, haul the wood to Jerusalem, and begin construction on the Temple. This is the way God is. He provides everything that is needed to do his will. The construction delay had been due to lack of encouragement not lack of materials.

Notice that it was the Lord who stirred up the spirit of Zerubbabel, Joshua, and "all the remnant of the people." The work of the Holy Spirit was what was causing them to respond to the Word of God. He stirred them up through his Word and his Spirit so that they stopped delaying the work on the house of the Lord of hosts, their God.

Notice also that Haggai calls the Lord "their God." He used this phrase three times in three verses (12–14). The opposition of their enemies, drought, and poor crops were enough to make some wonder if they had a God. The Lord assured them over and over again that they did.

There are times when things are not working out. It is easy to get discouraged and wonder if God has forgotten his people. But the problem just might be that his people are not doing his work. Some may believe that their church is not growing because God has withdrawn his blessing from them. It is not wrong to ponder and pray to see if it may be because church members are not attending, giving, praying, and **witnessing**. Could it be that many church members are preoccupied with other things and not doing what God wants them to do? Could it be that some are **lukewarm**? Could it be that many need to renew their commitment to the Lord and his work?

Why Do People Miss Out on God's Blessings?

- ***Materialism***—The tendency to put worldly things before spiritual things.
- ***Procrastination or Falling Away***—The tendency to stop doing God's work.
- ***Apostasy***—The tendency to tolerate leaders who don't give out the Word of God.
- ***Discouragement***—The tendency to think the task is too great.
- ***Lack of Faith***—The tendency to doubt God.

God is not opposed to people having worldly goods and pleasures. He is the Source of these things. People who try to find their peace and contentment in those things will find they are coming up empty. The true blessings of remaining near to him by making him our first priority always yields the everlasting fruit of a life that points others to him.

Chapter Wrap-Up

- The Jews were saying it was not time to build the Temple because times were hard, but God noted that this had not stopped them from building paneled houses for themselves.
- God told the Jews they should repent because their attitude caused him to send the hard times.
- God told the Jews to gather wood for the Temple and said he had sent a drought to discipline them for not rebuilding the Temple.
- The Jews decided to obey and respect God. In response, he promised to be with them.
- Encouraged by God's words, the Jews started construction of the Temple on the twenty-fourth day of the sixth month of the second year during the reign of King Darius.

Study Questions

1. What were the people saying and why were they saying it? Why was this hypocritical?
2. What did God advise the people to do? What indication did he give that they would be wise to take his advice?
3. What did God tell the Jews to do to please him? What had he done to discipline them and why?
4. What two attitudes did God's discipline provoke? What did God say he would do?
5. How did the people respond?

Haggai 2 Three More Messages

Chapter Highlights:
- The Second Message
- The Lord Wants to Know
- God's Prescription
- You're Not Alone

Let's Get Started

The Holy Spirit stirred up Zerubbabel, Joshua, and all the people. They immediately started working on the Temple with much enthusiasm. Like most revivals today, however, it didn't last very long. Their high hopes and great expectations were not being met. They quickly became discouraged. God, on the other hand, had promised to be with them, and nothing is more obvious in the Scriptures than the fact that he does what he says he will do. This is also evident by the fact that with great patience and love, he continued to speak to them through Haggai the prophet. This encouraged the Jews to forge ahead until the project was completed. In addition to this, his messages also reveal several amazing things about the future.

Messianic
about Jesus, the Messiah, and future things

what others say

Henry H. Halley

This is distinctly a **Messianic** vision. Haggai's mind was on that Temple, which he was helping Zerubbabel to build. But his words were God's words; and God's mind, in a sense deeper perhaps than even Haggai himself realized, was on Another Temple, yet to be, of which Solomon's Temple and Zerubbabel's Temple were but dim pictures.[1]

The Second Message

HAGGAI 2:1–2 ***In the seventh month, on the twenty-first of the month, the word of the LORD came by Haggai the prophet, saying: "Speak now to Zerubbabel the son of Shealtiel, governor of Judah, and to Joshua the son of Jehozadak, the high priest, and to the remnant of the people, saying:*** **(NKJV)**

The Jews started working on the Temple on the twenty-fourth day of the sixth month, and this message was given on the twenty-first day of the seventh month, so it is easy to determine that less than a month passed between the two messages. This was the last day of the Feast of Tabernacles, a holiday the Jews regularly celebrated to remember God's provision for their ancestors when Moses was leading them through the wilderness. They were probably celebrating his goodness and provision when he told Haggai to speak to the same people he had delivered the first message to: Zerubbabel, Joshua, and all the others.

what others say

Mark J. Boda

The date of this prophetic message corresponds to another important event in the history of Israel. It was during this festival over four centuries earlier that Solomon dedicated the temple (1 Kings 8:2). The many allusions to this great Solomonic temple in this prophetic message show clearly that Haggai and his people have this event in mind, so that comparisons with the earlier project may have led to discouragement. In other words, as God's people are overwhelmed by their external circumstances and their internal expectations, Haggai is moved to deliver his second oracle.[2]

The Lord Wants to Know

Haggai 2:3 ***'Who is left among you who saw this temple in its former glory? And how do you see it now? In comparison with it, is this not in your eyes as nothing? (NKJV)***

After the Jews gathered the timber to rebuild the Temple, they started to work on what was clearly a difficult and expensive project. Once they had worked on it for almost a month, they got discouraged. This is when God spoke through Haggai to ask three penetrating questions. First, "Who is left among you who saw this temple in its former glory?" He was referring to the fact that some of the older Jews could remember seeing the first Temple that Solomon built. It took almost two hundred thousand men roughly seven years to build it and cost perhaps the equivalent of three to four billion dollars today. It was a magnificent gold-adorned place of worship. Some called it the most beautiful building in the world. Second, "And how do you see it now?" God knew that the returnees were comparing Solomon's Temple with the one they had under construction. He was asking them to focus on this second one. Third, "In comparison with it, is this not in your eyes as nothing?" He knew that they did not think this second Temple was much in comparison to the first. It was a smaller and less glorious building. It was about half as tall as

Solomon's Temple. It had much less silver and gold. It did not house the Ark of the Covenant and did not have the holy fire. This is why the older Jews were discouraged. Aware of these shortages, they grumbled and complained. Their discouragement ran deeper still. Ezra recorded that "many of the priests and Levites and heads of the fathers' houses, old men who had seen the first temple, wept with a loud voice when the foundation of this temple was laid before their eyes" (NKJV). It must have been a heartbreaking sight to see many men in their eighties or older weeping so loudly.

loud voice
Ezra 3:12

Doubts do not solve problems or help people succeed, but they do cause people to give up before they ever get started or before the work is completed. In this case, doubts were like a wet blanket on the fire of enthusiasm that God's first message had generated. The success of the whole project was being jeopardized by the fond memories of elderly people who could remember the first Temple. They had hopes of building a more magnificent building for their good God.

key point

God's Prescription for a Discouraged People

HAGGAI 2:4 ***Yet now be strong, Zerubbabel,' says the LORD; 'and be strong, Joshua, son of Jehozadak, the high priest; and be strong, all you people of the land,' says the LORD, 'and work; for I am with you,' says the LORD of hosts. (NKJV)***

This is God's response to discouraged people who were trying to do his will. He told Zerubbabel, Joshua, and all the people five things. He said:

- Be strong, Zerubbabel.
- Be strong, Joshua.
- Be strong, all you people.
- Go to work.
- I am with you.

"Be strong . . . Be strong . . . Be strong" shows that the discouragement ran from the top to the bottom of this group of returnees. God deemed it necessary to speak to every one of them. When he says something once, it's very important. When he says something three times it's very, very, very important.

When God's people don't think they are accomplishing very much, God says, "Be strong." When God's people don't think they have what they need, God says, "Go to work." And when God's people get discouraged, God says, "I am with you." You say you don't have many members in your church; do your part and leave the results up to God. You say you don't have much money in your church; give your part and leave the results up to God. He will always do his part.

God's people are better off in a run-down barn with God on their side than they are in a large gold-adorned sanctuary with God against them. There is nothing wrong with big beautiful buildings if they are not built at the expense of first determining and fulfilling what is highest on God's list of priorities.

You're Not Alone

Haggai 2:5 ***'According to the word that I covenanted with you when you came out of Egypt, so My Spirit remains among you; do not fear!'*** (NKJV)

God gave assurance to the former exiles by reminding them of the covenant he had made with their ancestors in the wilderness. He promised their ancestors that they would be his treasured people, and they were. He promised them that he would dwell among them, and he did. And here God was telling the Jews to recall that he kept his promises to their ancestors when they came out of Egypt and to rest assured that he would do the same for them. They didn't have to have a large gold-adorned Temple, the Ark of the Covenant, or the holy fire to be his treasured people or for him to be with them. They need not be afraid, for the Holy Spirit would be with them.

covenant
Exodus 19:5–6

treasured
Deuteronomy 7:6

dwell
Exodus 29:45–46

what others say

Matthew Henry

The presence of God with us, as the *Lord of hosts*, is enough to silence all our fears and to help us over all the discouragements we may meet with in the way of our duty. The Jews had hosts against them, but they had the Lord of hosts with them, to take their part and plead their cause. He is with them; for, He adheres to his promise. His covenant is inviolable, and he will be always theirs, and will appear and act for them.[3]

A Whole Lot of Shaking

HAGGAI 2:6 ***"For thus says the LORD of hosts: 'Once more (it is a little while) I will shake heaven and earth, the sea and dry land; (NKJV)***

Mount Sinai
Exodus 19:18

thousand years
2 Peter 3:8

"Once more" refers back to verse 5 and the covenant God made with the Jews in the wilderness when he gave them the Ten Commandments. He descended upon Mount Sinai in fire and the whole mountain smoked like the smoke of a furnace and quaked greatly. "In a little while" means a short time from now. This is from the perspective of how God accounts time. Peter said, "But, beloved, do not forget this one thing, that with the Lord one day is as a thousand years, and a thousand years as one day" (NKJV). Here, in verse 6 God is speaking of a future judgment. It will be a judgment so severe that it will not only shake Mount Sinai, but will shake the entire creation.

Tribulation
the Tribulation Period, seven years of God's wrath against the wicked on earth

Millennial Kingdom
the thousand-year reign of Christ on earth

what others say

Irving L. Jensen

Now interpret 2:6–9 as referring to the end times, centered about the person of Christ as Messiah. Such an interpretation would involve the following: First will come the **Tribulation** (note the repeated word "shake"). See Revelation 16:18–20 and 19:11–21 for two descriptions of such judgment. At the end of the Tribulation, Christ, the "desire of all nations," will come to rule and be worshiped in His house.[4]

David M. Levy

The writer of Hebrews interpreted Haggai 2:6 in context of God's shaking the earth and nations at the Second Coming of Christ (Hebrews 12:26–27). He went on to say that after the **Millennial Kingdom**, God will again shake the heavens and the earth, which will bring about the total destruction of the universe (2 Peter 3:10, 12; Revelation 20:11). Then a new heaven and a new earth will appear (2 Peter 3:13; Revelation 21:1).[5]

There is widespread disagreement over the interpretation of this verse. Some scholars believe this shaking refers to a tremendous earthquake. Others believe it means great turmoil on earth or that the wicked will be troubled at the second coming of Jesus. When contemplated in light of other passages of Scripture, it could be both.

Zerubbabel's Temple
the name historians call the Temple that was being built (Zerubbabel was the governor and helped build it)

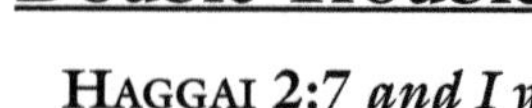

Double Trouble

HAGGAI 2:7 ***and I will shake all nations, and they shall come to the Desire of All Nations, and I will fill this temple with glory,' says the LORD of hosts.*** *(NKJV)*

God repeated his intention to shake all nations. Doing this will cause them to turn to the "Desire of All Nations." Some say this is Jesus, the coming Deliverer, but others say he will never be desired by all nations. Some say it is the silver and gold mentioned in the next verse and others say it is the peace on earth mentioned in verse 9. There seems to be no way to settle the issue, but the first view is the most widely accepted: It is a prophecy about Jesus. When God said, "I will fill this temple with glory," he was referring to the fact that Jesus would visit the Temple being built and also the future Millennial Temple. It is true that all nations do not desire him today, but it will be different during the Millennium.

It seems that God has made a reference to the Trinity in the last three verses. What do you think?

- "My Spirit remains among you" (verse 5).
- "For thus says the LORD of hosts" (verse 6).
- "They shall come to the Desire of All Nations" (verse 7).

what others say

Irving L. Jensen

A prominent principle of Old Testament prophecy is that of multiple fulfillment. An example of this is Haggai 2:7, "I will fill this house with glory." This was a conditional prophecy about **Zerubbabel's Temple**, but more gloriously about the Temple of the Messianic Kingdom of the end times.[6]

The Real Owner

HAGGAI 2:8 ***'The silver is Mine, and the gold is Mine,' says the LORD of hosts.*** *(NKJV)*

Everything individuals possess actually belongs to God. It is not my silver and gold, or my house and goods. It is God's silver and gold, and God's house and goods. The point is that those who were discouraged because the Temple was small and because they didn't have much silver and gold were not mindful of the fact that God owns everything and was orchestrating the building of the Temple. He could have ensured that plenty of silver and gold went into the Temple, but was choosing to do something else.

It Will Be Greater Than You Can Imagine

Haggai 2:9 ***'The glory of this latter temple shall be greater than the former,' says the Lord of hosts. 'And in this place I will give peace,' says the Lord of hosts." (NKJV)***

God was saying, "You don't think you are going to have much of a Temple, but your rebuilt Temple will be greater than the first one because I will be there and I will grant you peace." People may get discouraged because their church is small or old, or they don't have many members. They get discouraged because they don't have much money or because they or their loved ones are sick. However, when our priorities are in order, we realize that God being with us is of much greater importance than having elaborate buildings, lots of money, good health, or a life of ease.

God was saying, "The glory of the Temple that you are building and the glory of the Temple at the end of the age will be greater than the one built by Solomon." There had been a famine and the returnees were poor, but the riches of the earth belong to God and adornments could be provided if that was what he desired. Although the returnees were surrounded by their enemies, the all-powerful God would protect them. The glory of the Lord would make the Temple more valuable than their ridiculers were capable of recognizing at that time.

what others say

Jack W. Hayford

This was truer than anyone could have imagined, for it was into this building Jesus Himself entered centuries later! Though it was an expanded structure, embellished by Herod's enterprise, God's glory incarnate, "full of grace and truth" arrived in fullest splendor as prophesied.[7]

The Jews were discouraged because the Temple was small and they didn't have much silver and gold to use for decorations. But over the years people kept giving, and the provisions for adding to the Temple grew more and more over time. Then, Herod spent a large sum on it and added to it so that it was larger and more beautiful than the one Solomon built. Historians say it was one of the most beautiful buildings on earth. The people had a saying, "If you have never seen the Temple, you have never seen beauty." They eventually put a band of pure gold all the way around the top of the building on the outside. We cannot imagine the cost.

When Jesus visited the Temple for the last time he said, "Not one stone shall be left here upon another; that shall not be thrown down" (NKJV). Do you remember what happened? There was so much gold in the Temple that when the Romans came in and set Jerusalem on fire in AD 70, the Temple burned, and all that gold melted and ran down between the rocks of the Temple. Then, after the gold had cooled, they came back and pried the rocks apart to get the gold.

The Third Message

HAGGAI 2:10–11 ***On the twenty-fourth day of the ninth month, in the second year of Darius, the word of the LORD came by Haggai the prophet, saying, "Thus says the LORD of hosts: 'Now, ask the priests concerning the law, saying, (NKJV)***

The second message from God was given on the twenty-first day of the seventh month, and this message was given about three months later on the twenty-fourth day of the ninth month. All of the messages were given in the second year of Darius. This time God wanted Haggai to ask the priests two questions about something found in the **Law**.

What Do You Think?

HAGGAI 2:12–13 ***"If one carries holy meat in the fold of his garment, and with the edge he touches bread or stew, wine or oil, or any food, will it become holy?"'" Then the priests answered and said, "No." And Haggai said, "If one who is unclean because of a dead body touches any of these, will it be unclean?" So the priests answered and said, "It shall be unclean." (NKJV)***

go to

stone
Matthew 24:2

Law
the Law of Moses

consecrated
holy, set aside for God's special purpose

These questions are tough to understand so here is a paraphrase that may help: The first question God asked was, "If a defiled person carries **consecrated** food in his pocket and it touches other food, does the other food become consecrated? And the priests correctly answered, "No!" The second question God asked was, "If a defiled person touches consecrated food, does the food become defiled?" And the priests correctly answered, "Yes, it becomes defiled!" Here are two more questions that may help: First, if a church member sins does that make sinning right? The answer is no. Second, if a church member sins, does that defile the church member's work? The answer is yes.

fire
Proverbs 6:27–28

holiness
sincere conformity to the nature and will of God

what others say

Chuck Missler

So **holiness** cannot be communicated by contact, but unholiness can. Dirty water will discolor clean water. By pouring clean water in a glass of dirty water does the dirty water become clean? Not really. Measles is communicated by contact. Can the absence of measles be communicated by contact? That's the analogy. It may be a clumsy one, but that's the analogy. And by the way, ceremony cannot cleanse a sinner. You cannot run with the wrong crowd and stay clean.[8]

The Problem Is Sin

HAGGAI 2:14 ***Then Haggai answered and said, "'So is this people, and so is this nation before Me,' says the LORD, 'and so is every work of their hands; and what they offer there is unclean. (NKJV)***

The two questions God asked illustrate what the Jews were doing. They were working on the Temple but continuing in sinful practices. Their poor lifestyle was tainting the good work they were doing. Serving God involves more than building a Temple, more than working on church projects, or more than helping other people. People can lay stones, paint, preach, teach, and even give to the poor, but their gifts are unclean if their hearts and lives are impure. Their hypocrisy may even harm immature Christians or unbelievers who jump to the conclusion that the life of sin is somehow made permissible or excused by good works.

Solomon asked, "Can a man take fire to his bosom, and his clothes not be burned? Can one walk on hot coals, and his feet not be seared?" (NKJV). Scooping fire into your lap will burn your clothes. Walking on hot coals will burn your feet. The point is that sin in your

house
Haggai 1:12–14

life will not only make your sacrifices unclean and taint all the good deeds you do, but it will also harm you in the process.

what others say

David M. Levy

There is a growing sense that many Christian workers are serving God with unclean hearts and hands. They live as if God has winked at their sin, and because they are working for the Lord He will continue to bless them. Blessing may come to an individual or his or her organization for a season, but it comes more because of a praying spouse, family, or committed followers. Eventually a person's ungodliness is revealed, the Lord's discipline ensues, and judgment falls.[9]

Chew on This

HAGGAI 2:15 *'And now, carefully consider from this day forward: from before stone was laid upon stone in the temple of the LORD—(NKJV)*

God asked the Jews to let their minds drift back to the situation that existed before they ever did any work of any kind on the Temple and to remember it from this day forward. He wanted them to remember the hard times, hard work, meager incomes, and drought. He told them to compare the way things were in those days to the way they will be after this twenty-fourth day of the ninth month of the second year of the reign of Darius. He was saying, "Because you have obeyed and respected me and worked on my house, change is coming. Mark this day so you can compare the way things were with the way things will be."

This Is the Way It Was

HAGGAI 2:16 *since those days, when one came to a heap of twenty ephahs, there were but ten; when one came to the wine vat to draw out fifty baths from the press, there were but twenty. (NKJV)*

God reminded the Jews that before they had started the work on the Temple, a pile of harvested grain worth twenty measures was worth only ten. Also, that vat of wine they thought contained fifty measures only contained twenty. This explains verse 9 of chapter 1:

"You looked for much, but indeed it came to little; and when you brought it home, I blew it away" (NKJV).

Some people want to know how much a ephah is, but the real answer is vague. However, that is not the point. The answer is not really important because God wanted them to remember that before they had started to work on the Temple, their work had yielded less than half of what they had expected.

God Chastens His Children

> HAGGAI 2:17 *I struck you with blight and mildew and hail in all the labors of your hands; yet you did not turn to Me,' says the* LORD. *(NKJV)*

This is a list of other things God did to the Jews before they started to work on the Temple, things he wanted them to be sure to remember. They planted their crops, but he struck them with **blight**, **mildew**, and **hail**. He was trying to get them to **repent**, but they did not.

God loves people, and his Word says he uses disasters such as drought, disease, hail, earthquakes, and a poor economy to discipline those he loves. Our ancestors called these things the "acts of God." Many people today do not believe God would do things like this. Oftentimes they do not believe this until disaster strikes them. It is often during these times that these same people turn their attention toward God and ask why he allowed this to happen.

discipline
Hebrews 12:5–6

blight
probably the result of the drought

mildew
probably the result of too much rain at times

hail
He beat the plants down and broke them off.

repent
turn away from their sin and turn toward him

Mark This Day on Your Calendar

> HAGGAI 2:18 *'Consider now from this day forward, from the twenty-fourth day of the ninth month, from the day that the foundation of the* LORD*'s temple was laid—consider it: (NKJV)*

Here God was saying the day of the Jews working hard and getting nowhere are over. The drought and poor crops are things of the past. The use of discipline to encourage repentance has been suspended. He was saying that from this day on things are going to be different. He is asking them to be sure to compare their present financial state with what it will be in the days ahead.

Lord
Revelation 19:16

expended
used up

Blessings Are Coming

Haggai 2:19 *Is the seed still in the barn? As yet the vine, the fig tree, the pomegranate, and the olive tree have not yielded fruit. But from this day I will bless you.'"* (NKJV)

First, God reminded the Jews that none of their previous crop was left. The grain they'd harvested the year before had already been **expended**. Second, he reminded them that the grape vines, fig trees, pomegranates, and olive trees had not yet produced. Third, he promised to bless them, starting on that very day. They had no signs of prosperity in the past, but because they had changed their attitude toward him and made his priority theirs, he was promising them abundance in the future.

what others say

David M. Levy

Life is full of turning points for Christians. Often they stand at a fork on life's road, needing to make decisions that will affect themselves and those around them. If they make decisions that are self-serving and outside of God's will, their lives will be full of weariness and waste for years to come. But by walking down the path of righteousness, believers find the way of blessing.[10]

The Fourth Message

Haggai 2:20–21 *And again the word of the Lord came to Haggai on the twenty-fourth day of the month, saying, "Speak to Zerubbabel, governor of Judah, saying: 'I will shake heaven and earth.* (NKJV)

This fourth message was addressed specifically to Zerubbabel, but it is really for everyone. It was delivered on the same day as the third message: the twenty-fourth day of the ninth month. It is a repeat of something God said in his second message, that he plans to shake the heavens and the earth. This is a reminder that day of judgment is coming, a day when God will deal with all the nations that think they can get along without him. It is also a statement that he has plans for justly dealing with Israel's enemies.

Everything God says is important. He is the Creator, the King of kings and Lord of lords, and he only needs to say something once.

However, when he says something more than once, he is warning us to pay very close attention to it.

wars and rumors of wars
Matthew 24:6–7

fiery red
Revelation 6:4

Tribulation Period
seven years of God's wrath against the wicked on earth

God's Plan for the Nations

> HAGGAI 2:22 *I will overthrow the throne of kingdoms; I will destroy the strength of the Gentile kingdoms. I will overthrow the chariots and those who ride in them; the horses and their riders shall come down, every one by the sword of his brother.* (NKJV)

At some future time God plans to bring down the leaders of many Gentile nations. They will think they are powerful with their nuclear bombs, planes, ships, and missiles, but God plans to bring their power to nothing. He plans to destroy all these weapons and those who operate them. Notice how he plans to do it. He plans to stir up nation against nation so that they will be mutually destructive.

Government without God will not ultimately succeed. Even though government leaders may try to legislate him out of national relevance, God is always relevant and has appointed a time when he will hold the people and nations accountable for how they responded to his call for them to humble themselves before him and not hinder others from bowing to him.

Jesus predicted that there would be a time at the end of this age when people will hear of wars and rumors of wars. It will be a time when nation will rise against nation and kingdom against kingdom. In the book of Revelation, John wrote about a time when God will give the rider on the fiery red horse the power to remove peace from the earth and make men slay one another. Students of Bible prophecy usually refer to this as the **Tribulation Period**.

At the End of the Age

> HAGGAI 2:23 *'In that day,' says the LORD of hosts, 'I will take you, Zerubbabel My servant, the son of Shealtiel,' says the LORD, 'and will make you like a signet ring; for I have chosen you,' says the LORD of hosts."* (NKJV)

"In that Day" is a term often used in reference to the Tribulation Period and/or the Millennium. This day has not yet arrived, even though Zerubbabel passed away hundreds of years before Christ.

Zerubbabel
Luke 3:27

signet ring
a symbol of authority

When this day arrives and God overthrows the godless Gentile nations, he plans to make Zerubbabel like a **signet ring**. The meaning of this is unclear, but most authorities believe "like a signet ring" is a reference to Zerubbabel's descendant Jesus Christ. If this is correct, it means God has chosen the house of Zerubbabel to produce a descendant who will exercise all the authority of God. Zerubbabel was an ancestor of Jesus. He was also a descendant of King David, and Jesus was called the Son of David.

Dealing with Discouragement

Have faith in God. Forget about the past. Focus on the present and future.

- Past—Be honest about your sins (God forgives).
- Present—Be involved now (God provides).
- Future—Believe the best is yet to come.

Chapter Wrap-Up

- When God's people started rebuilding the Temple, they soon realized that it would be smaller and less glorious than the one Solomon had built. God told them to be strong and go to work because he would be with them like he was with their ancestors when he led them out of Egypt. He told them that in the future he will shake all nations, the Savior will come, the Temple will be filled with his glory and will be greater than the first one, and he will give them peace.
- God had Haggai ask the priests the question: If something holy touches something unclean, will the unclean object become holy? The priests correctly answered no. God had Haggai then ask them: If something unclean touches something holy, will the unclean thing make the holy thing unclean? The priests correctly answered yes. Haggai then explained to the people that sin in their lives dirtied their good works and sacrifices. He told them to remember the day they started to work on the Temple because it was the dividing line between past hardships and future blessings.

- God's fourth message predicted a time of great turmoil on earth when Gentile kingdoms will be destroyed through war, and at the end of the age a descendant of Zerubbabel will reign on earth.

Study Questions

1. In God's second message, what did the Jews realize that was so discouraging to them? What covenant did God recall that encouraged them?
2. What will make the final Temple greater than the one Solomon built? What will God give at that Temple?
3. In God's third message, what was defiling the work the Jews were doing on the Temple?
4. Why did God want the Jews to remember the day they started to work on the Temple?
5. In God's fourth message, what does he plan to do to the wicked Gentile nations in the future?

Part Four
THE BOOK OF ZECHARIAH

Introduction—Zechariah Visions and Messages

Few people doubt that Zechariah wrote this book, but extensive efforts have been made to identify the correct Zechariah because the Old Testament mentions at least twenty-nine different ones. This Zechariah was a **contemporary** of Ezra, Nehemiah, and Haggai. He is even mentioned by Ezra and Nehemiah in the books they wrote. His name means "the Lord remembers," or "Jehovah remembers." He was a prophet and a priest whose father was named Berechiah and whose grandfather was named Iddo. He was in the first wave of returnees that moved to Israel with Zerubbabel. He was a very young man at the time. He settled in Jerusalem and prophesied from there. At some point, he became a member of the Great Synagogue, which was a group of 120 leaders. This association was founded by Nehemiah and headed by Ezra. It was also a forerunner of the famous Jewish Sanhedrin that was noted in the New Testament. Zechariah was primarily concerned about the rebuilding of the Temple, but his prophecies are far more extensive than that. He has many words of encouragement and much to say about repentance, salvation, and holy living. He mentions the coming Messiah so many times that some have referred to him as the messianic prophet of the Old Testament.

Zechariah
Ezra 5:1; 6:14

Berechiah
Zechariah 1:1

young
Zechariah 2:4

contemporary
lived at the same time

He had an effective ministry among the returnees for a while and was very instrumental in the rebuilding of the Temple. However, somewhere along the way things turned sour for him and he was murdered by his own people. When Jesus condemned the Pharisees for their unbelief, he compared them to those who had killed Zechariah. He said, "Therefore, indeed, I send you prophets, wise men, and scribes: some of them you will kill and crucify, and some of them you will scourge in your synagogues and persecute from city to city, that on you may come all the righteous blood shed on the earth, from the blood of righteous Abel to the blood of Zechariah, son of Berechiah, whom you murdered between the temple and the altar" (Matthew 23:34–35 NKJV).

Most commentators divide Zechariah's book into two parts: The first is chapters 1–8 and the second is chapters 9–14. The first part

Minor Prophets
the twelve shortest prophetic books in the Old Testament

of Zechariah was probably written around 520–518 BC, before the Temple was rebuilt. The second part of Zechariah has an unknown date of origin, but it was written after the rebuilding of the Temple was complete in 516 BC. This commentary divides the book into three parts:

- The Visions of Zechariah (Chapters1–6).
- Two Messages from God (Chapters 7–8).
- Future Things (Chapters 9–14).

Zechariah divided the Future Things (the last six chapters) into two burdens, each of which is a chapter long.

The Visions of Zechariah

Zechariah was an Israelite, but he was born in Babylon during the Captivity. Here are some interesting facts about his book:

- It is the longest book in the **Minor Prophets** (211 verses).
- It is about 70 percent prophecy (144 verses).
- It contains more prophecies about Jesus than any of the Minor Prophets (the book of Isaiah, a Major Prophet, has more).
- It is quoted more than seventy times in the New Testament (one-third of the time in the Gospels, with most of the remainder in the book of Revelation).
- It contains several difficult-to-interpret visions that are similar to those found in the books of Daniel and Revelation. It is sometimes called apocalyptic literature.
- It contains several amazing prophecies of things to come—the Antichrist, the Tribulation Period, the second coming of Jesus, and the Millennium, to name a few.
- It mentions almost a dozen times that the Lord will eventually reign over the entire world.
- It claims to speak for God, using "Lord of hosts" more than fifty times and "thus saith the Lord" more than sixty times.
- It contains several prophecies about the city of Jerusalem, mentioning Jerusalem almost forty times and calling it the chosen city three times.

- Several times it mentions that the Jews will come to a saving knowledge of the Lord.
- It opens with a series of eight visions. These are followed by two messages from God and then by several prophecies about future events.

double prophecies contain both an immediate partial fulfillment and a future complete fulfillment

All of the first eight visions occurred in the same night and Zechariah carefully linked them together. Notice this in the following chart.

Zechariah's Eight Night Visions

Vision	Connecting Phrase	Chapter & Verse
1	"I saw by night" (NKJV).	1:8
2	"Then I raised my eyes and looked" (NKJV).	1:18
3	"Then I raised my eyes and looked" (NKJV).	2:1
4	"Then he showed me" (NKJV).	3:1
5	"I am looking" (NKJV).	4:2
6	"Then I turned and raised my eyes, and saw" (NKJV).	5:1
7	"Lift your eyes now, and see" (NKJV).	5:5
8	"Then I turned and raised my eyes and looked" (NKJV).	6:1

Zechariah 1 First Two Visions

Chapter Highlights:
- When Was It?
- Don't Make God Angry
- Something to Tell Everyone
- Beware of Tribulation

Let's Get Started

The Bible records scores of people who had **visions**: Abraham, Amos, Daniel, Ezekiel, Isaiah, and Jeremiah in the Old Testament, and Peter, John, and Paul in the New Testament, to name just a few. Concerning the last days of the church, God said, "Your sons and your daughters shall prophesy, your young men shall see visions, your old men shall dream dreams" (Acts 2:17 NKJV). People don't have to be religious to have visions, but they are very common among the prophets. Zechariah had at least eight, several of them in one night.

visions
dreams, trances, and pictorial revelations that stimulate the mind and are regarded as omens of future events whether good or bad

Messiah
Jesus

what others say

Bible Dictionary

A supernatural appearance; something seen by means other than ordinary sight. Visions often came in dreams and were considered revelations from God. God came to Abraham and to Jacob in visions (Genesis 15, 46). Biblical visions concerning the kingdom of God were reported by the prophets.[1]

The Prophecy Bible

The first eight chapters [of Zechariah) frequently allude to the temple and encourage the people to complete their work on the new sanctuary. As they build the temple, they are building their future, because that very structure will be used by the **Messiah** when He comes to bring salvation.[2]

When Was It?

ZECHARIAH 1:1 *In the eighth month of the second year of Darius, the word of the* LORD *came to Zechariah the son of Berechiah, the son of Iddo the prophet, saying,* (NKJV)

Haggai's first message from God came on the first day of the sixth month in the second year of King Darius. His second message came on the twenty-first day of the seventh month of the same year. His other two messages came on the twenty-fourth day of the ninth

Jerusalem
2 Chronicles
36:15–22

month. This message to Zechariah came in the eighth month of the same year. Among other things it shows that Zechariah lived at the same time as Haggai and that the opening words of this book were given between Haggai's second and third messages.

Zechariah calls this *the word of the LORD*. It's something he said over and over again. He mentioned the Lord seven times in the first four verses. These words are not Zechariah's words. They came to him from God by the inspiration of the Holy Spirit.

The names of Zechariah (the Lord remembers), his father, Berechiah (the Lord will bless), and his grandfather Iddo (at the set time) are messages in themselves and not a bad summary of Zechariah's book: The Lord will remember and bless (Israel) at the set time.

Don't Make God Angry

ZECHARIAH 1:2 ***"The LORD has been very angry with your fathers. (NKJV)***

Many people do not believe in the anger of God, but their unbelief is not because the Bible does not teach it. It's because they do not accept the plain teaching of the Scriptures. The prophet Zechariah clearly said that God got angry with Israel's forefathers. But he didn't leave it there. He said God got *very* angry with them. This explains why he allowed King Nebuchadnezzar to attack and destroy Israel, Jerusalem, and the Temple. He is a holy and patient God, but he cannot ignore sin forever. The time came when he felt strongly compelled to deal with Israel's sin.

what others say

Dave Breese

Heritage is a very popular word in our time, but it's not worth much if a person's heritage is corrupt. Then, what he must do is reject his heritage. He must follow a new one that is not like the old one.[3]

Something to Tell Everyone

ZECHARIAH 1:3 ***Therefore say to them, 'Thus says the LORD of hosts: "Return to Me," says the LORD of hosts, "and I will return to you," says the LORD of hosts. (NKJV)***

Notice that Zechariah said three times that "the LORD of hosts" is speaking. Saying this once means the message is important, but repeating this again and again adds a sense of urgency.

people
2 Chronicles 7:14

God was saying he wanted to set his great anger with Israel's ancestors aside. He wanted the returnees' repentance to be based on a response to his promise to establish a new and better relationship with them, not on the threat of judgment. If they would be his people, he would be their God. In exchange for repentance, he was offering forgiveness and grace.

Zechariah called God "the LORD of hosts" more than fifty times. He has unlimited power and resources. Later, Zechariah will reveal that Jesus is coming back as a conquering King. The Lord of hosts, then, is a fitting title.

what others say

Merrill F. Unger

> The Lord cannot return in manifest fellowship and blessing to His people until they manifest their faith in Him by repentance, for He is approachable by man only on the basis of faith (Hebrews 11:6).[4]

Beware of Tradition

> ZECHARIAH 1:4 ***"Do not be like your fathers, to whom the former prophets preached, saying, 'Thus says the LORD of hosts: "Turn now from your evil ways and your evil deeds."' But they did not hear nor heed Me," says the Lord.*** (NKJV)

The returnees were urged not to make the same mistake their rebellious ancestors made. Before the Babylonian captivity God sent his prophets to tell them to stop sinning and to start living right. Isaiah, Habakkuk, Jeremiah, Ezekiel, Zephaniah, and many others pleaded with them over and over again, but they were obstinate. Because they steadfastly refused to heed what God's prophets said, the severe judgment of God eventually fell upon their nation. Zechariah was imploring them to learn from history and not repeat the mistakes of their ancestors who did not listen to the prophets.

Every generation has people who supposedly devote themselves to teaching the Word of God but have lost their own way and departed from doing what the Scriptures say to do. When these people are put

Word
John 1:1

revival
renewed zeal to obey God

into positions of leadership after moral failure, for instance, they may not want to return to the true Word of God. Some even use their authority to oppose others' calls for repentance. Following traditions that contradict the Scriptures is a step in the direction of stirring God's anger. Just as the returnees were encouraged to learn from the experiences of their ancestors, we are called to do the same. Failing to obey God's Word and not twist their meaning to fit our own contorted opionions is sure to bring harm to our relationship with God, to ourselves, and to God.

Today, many people do not want the Bible read in school, and they do not want the Ten Commandments posted at schools, courthouses, or public buildings. The Bible says, "In the beginning was the Word, and the Word was with God, and the Word was God" (NKJV). It is clear that those who reject the Word of God are rejecting God himself. That's the mistake the Jews made before the Babylonian captivity. They thought they were rejecting what the prophets said, but they were actually rejecting what God said. Nine out of ten Americans own at least one Bible and the average American household owns three, but more than half are almost totally in the dark about what the Bible teaches. Few stop to think about the fact that ignoring the Scriptures is the same thing as ignoring God.

Gone! Gone! All Gone!

ZECHARIAH 1:5 ***"Your fathers, where are they? And the prophets, do they live forever? (NKJV)***

By asking, "Where are your fathers?" God was implying that they were dead. The same was true of his faithful prophets of earlier days. God was patient with his rebellious people, but had no plans to send his prophets to them forever. Everyone he sent eventually died or was killed. The call for repentance came to an end and the judgment of God fell.

what others say

Irving L. Jensen

The immediate goal of Zechariah's prophecy is to bring about spiritual **revival** and to motivate and encourage the people to complete the temple. But a second reason God gave us the book of Zechariah was to officially "register" some unmistakable prophecies about the coming Messiah.[5]

David Wilkerson

I tell you, it is absolutely fatal for any nation to reject the Bible's authority, and to ignore the warnings and pleadings of God's watchmen. America may be judged for other particular sins—but by rejecting God's word as our standard, we'll surely bring judgment upon our land.[6]

Nebuchadnezzar
Daniel 1:1

The Prophets Were Right

ZECHARIAH 1:6 ***Yet surely My words and My statutes, which I commanded My servants the prophets, did they not overtake your fathers? So they returned and said: 'Just as the LORD of hosts determined to do to us, according to our ways and according to our deeds, so He has dealt with us.'"'"*** *(NKJV)*

God was asking, "Were the words and decrees that I commanded through my prophets fulfilled?" The implied answer is, "No, your ancestors did not heed my warnings, so I delivered them into the hands of their enemies, including Nebuchadnezzar king of Babylon." God was also saying here that he did not need to ask the returnees this question because their own ancestors eventually acknowledged that they were wrong and got what they deserved when God did what he said he was going to do if they did not turn from their wicked ways.

God's love and righteousness come into play in situations of yesterday and today. He loves everyone because he chooses to love everyone. He deals righteously with everyone because he chooses to deal righteously with everyone. However, his love does not compel him to ignore sin, but his righteousness and justice compel him to keep his Word. If a sinful nation will not repent, God must do what his Word says he will do. People can choose to ignore his Word, but God cannot choose to ignore his Word. The situation the returnees were in may be summarized like this:

- Their ancestors were dead.
- The prophets of old were dead.
- The Word of God was alive.

Darius
Haggai 1:1, 15; 2:10

Angel of the Lord
Zechariah 1:11

Angel
Genesis 16:10–13; Exodus 3:2–6

fig tree
Jeremiah 24:1–5; Hosea 9:10

Shebat
our January/February

man
the Angel of the Lord

hollow
a ravine, narrow gorge, or valley

pre-incarnate Christ
Jesus before he was born as a baby in the flesh

This Is When I Had the Visions

ZECHARIAH 1:7 ***On the twenty-fourth day of the eleventh month, which is the month Shebat, in the second year of Darius, the word of the LORD came to Zechariah the son of Berechiah, the son of Iddo the prophet:*** *(NKJV)*

The first six verses of this chapter were given in the eighth month of the second year of Darius. Three months later this message was given in the eleventh month of the same year. It was in the month of **Shebat**. In fact, all the messages recorded from here on in the first six chapters of this book were given in the same night. These visions contain the Word of God as given by God to Zechariah.

The second year of Darius is the same year Haggai received his four messages. In fact, these messages were given about two months after Haggai's last message. Since this was in January or February, the year would have changed over from 520 to 519 BC.

The First Vision: Man Under the Myrtle Trees

ZECHARIAH 1:8 ***I saw by night, and behold, a man riding on a red horse, and it stood among the myrtle trees in the hollow; and behind him were horses: red, sorrel, and white.*** *(NKJV)*

Zechariah's first vision occurred during the night when he saw a **man** sitting on a red horse that was standing in the shade of a group of myrtle trees in a **hollow**. This man was the Angel of the Lord, and behind him were other angels, perhaps a whole army of angels sitting on horses, some red, some light reddish brown (could also be speckled or mixed color), and some white.

The Angel of the Lord is a mysterious personality who often appears in the Bible. In some Old Testament Scriptures this Angel is clearly God, and in others he takes the form of a man. Because this angel often appears to be God in the flesh, some scholars believe he is the **pre-incarnate Christ**.

Trees are sometimes used as symbols of nations in the Bible. Jesus told his disciples, "Look at the fig tree, and all the trees. When they are already budding, you see and know for yourselves that summer is now near. So you also, when you see these things happening, know that the kingdom of God is near" (Luke 21:29–31 NKJV). In this case, the fig tree is Israel and the other trees are the Gentile nations.

But some authorities say the myrtle tree in this chapter is a symbol of Jerusalem or Israel. It thrives in low places such as the Kidron Valley near Jerusalem, and its branches are used to make booths during the Feast of Tabernacles. It is a short tree representing a small nation growing in a hollow or occupying a lowly position on the face of the earth. Jerusalem and Zion are mentioned seven times in this vision.

angels
Matthew 13:41; 16:27; 24:31

Horses are often associated with war and judgment. Revelation chapter 6 presents what is commonly called the Four Horsemen of the Apocalypse. The second horse is fiery red, the color of blood, "and it was granted to the one who sat on it to take peace from the earth" (Revelation 6:4 NKJV). The riders on the other horses—red, sorrel, and white—are under the authority of the first rider on a red horse. In a sense they are his assistants or troops. White horses symbolize conquest as depicted by the Antichrist and the Christ in Revelation 6 and 19. Riders on sorrel horses are a mystery.

Ask and You Will Receive

> ZECHARIAH 1:9 ***Then I said, "My lord, what are these?" So the angel who talked with me said to me, "I will show you what they are."*** *(NKJV)*

The word "lord" in lowercase letters indicates that Zechariah was not addressing The Lord. He was addressing an angel. Zechariah referred to him eleven different times as "the angel who spoke to me" (Zechariah 1:9, 13, 14, 19; 2:3; 4:1, 4, 5; 5:5, 10; 6:4). Calling him "lord" is simply an Old Testament way of showing respect. Commentators commonly call this angel "the interpreting angel" because he constantly explains things.

Zechariah asked the interpreting angel the significance of the things he saw in his vision. In response, the interpreting angel said he would receive an explanation. It is important to keep in mind the fact that Jesus has an army of angels to serve him.

You Wanted to Know

> ZECHARIAH 1:10 ***And the man who stood among the myrtle trees answered and said, "These are the ones whom the LORD has sent to walk to and fro throughout the earth."*** *(NKJV)*

The interpreting angel said, "I will show you what they are," but before he did that, the man who stood among the myrtle trees, the One identified as the Angel of the Lord, said the riders on the red, sorrel, and white horses were the ones that God sent to patrol the whole earth. They were his assistants or an angel patrol that was sent to monitor the earth.

The idea that both good and evil angels are presiding over nations and watching over events on earth is well established in the Scriptures. Some events that take place on earth do so because there is **supernatural** involvement in the affairs of people. Satan walks back and forth on the earth "like a roaring lion, seeking whom he may devour" (NKJV). For this reason, Christians need to put on the whole armor of God.

Peace on Earth

ZECHARIAH 1:11 ***So they answered the Angel of the LORD, who stood among the myrtle trees, and said, "We have walked to and fro throughout the earth, and behold, all the earth is resting quietly." (NKJV)***

This verse identifies the man on the red horse standing among the myrtle trees as being the Angel of the Lord. The angel patrol reported to the Angel of the Lord, who may well have been Jesus, and told him that they had traveled all over the earth. They had what many would consider good news: peace prevailed wherever they went. There was no war on earth. This is an amazing thing considering the fact that in the last 3,500 years there have been only 227 years when there was not war somewhere on the earth. There was peace on earth, however, in Zechariah's vision.

angels
Daniel 4:17

Satan
Job 2:2;
1 Peter 5:8

whole armor
Ephesians 6:10–17

seventy years
Jeremiah 25:11; 29:10;
2 Chronicles 36:10–21

supernatural
something from another realm

Let's Have a Little Talk with God

ZECHARIAH 1:12 ***Then the Angel of the LORD answered and said, "O LORD of hosts, how long will You not have mercy on Jerusalem and on the cities of Judah, against which You were angry these seventy years?" (NKJV)***

Following the angel patrol's report of peace on earth, the Angel of the Lord decided to ask God a question. Seventy years had passed since God allowed King Nebuchadnezzar to destroy Jerusalem and the surrounding cities of Judah. Almost fifty thousand exiles had returned, but the Holy City had not been rebuilt and the Angel of the Lord wanted to know how long it would be before God started blessing the people and the city again.

Jesus is coming back as King of kings and Lord of lords. He will establish his throne in Jerusalem. His Word will go out from the Holy City and he will reign on earth for a thousand years. It is natural that the Angel of the Lord would be interested in how long it would be before God planned to start blessing the city again. *How long* is the cry of a longing heart. It reveals the deep love Jesus has for his people and the Holy City.

what others say

King James Bible Commentary

This verse records a most wonderful truth—the intercession of the angel of the Lord (the Second Person of the Trinity) with the Lord of hosts (the First Person of the Trinity) on behalf of His people, Israel. The doctrine of the intercession of Christ is not the sole product of New Testament revelation (cf. Hebrews 7:25; I John 2:1) nor is the fact of the Trinity, for that matter.[7]

I Liked What I Heard

ZECHARIAH 1:13 ***And the LORD answered the angel who talked to me, with good and comforting words.*** *(NKJV)*

The "LORD" here is the Lord of hosts, God the Father. Zechariah heard him speak directly to the interpreting angel. He spoke kindly and his words were comforting. In the next four verses the interpreting angel will reveal what he said, but Zechariah already knew that it was very good news for Jerusalem and the towns of Judah. It was just what God's hurting people needed to hear. It reveals God's everlasting love for the Jews who follow him and his plans for Jerusalem in the Millennium.

Jerusalem
Micah 4:1–7;
Psalm 132:13–16

thousand years
Revelation 20:1–6

God Was Jealous

ZECHARIAH 1:14 ***So the angel who spoke with me said to me, "Proclaim, saying, 'Thus says the LORD of hosts: "I am zealous for Jerusalem and for Zion with great zeal.*** *(NKJV)*

New Jerusalem
Revelation 21:1–27

zealous
He has a deep and special love.

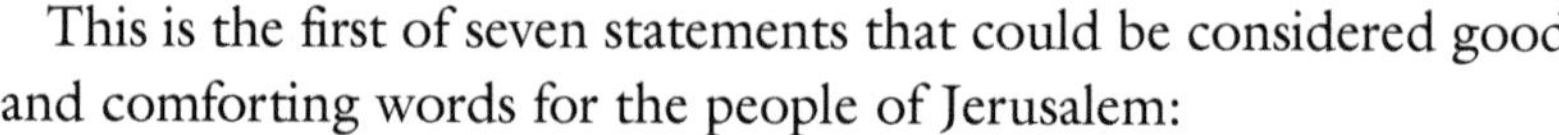

This is the first of seven statements that could be considered good and comforting words for the people of Jerusalem:

- God was zealous for Jerusalem and Zion.

The interpreting angel told Zechariah to proclaim that God is very **zealous** for Jerusalem and Zion. It can be said that he is zealous with great zeal or jealous with great jealousy. Why would he not be? Why would he not want to keep the covenants and promises he made to Abraham, Isaac, Jacob, and all the others? His holiness and righteousness require him to tell the truth and to protect his reputation.

This is bad news for those who oppose Israel today. Jerusalem occupies a special place in the heart of God. He has a plan for the Holy City. It cannot be permanently destroyed, and it cannot be permanently occupied by any entity other than the Jews. The efforts of people to do otherwise will fail because what they do is in opposition to God's plan and will eventually trigger an angry and protective response from him.

Zion is mentioned over and over again in the Bible, but it means different things at different times. Originally, it referred to a scarp of rock near Jerusalem. Then, it referred to the entire ridge Jerusalem was built upon. Then, it became a poetic name for the City of David, or Jerusalem itself. But Zion sometimes refers to the Temple or Temple Mount, it sometimes refers to Jerusalem during the Millennium, and it sometimes refers to the New Jerusalem.

what others say

Ralph L. Smith

Jealousy in essence is an intolerance of rivals. It can be a virtue or a sin depending on the legitimacy of the rival. God would allow no rivals in the covenant between him and Israel. He bound Israel exclusively to his service and he swore to protect her against all enemies.[8]

God Was Angry

ZECHARIAH 1:15 ***I am exceedingly angry with the nations at ease; For I was a little angry, and they helped—but with evil intent."*** *(NKJV)*

This is the second of seven statements that could be considered good and comforting words for the people of Jerusalem:

• God was very angry with the nations that were at peace.

He was only a little angry at first. Babylon actually helped him carry out his decree to put the Jews off the land, but the nations added to the Jewish people's miseries while they were captives in Babylon, and God didn't like that. He wanted the Jews punished, but he didn't want the punishment to exceed his decreed amount.

pray
Psalm 122:6

God was so angry with Israel for stealing seventy crops (not letting the land rest every seventh year so they could grow crops for the entire 490 years) that he decided to put the people off the land for seventy years to get the seventy crops back. The problem is that God has an everlasting covenant with Israel, and he will not permanently abandon the nation. He clearly intended for the Jews to be off the land for a full seventy years, but he did not want the people punished more than the seventy years he decreed. For example, they did not steal seventy-one crops so he did not want them put off the land for seventy-one years. He is just and righteous, and his punishment suits the sin. But Israel's ever-present enemies rejoiced over Israel's being put off the land, exploited the people, tried to prevent the nation from coming back into existence, and then tried to prevent the rebuilding of the Temple, Jerusalem, and the city wall. If their will had been accomplished, God would not have kept his covenant. The Scriptures would not be true, his reputation would be ruined, and his name would be blasphemed. These are things he could not allow. Without the Temple and Jerusalem, many prophecies could not be fulfilled. For example, the baby Jesus could not be presented at the Temple near where he would be crucified and Jesus could not suddenly appear there to make his triumphal entry. This satanic threat to set aside God's covenants, and prophecies angered him. World peace without God's plan of redemption through the Cross is world peace on Satan's terms, and must be exposed for the lie it is.

World peace is the wonderful dream of many and God can grant it, but he will not grant it as long as Israel is in turmoil and as long as that nation and the Holy City are divided. The security of Israel depends upon that nation's obeying the Word of God, but the security of the Gentile nations depends upon their attitude toward Israel and Jerusalem. The nations should pray for the peace of Jerusalem, guarantee the safety of Israel, and work to establish the borders given in the Scriptures. Unless these things are done, God will be angry with the nations in the future after the Rapture, and he will

rider
Revelation 6:4

send the rider on the fiery red horse to remove peace from the earth. God intends for Jesus to sit on the throne in Jerusalem, for the Jews to serve him, and for the Jews to have a certain amount of territory. The world can try to divide the land and give it to others, but God will not grant world peace on Satan's terms.

God Will Do Things for Israel

ZECHARIAH 1:16 ***'Therefore thus says the LORD: "I am returning to Jerusalem with mercy; My house shall be built in it," says the LORD of hosts, "and a surveyor's line shall be stretched out over Jerusalem."'*** *(NKJV)*

Here are the third, fourth, and fifth statements of the seven that could be considered good and comforting words for the people of Jerusalem:

- God promised to dwell in Jerusalem again and to be merciful toward the people.
- God promised that the Temple would be rebuilt.
- God promised that the measuring line used to measure the length and breadth of Jerusalem would have to be stretched out to measure an even larger city.

The return of God's divine presence was not based on Israel's goodness, but on God's mercy. The Temple, which had languished for about sixteen years since the laying of the foundation, would be completed in Jerusalem. The city, which was still a massive pile of rubble, would be rebuilt and enlarged.

Kind and Comforting Words About Israel's Future

ZECHARIAH 1:17 ***"Again proclaim, saying, 'Thus says the LORD of hosts: "My cities shall again spread out through prosperity; the LORD will again comfort Zion, and will again choose Jerusalem."'"*** *(NKJV)*

Here are the sixth and seventh statements of the seven that could be considered good and comforting words for the people of Jerusalem:

- Prosperity would result in the rebuilding and growth of many Jewish cities.
- God will again comfort Zion and choose Jerusalem one final time.

horns
Daniel 7:7–28; Revelation 17:12

History demonstrates a partial fulfillment of these good and comforting words up until the first coming of Jesus. God demonstrated his love for Israel and Jerusalem. He dealt with the nations that angered him because of their opposition to Israel. His presence returned to Jerusalem, but only partially, because the Shekinah glory was absent from the Temple. The Temple was completed about four years later, but it was not as glorious as expected. Jerusalem was rebuilt about eighty years later along with many cities and towns. Then, the Messiah appeared, seemingly to bring about a complete fulfillment. The Jews rejected him, however, causing a break in the fulfillment. About thirty-eight years later, Jerusalem, the Temple, and the cities were destroyed. Although these good and comforting words were partially fulfilled, there seems to be a greater and more complete fulfillment in the future after the second coming of Jesus. The "agains" in this verse are yet to be completely fulfilled. This is why Jerusalem and the cities have been rebuilt, why they are growing, and why there is a desire to rebuild the Temple. All of this is in preparation for the final fulfillment of these promises. The Jews will accept Jesus when he comes back, and these wonderful words will be brought to fruition.

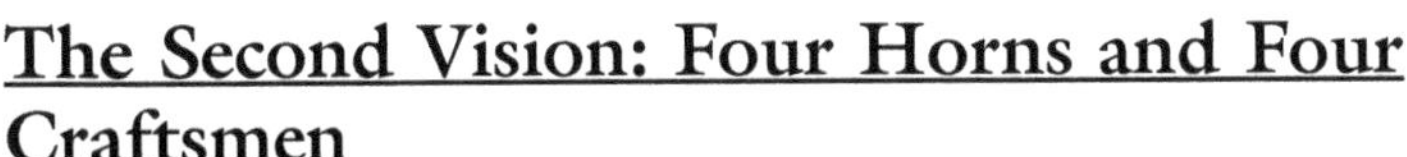

The Second Vision: Four Horns and Four Craftsmen

> **ZECHARIAH 1:18–19** ***Then I raised my eyes and looked, and there were four horns. And I said to the angel who talked with me, "What are these?" So he answered me, "These are the horns that have scattered Judah, Israel, and Jerusalem."*** *(NKJV)*

After his first vision, Zechariah raised his eyes and saw a second vision of four horns in front of him. Horns are often used as symbols of nations (kingdoms) in the Bible. Zechariah, however, did not know what these horns meant, so he asked the interpreting angel, "What are these?" The interpreting angel told him, "These are the horns [nations or kingdoms) that have scattered Judah, Israel, and Jerusalem."

The attempts to identify the four horns are many and varied. One group says they are four powers that existed prior to Zechariah's vision: Egypt because she enslaved the Jews before Moses, Assyria because she destroyed the Northern Kingdom of Israel in 721 BC, Babylon because she destroyed the Southern Kingdom of Judah in 586 BC, and the Medes and Persians because they were in power during Zechariah's day. A second and larger group, on the other hand, believes they are the four powers in Nebuchadnezzar's dream (Babylon, Medo-Persia, Greece, and Rome) found in Daniel, chapter 2. Those who take the latter view believe the Roman Empire will be revived and be led by a little horn called the Antichrist, who will oppose a revived Israel just before the second coming of Jesus. The emerging European Union seems to fit this latter interpretation.

The Four Craftsmen (Smash Those Terrorist Horns)

ZECHARIAH 1:20–21 ***Then the LORD showed me four craftsmen. And I said, "What are these coming to do?" So he said, "These are the horns that scattered Judah, so that no one could lift up his head; but the craftsmen are coming to terrify them, to cast out the horns of the nations that lifted up their horn against the land of Judah to scatter it." (NKJV)***

Next, Zechariah saw four craftsmen (some translations say carpenters), and he needed another explanation. He was told that it was the duty of these craftsmen to terrify and destroy the horns or nations that had opposed God's people. The exact identity of these four craftsmen is not revealed, but it is clear that they are God's instruments of judgment in the world. They represent things that exist at the same time as the four horns and that God will use to bring down powers that terrorize the Jews. Those who use terrorism against the Jews so that "no one could lift up his head" will find that God will use terrorism against them. Long ago God told Abraham and his descendants, "I will bless those who bless you, and I will curse him who curses you" (Genesis 12:3 NKJV). Terrorism against the Jews will ultimately lead to the Battle of Armageddon with all the nations gathered against tiny Israel. Then, they will find out what real terrorism is and they won't stand a chance.

Medes and Persians
Daniel 5:1–31

When the Gentile Age draws to a close, the Antichrist will suddenly rise to power. He will decide to destroy Israel, but God will use four things to oppose him: war, famine, plagues, and wild beasts. Every horn (nation or kingdom) that opposes Israel will be opposed by God's craftsmen (possibly war, famine, plague, or wild beasts). Every nation will reap what it sows with regard to its treatment of Israel: an eye for an eye and a tooth for a tooth, good for good and evil for evil.

famine
Revelation 6:1–8

what others say

H. A. Ironside

For every horn there is a carpenter, and as they have agreed together to oppress and destroy Israel and Judah, so shall God use these carpenters to destroy them. Israel's enemies are God's enemies and must be frayed and broken when their appointed course is run, with a view to the full deliverance of the remnant of the people of His choice.[9]

Chapter Wrap-Up

- God expressed displeasure with the Jews who lived before the Babylonian captivity. Then he called upon the former exiles to turn to him and promised to bless them if they would. He reminded them that their ancestors had ignored his calls for repentance and the result had been that they had died in a foreign land. Finally, he pointed out that the Jews eventually admitted that God was just in his dealings with them.
- In his first vision Zechariah saw a man who was the Angel of the Lord. He was with several other angels and all of them were on horses under a myrtle tree. The angels had patrolled the earth and reported to the Angel of the Lord that they had found peace on earth. But Jerusalem had been in ruins for seventy years and God was not happy. He loved Jerusalem, promised to restore it, promised the Temple would be rebuilt, and promised to cause Jerusalem and the surrounding towns to grow and prosper.
- In his second vision, Zechariah saw four horns that represented the nations that scattered Jerusalem, Israel, and Judah. Then he saw four craftsmen, who represented the judgments God uses to destroy Israel's enemies.

Study Questions

1. What would God do for the Jews if they would repent of their sins and return to him? Why did their ancestors die in a foreign land?
2. Who was the rider under the myrtle trees and who was with him?
3. Why did the report of peace on earth disturb the Angel of the Lord?
4. What did God promise to do for Israel?
5. Identify the four horns and the four craftsmen.

Zechariah 2
The Third Vision

Chapter Highlights:
- **Jerusalem Will Be Rebuilt**
- **Israel Will Be Regathered**
- **God Will Dwell There**

Let's Get Started

In Zechariah's first vision, which is found in chapter 1, God made seven statements that were considered good and comforting words for the people of Jerusalem. The third, fourth, and fifth statements are found in verse 16 (NKJV). God said:

- "I am returning to Jerusalem with mercy;
- My house shall be built in it,
- and a surveyor's line shall be stretched out over Jerusalem."

This chapter contains Zechariah's third vision. It expands on and confirms the good and comforting words in chapter 1 that are about a surveyor's line.

This message must have been a source of hope and encouragement to the former exiles. In essence, they were being told to go ahead with the rebuilding of Jerusalem and to not have any doubts about the success of what they were doing. Why? Because Jerusalem is destined to become a very large city, God will dwell in their midst, and much more. The scope of this vision extends from a limited partial fulfillment about 2500 years ago to a coming total fulfillment in the future during the **Millennium**. The reestablishment of Israel in 1948 is paving the way for this.

Millennium
thousand-year reign of Christ on earth

The Third Vision: The Measuring Line

ZECHARIAH 2:1–2 ***Then I raised my eyes and looked, and behold, a man with a measuring line in his hand. So I said, "Where are you going?" And he said to me, "To measure Jerusalem, to see what is its width and what is its length." (NKJV)***

After Zechariah's second vision about the four horns and four craftsmen, he raised his eyes and saw a man with a measuring line in his hand. It seems natural for the vision to move from four craftsmen, or carpenters, who will tear down to a man with a measuring line who will build up. The identity of this man is not revealed, but he appears to be the Angel of the Lord (probably the carpenter's Son named Jesus) mentioned in chapter 1. Zechariah was curious to know where this man was going. This man readily replied that he was going to measure the width and length of Jerusalem. Since the Holy City didn't exist at this time, this vision signals its future rebuilding. So this is a prophecy about the rebuilding of Jerusalem and this man has something to do with laying it out, determining how big it will be, determining what is needed, constructing it, and such. A master builder or carpenter needs a plan and materials to build a house or city.

A Great City

Zechariah 2:3–4 ***And there was the angel who talked with me, going out; and another angel was coming out to meet him, who said to him, "Run, speak to this young man, saying: 'Jerusalem shall be inhabited as towns without walls, because of the multitude of men and livestock in it.*** *(NKJV)*

The interpreting angel who was talking to Zechariah in chapter 1 started walking away from him, but a second angel approached the interpreting angel and told him to run and tell that young man that Jerusalem will grow beyond its wall and be like an unwalled city with multitudes of people and animals. The identity of this young man is not revealed. The second angel may be giving the direction to speak to the man with the measuring line, the Angel of the Lord, but most commentators believe he was giving the direction for this to be spoken to this young man called Zechariah. This is one reason why many commentators think Zechariah was a young man when he left Babylon and moved to Jerusalem. Another reason is the fact that he lived and prophesied in Jerusalem for many years after he moved there. But, at this time, Zechariah was probably inexperienced. He probably had a limited understanding of the greatness of God. In light of this, the angel may have been saying that information was to be given to him. He was to be told to expect a large city with more people and animals than the wall could encompass. In the future, Jerusalem won't be a small city; it will be a large and great one.

Jerusalem has been a "disputed city" since Israel became a nation in 1948. The Jews claim all of Jerusalem to be the capital of Israel, but the Palestinians claim east Jerusalem as the capital of a future Palestinian state. Most world leaders want to divide the city between the two groups. Jerusalem is growing, however, because the carpenter's Son is rebuilding it for the Jewish people and for his home during the Millennium.

pillar
Exodus 13:21–22

millennial kingdom
the kingdom Christ will establish on earth during the Millennium

what others say

Paul E. Grabill

While Jerusalem did experience growth prior to the Christian era, Zechariah's prophecy has in view the **millennial kingdom** of Christ, as the context of the book shows (6:13–15). Gentiles will be under Christ's protection and care, and He will reign in peace over all the earth (3:10).[1]

A Great Wall

ZECHARIAH 2:5 ***For I,' says the LORD, 'will be a wall of fire all around her, and I will be the glory in her midst.'"*** *(NKJV)*

The focus of the vision switched away from the city, its people, and animals and to the wall and God. In the future, the wall of Jerusalem will not be needed and the Jews will not need peace treaties with the nations around them. The city will be secure because God will surround it with his presence and will be like a wall of fire ready to consume any enemy that tries to harm his people. And notice, too, that God will be the glory of the city. He will return to dwell there with all the people and animals.

The language here recalls God's presence with the Hebrews in the wilderness as a pillar of cloud and a pillar of fire to guide and protect them. It's reminiscent of Moses's going up on Mount Sinai: "Now the glory of the LORD rested on Mount Sinai, and the cloud covered it six days. And on the seventh day He called to Moses out of the midst of the cloud. The sight of the glory of the LORD was like a consuming fire on the top of the mountain in the eyes of the children of Israel" (Exodus 24:16–17 NKJV). During the Millennium, God will be in Jerusalem with Israel like he was in the days of Moses.

future years
Ezekiel 38:1–23

far north
Ezekiel 38:6, 15

Zerubbabel
Ezra 2:1–67

Babylon
Jeremiah 25:1–14

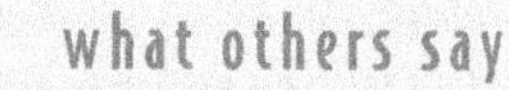

Robert E. Wenger

Whether or not His protective presence will appear as real fire we cannot say. But since He is said to be "a consuming fire" (Hebrews 12:29) and has appeared in this form previously (Exodus 3:2; 19:18), we have reason to believe He will do so again.[2]

In the future years an army that many believe will be Russia and a group of Islamic allies will march out of the far north to invade the Promised Land. The sovereign Lord says: "On that day it shall come to pass that thoughts will arise in your mind, and you will make an evil plan: You will say, 'I will go up against a land of unwalled villages; I will go to a peaceful people, who dwell safely, all of them dwelling without walls, and having neither bars nor gates'" (Ezekiel 38:10–11 NKJV). This army will attack, not realizing that God is providing a wall around the city. This will be understood when that army is destroyed.

Listen Up

ZECHARIAH 2:6–7 ***"Up, up! Flee from the land of the north," says the LORD; "for I have spread you abroad like the four winds of heaven," says the LORD. "Up, Zion! Escape, you who dwell with the daughter of Babylon." (NKJV)***

"Up, up!" is God's way of getting the people's attention in Zechariah's day. Approximately two to three million Jews lived in Babylon, but less than fifty thousand returned with Zerubbabel. Here, God is telling those Jews who remained in Babylon in Zechariah's day that he is the One who brought Babylon out of the north to scatter them, and now he is the One who is calling them to leave Babylon and return home. Babylon is east of Israel, but in those days people traveled the Fertile Crescent, which caused them to approach Israel from the north.

God's scattering the Jews abroad "like the four winds of heaven" is a reference to Nebuchadnezzar's violent attacks that caused them to rapidly flee in every direction. God was saying he scattered them, but the decision to return was theirs.

Here, God issued a second call, saying, "Up, Zion! Escape." This refers to a plea for the Jews to return to Israel in the future. In Revelation 17:5, John called the coming one-world religious system "Mystery Babylon the Great, the Mother of Harlots and of the Abominations of the Earth" (NKJV). Babylon is a mother and her daughters are harlots or prostitutes. During the future Tribulation Period a voice from heaven will say, "Come out of her, my people, lest you share in her sins, and lest you receive of her plagues. For her sins have reached to heaven, and God has remembered her iniquities" (Revelation 18:4–5 NKJV). Babylon was a pagan city known for its sin: pride, pleasure, riches, astrology, false worship, and more. The Jews who return are called Zion. The Jews who don't return are called the daughter of Babylon. This is a derisive term referring to future Jews who will find living in the world more desirable than living in Israel.

Jesus Is Coming

> **ZECHARIAH 2:8–9** ***For thus says the LORD of hosts: "He sent Me after glory, to the nations which plunder you; for he who touches you touches the apple of His eye. For surely I will shake My hand against them, and they shall become spoil for their servants. Then you will know that the LORD of hosts has sent Me.*** *(NKJV)*

Here is a paraphrase: "After God has sent his Son, and after his Son has broken the Gentile nations that have robbed Israel—for whoever has harmed Israel has stuck his finger in the pupil of God's eye—God will shake his fist at those Gentile nations. Israel who has been robbed will become the robber, and those who have robbed Israel will be plundered. Then, Israel will know that God has sent his Son." Notice these points:

- Me (capital M) is a Servant of the Lord of hosts.
- God will send his Servant (the rider on the red horse in chapter 1) to get glory from the nations that harm Israel.
- Every nation that hurts Israel hurts God.
- God is so powerful that all he needs to do to overthrow the Gentile nations is to shake his fist.
- When the Gentile nations are destroyed, Israel will know that God sent his Servant.

what others say

Dave Breese

Those who burden themselves with Israel will have to answer to Israel's God and it makes no difference who they are or claim to be. Woe to that person or nation who would dare to lift a finger against God's chosen people.[3]

It's Going to Be Good

ZECHARIAH 2:10–13 ***"Sing and rejoice, O daughter of Zion! For behold, I am coming and I will dwell in your midst," says the LORD. "Many nations shall be joined to the LORD in that day, and they shall become My people. And I will dwell in your midst. Then you will know that the LORD of hosts has sent Me to you. And the LORD will take possession of Judah as His inheritance in the Holy Land, and will again choose Jerusalem. Be silent, all flesh, before the LORD, for He is aroused from His holy habitation!" (NKJV)***

"Daughter of Zion" is an often-used phrase in the Scriptures. It refers to the Jews living in Jerusalem, and it can be complimentary or derisive depending upon the faithfulness or unfaithfulness of the Jews. Here it is complimentary and is used for comparison to the "daughter of Babylon" in verse 7. During the Millennium, the daughter of Zion will have a wonderful future in the Promised Land, but the daughter of Babylon will suffer for her sins.

Singing and rejoicing are in the daughter of Zion's (faithful Israel's) future. Why? Because God is coming in the person of his Son, Jesus. When this happens the Gentiles in many nations will turn to God and accept Jesus as their Savior. Jesus will dwell among his people in Jerusalem and Israel will know that God sent him. Israel and Jerusalem will belong to God. The entire world is urged to show awe and reverence to God because he will be involved in the administration of the world.

Jerusalem is a cup of drunkenness and a heavy stone for the world today because world leaders do not understand Jesus's intention to take possession of Israel and Jerusalem. They want to determine who gets Jerusalem, but God has decided that he won't leave the decision up to them. They will have to learn the hard way.

This is good news for Israel. Many Gentiles will turn to Christ, but God's covenant with Israel will still be firm. **Paul** said, "For I do not desire, brethren, that you should be ignorant of this mystery, lest you should be wise in your own opinion, that blindness in part has happened to Israel until the fullness of the Gentiles has come in. And so all Israel will be saved, as it is written: 'The Deliverer will come out of Zion, and He will turn away ungodliness from Jacob; for this is My covenant with them, when I take away their sins.' Concerning the gospel they are enemies for your sake, but concerning the election they are beloved for the sake of the fathers. For the gifts and the calling of God are irrevocable" (NKJV).

what others say

King James Bible Commentary

The fact that Gentiles will have a prominent part in the millennial kingdom should not come as a surprise to Israel since the Old Testament prophets consistently predicted it. In fact, Gentile inclusion in the kingdom will enable Israel to know that the Lord of hosts hath sent me (Messiah) unto thee (Israel).[4]

irrevocable
Romans 11:25–29

Paul
a famous missionary who knew Jesus personally

Chapter Wrap-Up

- Zechariah saw a man holding a measuring line, asked him where he was going, and was told he was going to measure Jerusalem. An angel told him that Jerusalem will be greatly expanded and that God will protect the enlarged city and dwell in it in the future.
- God urged the Jews to leave the places where he had scattered them and to return to Israel. This applies to Zechariah's time and a future return during the Millennium. God predicted his Son would come to obtain glory for the Father, said those who harm Israel harm him, and said he will shake his fist at them and cause them to be spoiled.
- Jerusalem should rejoice because God will dwell there. Many nations will turn to Christ and know that God sent him there. Israel and Jerusalem will be his personal possession.

Study Questions

1. Where was the man with the measuring line going? Why? What was the significance of this?
2. Will Jerusalem be an unwalled city in the future? How will it be protected? Who will cause this?
3. Why is it dangerous to oppose Israel? What will happen to those who harm Israel?
4. What did God tell Israel to rejoice about?
5. Who will the Gentiles serve during the Millennium?

Zecharia h 3
The Fourth Vision

Chapter Highlights:
- The High Priest
- Get Rid of Dirty Clothes
- Two Ifs and Three Promises
- God's Servant

Let's Get Started

This vision is full of symbolism that deals with a question: How can the sinful people and defiled priests in Israel be cleansed and restored without compromising the righteousness of God? This is a natural question. A holy Jesus cannot return and dwell in Jerusalem if the people and priests are defiled. The vision makes it plain that this issue is in the hands of a faithful and merciful God. He has a way to make things right. Paul said, "By grace you have been saved through faith, and that not of yourselves; it is the gift of God, not of works, lest anyone should boast" (Ephesians 2:8–9 NKJV). Paul was talking to the church, but Zechariah's fourth vision shows that God will treat Israel the same way during the Millennium. Israel's restoration and future salvation do not depend upon the people earning it. Her restoration and future salvation depend upon the grace of God. The Lord teaches this by picturing a man named Joshua standing before him to be judged. Joshua was a real person, but everything that happened to him in the vision is an example of what will happen to Israel. The first five verses of this chapter reveal the vision and the last five verses reveal the explanation.

The Fourth Vision: The High Priest

> ZECHARIAH **3:1–2** ***Then he showed me Joshua the high priest standing before the Angel of the LORD, and Satan standing at his right hand to oppose him. And the LORD said to Satan, "The LORD rebuke you, Satan! The LORD who has chosen Jerusalem rebuke you! Is this not a brand plucked from the fire?"*** *(NKJV)*

After God showed Zechariah the vision of the man with the measuring line, he showed him the vision of Joshua the high priest. The name Joshua causes most people with knowledge of the Bible to think about the Joshua who helped Moses lead the children of Israel in the wilderness. But that Joshua lived several hundred years before

nation
Exodus 19:6

priests
Isaiah 61:6

accuser
Revelation 12:10

right hand
Psalm 109:6

symbolic
Zechariah 3:8

anti-Semitic
hostility toward the Jews

this one. The names are the same, but the people are different. This Joshua joined Zerubbabel in the first wave of returnees from Jerusalem. He was standing before the Angel of the Lord, who was identified as the pre-incarnate Jesus in chapter 1. Joshua was the high priest of Israel, a position that allowed him to represent the entire nation before God. When the High Priest went into the Holy of Holies in the Temple on the great Day of Atonement, he did so as the representative of the entire nation. In this case, Joshua was in God's courtroom, where he was the defendant representing the entire nation as he stood before the Judgment Bar with Jesus on the throne. Unfortunately, Satan was there also because he showed up in the role of a wicked prosecuting attorney to accuse Joshua (Israel and the priests). This is normal for Satan. The Bible even calls him the accuser of our brethren. Standing at Joshua's right hand is this accuser. Obviously, this vision hasn't gotten to verse 8 yet, but keep in mind the fact that Joshua and his people are symbolic of things to come.

The vision doesn't reveal what Satan said, but it obviously had something to do with Israel and Jerusalem. It is also possible that the devil's (the word "devil" means "slanderer") accusation was correct, but it definitely did not fall upon friendly ears, because Jesus rebuked Satan twice. Jesus even announced that he had chosen Jerusalem and he had protected Israel. He called the Jews "a brand (burning stick) plucked from the fire." This is a figure of speech referring to the fact that Babylon captured Israel, burned Jerusalem and the Temple, and would have permanently destroyed the nation if God had not preserved the Jews in a foreign land, plucked them out, and brought them back into existence as a nation again.

what others say

Charles H. Dyer

Satan promotes much **anti-Semitic** activity today. He hates God, and he vents his hatred on the people chosen by God. Spiritual forces are at work to turn the world against the Jews. We must be sensitive to those forces at work around us, and we must pray for the Jews and for the nation of Israel.[1]

Thomas Edward McComiskey

His accusation is futile because God has already revealed his will for the people by delivering them from the captivity. If he had wished to let them perish for their sin, the Lord would have left them in Babylon; but by snatching them from the flames of exile, he revealed that his **grace** was greater than their guilt.[2]

filthy
Isaiah 64:6

grace
the undeserved favor of God

turban
the hat or mitre worn by the high priest

Get Rid of Those Dirty Clothes

> ZECHARIAH 3:3–5 *Now Joshua was clothed with filthy garments, and was standing before the Angel. Then He answered and spoke to those who stood before Him, saying, "Take away the filthy garments from him." And to him He said, "See, I have removed your iniquity from you, and I will clothe you with rich robes." And I said, "Let them put a clean turban on his head." So they put a clean turban on his head, and they put the clothes on him. And the Angel of the* LORD *stood by.* (NKJV)

While Joshua, as the representative of Israel and the priests, was standing before the Angel of the Lord (Jesus), the Lord told others who were there to remove Joshua's filthy clothes. Filthy clothes are a symbol of the believer's righteous acts. What the good believers do for the Lord is filthy because it is tainted by sin in their lives. This is verified by our Lord's comments to Joshua, "See, I have removed your iniquity from you, and I will clothe you with rich robes" (verse 4 NKJV). Then, Jesus told his helpers to put a clean **turban** on Joshua's head and to replace his clothes. Replacing his dirty clothes with clean clothes and putting the priest's hat on his head are symbols of clothing him in the righteousness of Christ and restoring him to the priesthood. This is a beautiful picture of God's forgiveness and restoration of Israel both in Zechariah's day and during the coming Millennium.

This vision pictures the Judgment Bar with Satan there to accuse God's people, but Jesus Christ the Righteous is there as an Advocate for God's people. He is there to counter and rebuke the accuser, to take away the sinner's unrighteousness, and to replace it with his own righteousness. The sinner can't do this for himself, but Jesus can do this for him because he died on the cross in the sinner's place. Cleansing and restoration are for the church, but also for Israel.

house
Hebrews 3:6

what others say

J. Vernon McGee

The garments of the high priest included a turban, and on that turban were the words: HOLINESS UNTO THE LORD, as in chapter 14 verse 20. This man Joshua didn't have a turban because in those dirty old garments he certainly was not holy to the Lord. But a turban is given to him now on which is inscribed "Holiness unto the Lord." He will be used of God now just as Israel will be used of the Lord in the future.[3]

Two Ifs and Three Promises

Zechariah 3:6–7 ***Then the Angel of the Lord admonished Joshua, saying, "Thus says the Lord of hosts: 'If you will walk in My ways, and if you will keep My command, then you shall also judge My house, and likewise have charge of My courts; I will give you places to walk among these who stand here. (NKJV)***

The Angel of the Lord (Jesus) lectured Joshua (Israel), saying the Lord of hosts (God) said that if he would walk in God's ways and keep God's commandments, God would do three things for him:

- Put Joshua (Israel) in charge of his house (let him make decisions concerning God's people).
- Put Joshua (Israel) in charge of his courts (the rebuilt Temple).
- Give Joshua (Israel) a place among those (the angels) standing in their presence, suggesting he would have immediate and special access to God.

Diligent obedience will bring great blessings. Since Israel has not done this in the past, it awaits a future fulfillment in the Millennium and beyond.

God's Servant (The Branch)

Zechariah 3:8–10 ***Hear, O Joshua, the high priest, you and your companions who sit before you, for they are a wondrous sign; for behold, I am bringing forth My Servant the BRANCH. for behold, the stone that I have laid before Joshua: Upon the stone are seven eyes. Behold, I will engrave its inscription,' says the Lord of hosts, 'and I will remove the iniquity of that land in one day. In that day,' says the Lord of hosts, 'every-***

one will invite his neighbor under his vine and under his fig tree.'" (NKJV)

Servant
Isaiah 53:1–11

Branch
Isaiah 11:1–9; Jeremiah 23:5–6; 33:15

Stone
Daniel 2:34–45

"Hear" means God wants people to notice that Joshua and his associates (fellow priests) were a wondrous sign. This vision not only had significance for Joshua's (Israel's) time, it also had significance for Joshua's future. It was a sign of things to come. God promised to send forth his Servant the Branch, a clear prophecy of the first coming of Jesus. Then, he set a Stone a clear prophecy about the second coming of Jesus as King, before Joshua. This Stone had seven eyes, a symbol that Jesus is omniscient, sees everything, and will watch over Israel. The Stone had an inscription on it that was a promise to remove Israel's sin in just one day. When that day arrives Israel will be so safe that the Jews will be able to invite their neighbors to visit and relax with them under their own vines and fig trees.

The Millennium will follow the second coming of Jesus. He will live and reign on earth. Satan will be bound and chained for a thousand years. The redeemed of Israel will be regathered, cleansed, and forgiven. The Jews will get the Promised Land, including all of Jerusalem and a whole lot more. The Millennial Temple will be rebuilt, and the Jews will finally be the nation of priests that God intended them to be. Multitudes of Gentiles will be saved and go to Jerusalem to worship. Peace, justice, righteousness, truth, and holiness will prevail. Prosperity will abound. Discrimination, oppression, poverty, and false worship will not be tolerated. It will be an ideal time to live and worship.

The word "Branch" is used in at least four different ways in the Old Testament with an amazing tie to the four New Testament Gospels. Jeremiah used the word "Branch" to refer to Jesus as a King (Matthew presents Jesus as a King). Zechariah used the word "Branch" to refer to Jesus in two ways: as a Servant, and as a Man (Mark presents Jesus as a Servant. Luke presents Jesus as a Man). Isaiah used the word "Branch" to refer to Jesus as the Branch of God (John presents Jesus as the Son of God). Men would not think to do this. It is confirmation of the divine authorship of the Scriptures in both the Old and the New Testaments.

Calvary
the site in Jerusalem where Jesus died

what others say

Walter C. Kaiser, Jr./Lloyd J. Ogilvie

> Such a cleansing of the land is typical of the spiritual cleansing that Messiah will accomplish on **Calvary**. This action is the key to the whole fourth vision. The "one day" promised here is "that day" of Zechariah 9–14, i.e., the "day" of Israel's national repentance when her people will look on Him whom they have pierced (Zechariah 12:10).[4]

Chapter Wrap-Up

- While Joshua, who represented Israel and the priests, was standing before Jesus, the devil appeared and began to accuse Joshua, but Jesus rebuked Satan and announced that Jerusalem was his chosen city and that the Jews were his chosen people whom he rescued from Babylon.
- Joshua's clothes were dirty, so Jesus had them removed to symbolize the removal of Israel's sins. Jesus replaced Joshua's dirty clothes with clean clothes and a priest's hat to symbolize the restoration of Israel as a nation of priests. Then the Lord told Joshua that if he would obey him and keep his commandments, God would let him rule his people, be in charge of the Temple, and have access to God.
- Joshua and his associates, who symbolize Israel and the priests, were told that they were symbols of things to come. They were also told that God's Servant, the Branch (Jesus), was coming.
- God said he was setting a Stone, Jesus, before Joshua. This Stone would have seven eyes, see everything, and bear an inscription, which is a promise to remove Israel's sin in one day. Then Israel will be secure and can enjoy living in the land.

Study Questions

1. How do we know that Satan's accusations against Joshua were also against Jerusalem?
2. What symbol indicates that Israel and the priests were guilty of sinning? What two symbols reveal that Israel and the priests will be cleansed and restored in the future?
3. What two things did Joshua need to do if he wanted to be in charge of God's people?
4. Who is specifically mentioned as standing and who as seated at this hearing before the Angel of the Lord?
5. When will the Jews have peace and be able to relax in their own land?

Zechariah 4
The Fifth Vision

Chapter Highlights:
- A Lamp and Two Trees
- God Is Great
- Temple Completed
- Messiah King and Priest

Let's Get Started

The main character in Zechariah's fourth vision was Joshua the high priest, Israel's religious leader. The main character in this fifth vision is Zerubbabel, the political leader. Zechariah was called to encourage the Jews to rebuild the Temple at a time when they were meeting some very stiff opposition. Under those difficult circumstances he received this vision that was a message to Zerubbabel. It has one overriding theme: No obstacle is too great if you have God's help. Jesus said it this way, "With God all things are possible" (NKJV). With God's help, nothing could keep the Temple from being rebuilt and nothing could prevent Israel from assuming its role as a vehicle for God's light in the world. Opposition cannot stop God's work when God's people have his help. This was true in Zechariah's day, it is still true today, and it will be true in the future. Israel defaulted on her light-giving role and was replaced by the church, but she can be given another chance.

possible
Matthew 19:26

what others say

J. R. Church

Prophetically, I think the passage looks into the far future to the generation in which we live to encourage the Jewish people once again to get on with the job of rebuilding their Temple. With Jewish demands for a presence on the Temple site (which have been increasing over the past decade), I feel that the time has come for the ultimate fulfillment of this prophecy. However, in order for the Jews to rebuild their Temple, the two olive trees pictured in this vision must make their appearance: They are called in Revelation 11 "two witnesses."[1]

The Fifth Vision: The Golden Lampstand and the Two Olive Trees

ZECHARIAH 4:1–3 ***Now the angel who talked with me came back and wakened me, as a man who is wakened out of his sleep.***

Word
Psalm 119:105

Yahweh
The English translation of the Hebrew word YHWH. It refers to God.

And he said to me, "What do you see?" So I said, "I am looking, and there is a lampstand of solid gold with a bowl on top of it, and on the stand seven lamps with seven pipes to the seven lamps. Two olive trees are by it, one at the right of the bowl and the other at its left." (NKJV)

Something made Zechariah sleepy, so he dozed off and the interpreting angel had to come back and wake him up. Following that, the angel showed him a vision of a strange-looking solid-gold lampstand between two unusual olive trees. The lampstand had a bowl at the top that was connected to seven burning lamps. The connection was seven pieces of tubing running from the bowl to each burning lamp for a total of forty-nine pieces of tubing. One of the olive trees was on the left side of the bowl and the other was on the right side.

what others say

Ralph L. Smith

The meaning probably is that the olive branches furnish golden olive oil through the golden pipes, presumably to the seven lamps. If this is the meaning, then the lamps represent Israel and not **Yahweh**. The two olive trees probably represent Zerubbabel and Joshua, the political and religious leaders.[2]

C. I. Scofield

In this vision the lampstand represents God's witness before the world. In the time of Zechariah this witness was maintained by Israel. In the Church Age it is maintained by the Church. Although the Church will be removed at the rapture, God will still maintain a witness in the world. The two olive trees represent two phases of God's government, one the priestly and the other the kingly. From these two olive trees the oil was carried to the lampstand. Oil is the uniform symbol of the Holy Spirit.[3]

Lampstands are used to give off light. This lampstand had seven lights on it, a figure of speech meaning it gave off the maximum amount of light. Light is a symbol of the Word of God. The Lord meant for a continuous unhindered supply of oil (the Holy Spirit) to flow through the lampstand (Joshua and Zerubbabel) and give off light (the Word of God). The lampstand could be portrayed as government and religion working together, or all of Israel.

You Have to Have Oil

work
Ezra 4:1–24

Holy Spirit
the third person of the Trinity, the invisible presence of God

capstone
last stone or the one that completed the project

> **Zechariah 4:4–8** ***So I answered and spoke to the angel who talked with me, saying, "What are these, my lord?" Then the angel who talked with me answered and said to me, "Do you not know what these are?" And I said, "No, my lord." So he answered and said to me: "This is the word of the Lord to Zerubbabel: 'Not by might nor by power, but by My Spirit,' says the Lord of hosts. 'Who are you, O great mountain? Before Zerubbabel you shall become a plain! And he shall bring forth the capstone with shouts of "Grace, grace to it!"'" Moreover the word of the Lord came to me, saying: (NKJV)***

Zechariah asked the interpreting angel for an explanation of the things he saw. This seemed to surprise the interpreting angel, but Zechariah replied that he didn't know what these things were. The interpreting angel didn't answer Zechariah's question, but he gave him a message to deliver to Zerubbabel. This was the governor of Israel who was supervising the work on the Temple. In essence, God told Zerubbabel that the Temple could not be rebuilt by human effort or strength alone, but it could be rebuilt with the help of the **Holy Spirit**. Apparently, Zerubbabel was trying to rebuild the Temple in his own strength and was facing a mountain of opposition and problems that brought the work to a standstill. But God said the mountain would be leveled, meaning the opposition and problems would crumble before the Holy Spirit, the Temple would be rebuilt, and Zerubbabel would set the **capstone** to the shouts and cheers of the people.

God was saying there was not enough power on earth to rebuild the Temple if he was not in it. He was also saying that there was not enough power on earth to stop it if he wanted it done. Zerubbabel and the fifty thousand returnees were not enough to build it without God's help. In turn, Israel's enemies, though they had the largest and most powerful army on earth, couldn't keep it from happening if he decided to get it done.

Another Message

> **Zechariah 4:9–10** ***"The hands of Zerubbabel have laid the foundation of this temple; his hands shall also finish it. Then you will know that the Lord of hosts has sent Me to you. For who***

word
Zechariah 4:6–7

foundation
Ezra 3:8–11

people
Haggai 2:1–9

anointed
a person chosen by God to do some special thing

has despised the day of small things? For these seven rejoice to see the plumb line in the hand of Zerubbabel. They are the eyes of the LORD, which scan to and fro throughout the whole earth." *(NKJV)*

Following the word of the Lord to Zerubbabel, God had a word for Zechariah: Zerubbabel was in charge of laying the Temple foundation, and he would still be in charge of the rebuilding project when the structure was completed. This was God's promise that construction of the Temple would not drag on beyond Zerubbabel's lifetime. Then, the angel added that fulfillment of this promise would also be evidence that God had sent him to Zechariah.

"Who has despised the day of small things?" probably refers back to the attitude of the people when they realized that the rebuilt Temple would be much smaller than the one Solomon had built. They were disappointed and ready to give up on the project, but God let them know that nothing he does is small. He let them know that others were rejoicing to see that Zerubbabel had the plumb line in his hand and construction had actually started. Along with this, he had perfect vision, saw everything, and was watching over them. If he was involved, it would be great. In fact, he considered it to be great, and his opinion was the only one that really mattered.

If at First You Don't Succeed, Try, Try Again

ZECHARIAH 4:11–14 ***Then I answered and said to him, "What are these two olive trees—at the right of the lampstand and at its left?" And I further answered and said to him, "What are these two olive branches that drip into the receptacles of the two gold pipes from which the golden oil drains?" Then he answered me and said, "Do you not know what these are?" And I said, "No, my lord." So he said, "These are the two anointed ones, who stand beside the Lord of the whole earth."*** *(NKJV)*

Up until this point, the interpreting angel had not explained the two olive trees to Zechariah. Even though Zechariah asked about them, he didn't wait for an answer. Zechariah also wanted to know about the branch on each olive tree with clusters of olives that dripped oil into a gold pipe leading to the lampstand. As before, the interpreting angel seemed surprised that Zechariah did not know what these were. He told Zechariah that these represented two men who were **anointed** to serve the Lord of the whole earth.

Most scholars agree that these two anointed ones were two men, the religious leader and the political leader of that day, namely, Joshua and Zerubbabel. They also agree that the oil dripping from their branches indicated that they were filled with the Holy Spirit. But there is more. Since Joshua and his associates were symbolic of things to come, there will be a future fulfillment when Jesus returns as Priest and King at his second coming. Joshua the high priest prefigures Jesus as a Priest after the order of Melchizedek. Zerubbabel the governor or political leader pre-figures Jesus as King of kings and Lord of lords. Joshua and Zerubbabel represent the combining of religion and government with one common goal under the anointing of the Holy Spirit to do God's work and this prefigures the second coming of Jesus to fulfill both positions (Priest and King). The big difference is that he won't just rule over Israel. He will be King of kings and Lord of lords over the whole earth.

Joshua
Zechariah 3:8

Chapter Wrap-Up

- The angel woke Zechariah up and asked him what he saw. He saw a lampstand supporting a bowl with seven lights, seven channels going to each light, and an olive tree on each side of the light.
- Zechariah asked what these things were and the angel seemed surprised he didn't know. Instead of answering Zechariah, the angel told him that God said to tell Zerubbabel that he needed the Holy Spirit to do God's work, God would neutralize the opposition to rebuilding the Temple, and the people would celebrate when the capstone was put in place.
- The angel told Zechariah that Zerubbabel had started the Temple and would complete it. This would be a sign that the angel had been sent by God. He urged the people to not be ashamed of the small Temple. He also told them that others were rejoicing because it was being rebuilt. He then let them know that God was watching over them.
- Zechariah wanted an explanation of the two olive trees that had branches dripping with oil that ran into the bowl on the lampstand. He was told these were the two anointed ones who served the Lord of all the earth. Most authorities agree that this referred to Joshua the high priest and Zerubbabel the governor.

There is also wide agreement that in the future, Israel will be ruled by a Priest-King who will be Jesus.

Study Questions

1. What did the lampstand, seven lights, and oil symbolize?
2. Why were light and oil needed in Zechariah's day?
3. What did God move to allow the Temple to be rebuilt? How do we know he moved it right away?
4. What was the purpose of the two olive trees? What two leaders did they represent?

Zechariah 5
The Sixth and Seventh Visions

Chapter Highlights:
- **The Flying Scroll**
- **Woman in a Basket**
- **It Wasn't a Genie in a Jar**
- **No Flying Nuns**

Let's Get Started

The visions in previous chapters teach that the returning Jews would experience grace, mercy, and forgiveness. The first vision in this chapter teaches that they could also experience judgment. God will forgive and bless people, but he expects those he forgives and blesses to keep his Word. Grace accepted means love and blessings, but it also carries the responsibility of obedience to the Giver of that love and those blessings. Grace rejected means severe punishment. God's guideline is his Word. His judgment of the acts of sin is in accordance with the Word of God.

The vision of the woman in the basket is short in words and long in meaning. It shows that God will eventually remove the cause of most, if not all, sin (as opposed to the acts of sin), or more specifically, the reasons why people sin. This had an immediate application for Israel, but like all of the previous visions, there is an end-of-the-age application that applies to Jews and Gentiles. During the Millennium, God will deal with the cause of all wickedness in all of the world.

The Sixth Vision: The Flying Scroll

> **Zechariah 5:1–4** ***Then I turned and raised my eyes, and saw there a flying scroll. And he said to me, "What do you see?" So I answered, "I see a flying scroll. Its length is twenty cubits and its width ten cubits." Then he said to me, "This is the curse that goes out over the face of the whole earth: 'Every thief shall be expelled,' according to this side of the scroll; and, 'Every perjurer shall be expelled,' according to that side of it." "I will send out the curse," says the Lord of hosts; "It shall enter the house of the thief and the house of the one who swears falsely by My name. It shall remain in the midst of his house and consume it, with its timber and stones."*** *(NKJV)*

After seeing the vision of the golden lampstand and the two olive trees in chapter 4, Zechariah turned, raised his eyes, and saw a flying

Tabernacle
Exodus 26:15–37

house
1 Peter 4:17

Tabernacle
a tent where God met with his people in the wilderness

scroll. It would be the equivalent of a flying carpet with writing on each side. There is wide agreement that the dimensions of this scroll were 30 x 15 feet if the measurements are converted from cubits to feet. Scholars are aware that these are the same dimensions as the Holy Place in the **Tabernacle**. For this reason, some suggest that the judgment of God will begin at the house of God. This definitely fits what Peter said in the New Testament.

There is no uncertainty about the significance of the scroll. The angel told Zechariah that it represented a curse flying over the face of the whole earth. The curse had an immediate application for Israel and a wider application for the whole world. This wider application suggests fulfillment during the Millennium when Jesus will rule the world with a rod of iron.

The scroll had writing on both sides. One side said God was prepared to banish all thieves. The other side said God was prepared to banish all perjurers or all who swear falsely by God's name. These are the two categories into which Jesus divided the Ten Commandments: sin against our fellowman, and sin against God. Sin is transgressing the Law or breaking the Ten Commandments. Breaking one of the commandments is an act of sin.

The size of the scroll, 30 x 15 feet, causes many to believe it was big enough to contain all of the Ten Commandments. In the Old Testament the returnees to Israel were expected to keep the Ten Commandments. During the Millennium the whole world will be expected to keep them.

The scroll was in the air for all to see. All of the Jews were well aware of the Ten Commandments and the judgments of God that preceded their release from Egypt. During the Millennium the whole world will be aware of the Ten Commandments and the judgments of God that will accompany severe transgressions.

God will send the curse into the houses of those who break his commandments and this curse will destroy everything there, including all the timber and even the stones. It will be somewhat like the death angel who entered the houses of unbelievers in Egypt to slay the firstborn. There was no place to hide and no way to escape. In summation, the curse represents the judgments of God found in the Word of God that will be pronounced upon those who disobey him. It's important to note here that God eventually used the Romans to remove the Jews from the land. During the Millennium, however, chronic violators will be removed from the earth by death. The judgments will be overwhelming and there will be no way to avoid them.

The fact that the scroll was flying indicates that the curse will be carried out very quickly. Someone said, "Justice delayed is justice denied." There will be no delay. These matters will not be dragged through the courts for years. Excuses won't be accepted. Jesus knows the thoughts of every individual and what is in their heart. He won't hesitate to act.

what others say

Steven C. Ger

On one side of the scroll is written the third commandment and on the opposite side is written the eighth commandment. The third and the eighth commandments would have been the middle commandments on each of the two stone tablets given to Moses. These middle commandments represent the entirety of the ten commandments, which, in turn, exemplify the entire Torah, the Mosaic law. In order for God to personally dwell in the midst of His people, they must be purged of covenantal impurity in preparation for His presence.[1]

Russell L. Penney

A curse or punishment will go out against those who violate His law, symbolized by those who steal (Exodus 20:15) and swear falsely (20:7). All those involved in such things will be purged from the covenant people (5:4). The severity and totality of the judgments suggests a fulfillment in the millennial kingdom when the Messiah will rule with a rod of iron (Psalm 2:9–12; Revelation 12:5; 19:15).[2]

Dave Breese

Why is something wrong that is wrong? It is wrong because the Bible says so. Why is something good and commendable? It is good and commendable not because it's practical or makes people happy, it may do that, but it is because the Bible says so. You must do what you do, say what you say, operate your life under the aegis of the flying scroll, the Word of God distributed now to all humanity.[3]

The Seventh Vision: The Woman in a Basket

ZECHARIAH 5:5–6 ***Then the angel who talked with me came out and said to me, "Lift your eyes now, and see what this is that goes***

measuring basket
a basket used to measure flour, barley, wheat, etc.

forth." So I asked, "What is it?" And he said, "It is a basket that is going forth." He also said, "This is their resemblance throughout the earth: *(NKJV)*

The foregoing vision dealt with the purging of acts of sin and purging the land and earth of those who commit them. This vision deals with the purging of the cause of sin or, in other words, the reasons why people sin.

Apparently the interpreting angel had stepped back to let Zechariah have a better view of the flying scroll, because he then stepped forward to point out another vision. Again, Zechariah wanted to know what this vision was. The angel told him it was a basket. A footnote in the NKJV reveals that the Hebrew word used here for basket is "ephah." It means a standard measuring container or a standard **measuring basket**. A real standard measuring basket was slightly larger than a bushel basket and probably large enough for a small child to squat down in. Such a container was used to measure standard amounts of commodities for sale or trade in the marketplace. It was used so often that it became an international symbol of commerce or trade. The interpreting angel further explained that the contents of the basket resembled something throughout the earth. This meant that the contents of the basket were a symbol of something that is all over the world.

It Wasn't a Genie in a Jar

ZECHARIAH 5:7–8 ***Here is a lead disc lifted up, and this is a woman sitting inside the basket"; then he said, "This is Wickedness!" And he thrust her down into the basket, and threw the lead cover over its mouth.*** *(NKJV)*

The interpreting angel raised the lead cover on the basket (symbol of commerce) so Zechariah could see inside, and there sat a woman. The interpreting angel told Zechariah this woman represented wickedness. She was wickedness personified, the very embodiment of wickedness. She must have tried to get out because the angel pushed her back into the basket and quickly covered the basket with the heavy cover made of lead. It is just speculation, but she was probably trying to escape because she had a premonition of her coming judgment. The difference between this vision and that of the flying scroll is that the flying scroll represented a curse upon individuals for acts of sin, whereas this woman represented the general spirit of wickedness or the reasons that cause people to sin. Sin is one thing, and the reason why people sin is something else. God not only intends to deal with sinners, but he also intends to deal with the worldwide systems that cause it.

They Weren't Flying Nuns

> ZECHARIAH 5:9–11 *Then I raised my eyes and looked, and there were two women, coming with the wind in their wings; for they had wings like the wings of a stork, and they lifted up the basket between earth and heaven. So I said to the angel who talked with me, "Where are they carrying the basket?" And he said to me, "To build a house for it in the land of Shinar; when it is ready, the basket will be set there on its base."* (NKJV)

Next, Zechariah looked up and saw two women, perhaps angels, with large wings like the wings of a giant stork. Flying with the assistance of the wind, they lifted the measuring basket (symbol of commerce) with its heavy lid and the woman inside (causes of sin personified). They held commerce and wickedness in the air between heaven and earth, and Zechariah wanted to know where they were going. The interpreting angel told him that the women were moving the measuring basket (symbol of commerce) and the woman (causes of sin personified) to the land of Shinar (Babylon, the first world government in the Times of the Gentiles), where a temple would be built so they could be properly displayed.

What is the meaning of this vision? Although it is difficult to say, it is important to keep a few things in mind:

- The Bible teaches that Babylon will be rebuilt.
- Nimrod tried to establish a one-world government and one-world religion at Babylon.
- Babylon, the nation that scattered the Jews in Judah, was the first one-world government in the Times of the Gentiles.
- The measuring basket was a well-known symbol of commerce in the ancient world.
- In the Bible a good woman often symbolizes true religion (Bride of Christ), and a bad woman often symbolizes false religion (Mystery, Babylon the Great; the Mother of Harlots).

- The woman in the parable of the leaven used false teachings to corrupt the kingdom of heaven.
- A spiritual adulteress named Jezebel taught false doctrines in the church at Thyatira.

In addition to saying that the cause of wickedness will be removed from Israel in the future, this could also be saying that Babylon will be rebuilt and become the center of globalism (one-world trade and one-world religion) during the Tribulation Period. The supporters of Antichrist will make Babylon their headquarters in the future. God will move them there and then destroy Babylon by fire in one hour for the entire world to see.

Notice that when the house is built in Babylon, the basket will be set there *on its base*. This seems to indicate that Babylon will be rebuilt in its original place. It's interesting that when Saddam Hussein started rebuilding Babylon, he uncovered the foundation and started building on top of what was already there (its base).

Chapter Wrap-Up

- Zechariah saw an unusually large scroll flying through the air. An angel told him it was a curse that will come upon all thieves and everyone who swears falsely by God's name. During the Millennium, chronic sinners against their fellowman or against God will be judged and punished according to the Word of God.
- Zechariah saw a measuring basket and was told it represented the sins of the Jews all over the nation. He looked inside and saw a woman called wickedness. When she tried to get out he pushed her down and covered the basket with a heavy lid.
- Zechariah saw two women fly down, pick up the basket with the woman inside, and start to leave. He asked where they were going and was told the women were taking the basket and the woman to Babylon, where a temple would be built to display these things.

Study Questions

1. What did the flying scroll symbolize? What was written on it and who should be concerned about it?

2. Concerning sin, how did the flying scroll differ from the measuring basket? How did the measuring basket differ from the wicked woman inside?

3. What is symbolized by moving the measuring basket and the wicked woman inside to Babylon?

Zechariah 6 The Eighth Vision and the Coming Messiah

Chapter Highlights:
- Worldwide Judgments
- A World Leader
- God's Chariot
- God's Priest King

Let's Get Started

Zechariah's visions have revealed much about God's plans for Israel at the end of the age, but the Lord's plans would be incomplete if they didn't include the Gentile nations. The full restoration of Israel includes judgment upon those who resist God's plans. This is the subject of Zechariah's final vision. He saw horses reminiscent of those mentioned in chapter 1. Others had been added to the group, and all were hooked up to war chariots. These horses will go forth to deal with the Antichrist and all those who have resisted God's authority.

After Zechariah's eight visions, the last of which includes the future overthrow of the one-world government led by the Antichrist, Jesus will be crowned as Priest and King over the one-world government that he will establish at his second coming. This is symbolized by the placing of a crown on the head of the high priest.

what others say

Peter C. Craigie

And though we may find the visionary words as difficult to grasp in detail as did the prophet's first audience, we may share with them the absolute conviction of the prophet's central message. God was and is sovereign in human history. And though the hand of God must always be difficult for the ordinary mortal to discern, we can share the prophet's faith that the passage of history is not a random process, but moves somehow towards the fulfillment of God's purpose in the world.[1]

The Eighth Vision: God's Chariots

ZECHARIAH 6:1–8 *Then I turned and raised my eyes and looked, and behold, four chariots were coming from between two mountains, and the mountains were mountains of bronze. With the first chariot were red horses, with the second chariot black horses, with the third chariot white horses, and with the*

bronze
Exodus 27:1–19

hooves bronze
Micah 4:13

brass
Revelation 1:15; 2:18

fourth chariot dappled horses—strong steeds. Then I answered and said to the angel who talked with me, "What are these, my lord?" And the angel answered and said to me, "These are four spirits of heaven, who go out from their station before the Lord of all the earth. The one with the black horses is going to the north country, the white are going after them, and the dappled are going toward the south country." Then the strong steeds went out, eager to go, that they might walk to and fro throughout the earth. And He said, "Go, walk to and fro throughout the earth." So they walked to and fro throughout the earth. And He called to me, and spoke to me, saying, "See, those who go toward the north country have given rest to My Spirit in the north country." *(NKJV)*

Following the vision of the woman in a basket, Zechariah turned, raised his head, looked, and saw one final vision. It began with four chariots that were mostly used as instruments of war in his day. Later, it will be revealed that these are spirit beings that look like war chariots.

These war chariots were coming out from their station before the Lord (verse 5) and going between two mountains of bronze. The Hebrew text actually reads "the mountains," meaning two specific mountains. "The mountains" were not identified, but because Zechariah was in Jerusalem when he had this vision, most scholars believe "the mountains" were two mountains near Jerusalem, perhaps Mount Zion and the Mount of Olives. One other possibility is the Temple Mount, also called Mount Moriah, but this does not seem to fit the text.

Bronze is a symbol of judgment in the Bible. In the Old Testament, God told Moses to make an altar of acacia wood overlaid with bronze to offer sin offerings on. The sacrificed animal signified God's judgment falling on a substitute (a type of Christ). He told the Hebrews he would make their hooves bronze so they could crush their enemies. In the book of Revelation, Jesus is pictured as having feet like brass, which is a reminder that he is the Judge of all mankind.

The horses were all very strong and their color seems significant:

- The first group was red (the red horse in Revelation 6:3–4 will remove peace from the earth).

- The second group was black (the black horse in Revelation 6:5–6 will cause economic disaster and famine).
- The third group was white (the white horse in Revelation 6:1–2 will go forth conquering and to conquer).
- The fourth group was dappled, which means spotted or mottled (the pale horse in Revelation 6:7–8 will go forth killing with war, famine, plagues, and beasts).

So the most common assumption is that these war chariots (spirit beings) were passing between Mount Zion and the Mount of Olives, and their mission was one of judgment. Their path would take them out to the Valley of Jehoshaphat where the **Battle of Armageddon** will be fought. The Mount of Olives is where Jesus will come back to at his second coming.

Zechariah asked for an explanation and was told that these were spirits of heaven, perhaps angels, sent from the presence of God to cover the whole earth. Only two directions are mentioned (north and south) because the Mediterranean Sea is on the west and the Syrian Desert is on the east, causing all traffic to flow north or south. These war chariots (spirit beings) were told to go throughout the earth. The chariot with black horses (economic disaster and famine) and the chariot with white horses (conquering and to conquer) joined forces and went north. The chariot with dappled horses (war, famine, plagues, and beasts) went south, but what they did is not revealed. There is also silence about the red horse (removes peace from the earth). Then, the chariots went all over the earth and what they did in the north country set God's Spirit at rest, an expression that means they appeased God's wrath by establishing his power and authority there.

The correct interpretation cannot be dogmatically stated, but it appears that the Four Horsemen of the Apocalypse and the Tribulation Period are in sight here. It also appears that God's judgments will go forth throughout the whole world until rebuilt Babylon, with its one-world government and one-world religion, is finally destroyed. These things have to happen before Israel is finally restored so that the Millennium can begin.

angels
Hebrews 1:13–14

Battle of Armageddon
a great battle on earth during the Tribulation Period

day of the Lord
another name for the Tribulation Period

what others say

C. I. Scofield

The symbol (chariots and horses) is in perfect harmony with this [judgment of God). Always in Scripture symbolism, they stand for the power of God earthward in judgment. The vision, then, speaks of the Lord's judgments upon the Gentile nations north and south in the **day of the Lord**.[2]

What Does the Future Hold?

Fact	What Will Happen
Fact 1	God will dwell in Jerusalem and be merciful toward his people. The Temple (Millennial Temple not Tribulation Temple) will be rebuilt. Jerusalem will be larger than ever. It will prosper and many Jewish cities will be rebuilt.
Fact 2	Israel's enemies will be God's enemies.
Fact 3	Jerusalem will grow beyond its walls and be like an unwalled city with multitudes of people and animals. God will dwell in Jerusalem, be like a wall of fire around Jerusalem, and be the glory of Jerusalem. The Jews will know God's Servant (Jesus). God will destroy the nations that harm Israel.
Fact 4	Israel's sin won't prevent God from cleansing and restoring Israel and her priests. Israel will be saved in one day and the world will have peace.
Fact 5	Jesus will combine religion and politics to rule the world as a Priest and King during the Millennium.
Fact 6	Jesus will rule with a rod of iron and remove chronic sinners from the earth during the Millennium.
Fact 7	Babylon will become the seat of one-world trade and one-world religion during the Tribulation Period.
Fact 8	The Four Horsemen of the Apocalypse, the Battle of Armageddon, and the destruction of Babylon must take place before Israel is fully restored.

God's Priest-King

ZECHARIAH 6:9–15 ***Then the word of the LORD came to me, saying: "Receive the gift from the captives—from Heldai, Tobijah, and Jedaiah, who have come from Babylon—and go the same day and enter the house of Josiah the son of Zephaniah. Take the silver and gold, make an elaborate crown, and set it on the head of Joshua the son of Jehozadak, the high priest. Then speak to him, saying, 'Thus says the LORD of hosts, saying: "Behold, the Man whose name is the BRANCH! From His place He shall branch out, and He shall build the temple of the LORD; yes, He shall build the temple of the LORD. He shall bear the glory, and***

shall sit and rule on His throne; so He shall be a priest on His throne, and the counsel of peace shall be between them both."' Now the elaborate crown shall be for a memorial in the temple of the LORD for Helem, Tobijah, Jedaiah, and Hen the son of Zephaniah. Even those from afar shall come and build the temple of the LORD. Then you shall know that the Lord of hosts has sent Me to you. And this shall come to pass if you diligently obey the voice of the LORD your God." (NKJV)

BRANCH
Zechariah 3:8

David
Jeremiah 23:5

Temple
Isaiah 2:2–4; Ezekiel 40–43

kingdom
Luke 1:32–33

Priest
Psalm 110:1–7

The captives (Jewish exiles) in Babylon took up an offering of silver and gold, and sent it to the Jewish returnees in Jerusalem. The Lord told Zechariah to take this offering of silver and gold to the house of Josiah. He instructed that it be used to make a crown. The crown was to be placed on the head of the high priest Joshua. This was an unusual event because one would normally expect Zerubbabel—the political leader and governor—to be crowned king, and not the high priest. It was also unusual because God had always kept the offices of high priest and king separate. In this vision, though, God gave instructions for the high priest to be crowned as king. Why? The answer is in what God said next. It contains five statements that clearly refer to the coming Messiah:

- "Behold, the Man whose name is BRANCH!" The word "Man" is capitalized and it refers to God's Servant, the coming King, a descendant of King David.
- "From His place He shall branch out." This means he will prosper or be successful at all he does.
- "He shall build the Temple of the LORD." This refers to the Temple that will be built during the Millennium. It does not refer to the Tribulation Period Temple.
- "He shall bear the glory, and shall sit and rule on His throne." This refers to his kingdom that will never end. He will receive glory and honor as a King.
- "He shall be a priest on His throne." This means he will be a Priest *and* a King.

After he placed the crown on Joshua's head, Zechariah was told to remove it and give it to the three exiles who brought the silver and gold and to Hen the son of Zephaniah. He said they should display it in the Temple as a memorial. Why? Because the symbolic act was over and there would be no Priest-King until Messiah came.

Man
John 19:1–5

Displaying it in the Temple would be a reminder that God will send a Priest-King. In that day, people from distant lands will go to Israel to work on the new Temple. All who obey him will be part of his kingdom.

The Lord said that the crown was to be set on Joshua's head and he was to be told: "Thus says the Lord of hosts, saying: 'Behold the Man whose name is the BRANCH!'" This is a scene that was repeated more than five hundred years later when the soldiers placed a twisted crown of thorns and a purple robe on Jesus. They said, "Hail, King of the Jews." They beat him, and when Pilate took him before the crowd, Jesus was wearing the crown of thorns and purple robe. When he did this, Pilate said, "Behold the Man!" (NKJV). He was a Man, but not just any man. The One who was crowned with thorns was the coming Priest-King.

Scholars have noticed eight "shall" statements in verses 13–15 that provide God's summary of Zechariah's eight visions of things to come. They are:

- He shall branch out.
- He shall build the Temple.
- He shall bear the glory.
- He shall sit and rule on his throne.
- He shall be a priest on his throne.
- The counsel of peace shall be between them both.
- The elaborate crown shall be for a memorial.
- Those from afar shall come and build the Temple of the Lord.

Quite often Bible names are very important. Consider what the names in verses 10 and 14 say about God:

- Heldai means "Jehovah's world," and it was changed to Helem (verse 14), which means "be strong."
- Tobijah means "Jehovah is good."
- Jedaiah means "Jehovah knows."
- Josiah means "Jehovah supports," and it was changed to Hen (verse 14), which means "gracious one" or "graciousness."
- Zephaniah means "Jehovah protects."

It's God's world. Be strong. He is good, knows everything, supports his people with grace, and protects them.

dispensational
the belief that God's plan for the earth is administered in set periods

what others say

John Phillips

A King-Priest; Jews coming from afar with gifts; a divine title; a double crown; a temple, being rebuilt; the crown placed in the temple "for a memorial"; a charge to "diligently obey the voice of the Lord"; God's pledge that "this shall come to pass"—all these were types and shadows that will be literally fulfilled at the second coming of Christ. Ezekiel's temple will be built. The King-Priest will reign. People will come from the ends of the earth to bring tithes and tributes to Jerusalem and worship in the temple.[3]

C. I. Scofield

Christ is now a Priest but is still in the holiest within the veil (Hebrews 9:11–14, 24; Leviticus 16:15) and seated on the Father's throne (Revelation 3:21). He has not yet come out to take his own throne (Hebrews 9:28). It was to keep alive this larger hope of Israel that these crowns were made for the symbolical crowning of Joshua; they were to be laid up in the Temple as a memorial.[4]

J. Randall Price

Since this prediction was not fulfilled by Zerubbabel the priest and builder of the Second Temple, it became a text awaiting fulfillment by the future coming Messiah. Orthodox and ultra-Orthodox Jews expect this fulfillment in the rebuilding of the Third Temple when the Messiah makes his appearance in Jerusalem. Christians (with a **dispensational** perspective) expect this when Jesus as Messiah erects the Millennial (Fourth) Temple at the beginning of the Kingdom age.[5]

Chapter Wrap-Up

- Zechariah saw four chariots that were probably coming out of the Valley of Jehoshaphat, where the Battle of Armageddon will be fought. These chariots were sent from God and were told to go throughout the earth. What they do in the North Country will appease God's wrath and establish his authority there.
- Zechariah was told to make a crown from the offerings of silver and gold that had been brought to the house of Josiah. He was told to crown Joshua. This made Joshua a type, or forerunner, of the Branch. He will rebuild the Temple, rule on his throne there, and be a Priest-King. Then Zechariah was told to remove the crown from Joshua's head, give it to the three exiles who had offered the silver and gold, and tell them to display the crown in the Temple. People will go to Jerusalem from distant lands to work on the Temple, and those who obey God will know that he sent his Son.

Study Questions

1. What did the four chariots symbolize? Where will they come from and where will they go?
2. How will their journey toward the North Country affect God's Spirits?
3. What is significant about putting a crown on the high priest's head? Why was it to be removed from Joshua's head and displayed at the Temple?
4. Who will build the last Temple? What position will he hold?

Zechariah 7 The People's Question and God's Answer

Chapter Highlights:
- **What God Wanted from Their Ancestors**
- **What Their Ancestors Did**
- **What God Did**

Let's Get Started

The next two chapters mark a turning point in the Book of Zechariah. They present two important messages he delivered to the people. Chapter seven is a call to straighten out some of the past problems. Chapter eight is a promise of a brighter future.

second year
Zechariah 1:7

fourth year
Zechariah 7:1

returned
Ezra 2:1–65

Almost two years had passed since Zechariah received the eight visions recorded in Chapters 1–6. He dated those eight visions in the second year of Darius. He dated the message in this chapter in the fourth year of Darius. During these two years the Jews had worked hard on the Temple. They knew they would complete it in about two more. When they started working on it, the drought that was going on stopped and there was an increase in God's blessings. Times were changing in Jerusalem. Things were looking up. But conditions were not so good in some of the surrounding towns and villages.

The People's Question

ZECHARIAH 7:1–3 ***Now in the fourth year of King Darius it came to pass that the word of the LORD came to Zechariah, on the fourth day of the ninth month, Chislev, when the people sent Sherezer, with Regem-Melech and his men, to the house of God, to pray before the LORD, and to ask the priests who were in the house of the LORD of hosts, and the prophets, saying, "Should I weep in the fifth month and fast as I have done for so many years?" (NKJV)***

Following the Babylonian captivity a remnant of the Jews returned home. They began to reestablish the nation of Israel, rebuild the cities and towns, to rebuild Jerusalem, and rebuild the Temple. Despite obstacles, they succeeded. They reestablished their nation and saw progress in Jerusalem. Progress was also made in several other towns, including Bethel. It seemed like God had started to bless Jerusalem. The people there were building houses, getting

fast
Zechariah 8:19

comfortable, and gaining wealth. Their future looked brighter. Conditions were much different in Bethel, however. Times were harder there and the future dimmer there. The people at Bethel wondered why Jerusalem was doing better than they were. They even wondered if it had something to do with their worship. Because they thought that perhaps the priests and prophets in Jerusalem could help them determine the source of the problem, they sent a committee to the Temple in Jerusalem to pray and to talk to the priests and prophets there. Their question was this: "Should I weep in the fifth month and fast as I have done for so many years?"

During the times when the people were captives in Babylon, they set aside certain days for weeping and fasting. God did not tell them to do this. They just did this on their own. It was something extra they wanted to do that was over and above what God had asked them to do. They thought God would be pleased with their extra sacrifices. Why not go through extra rituals? If one revival service a year is good, why not have two? If two revival services a year are good, why not have ten? If a four-night series of revival services is good, why not have a six-night series of services? The Jews thought that if fasting one time a year is good, why not fast four times a year? The Jews at Bethel noted that they had been weeping and fasting every year but with much less than they expected and certainly not nearly as much as they thought it was accomplishing in Jerusalem. The question they brought to the leaders in Jerusalem was as to whether they should keep up this practice. "As I have done these so many years" indicates that it had become ritual and they were growing tired of it.

Someone may ask, "What does this have to do with church members today?" They may say, "Church members don't weep and fast like the Jews did." No, but church members do things over and over again just like these people did. Many churches lack fresh vision from God because they have stagnated in doing the same things they have always done. Attendance drops each week rather than growing, and few, if any, people ever make a confession of faith in Christ. Change may be harder, but the slow death of a body of believers is even harder. To be truly effective, a body of believers must seek and adhere to God's strategies for accomplishing his purposes for that church now and in the future. This principle also holds true for individuals, families, communities, and nations.

God's Answer

> ZECHARIAH 7:4–7 *Then the word of the* LORD *of hosts came to me, saying, "Say to all the people of the land, and to the priests: 'When you fasted and mourned in the fifth and seventh months during those seventy years, did you really fast for Me—for Me? When you eat and when you drink, do you not eat and drink for yourselves? Should you not have obeyed the words which the* LORD *proclaimed through the former prophets when Jerusalem and the cities around it were inhabited and prosperous, and the South and the Lowland were inhabited?'"* (NKJV)

God instructed Zechariah to ask the people and the priests to examine why they were fasting and mourning. The fact that God asked them to state their motive or purpose for doing this indicates that their motives were selfish ones. It seems that their fasting and mourning were motivated by the desire to obtain something *from* God rather than by the desire to do something *for* God. Apparently, they thought their extra efforts would compel or obligate God to bless them. To address this, he told them to listen to the former prophets of the time when Jerusalem and the surrounding towns were inhabited and prosperous. He wanted them to take a look back at their history, especially that history prior to the destruction of Jerusalem. He wanted them to learn from the fact that their nation was destroyed during the time of their ancestors even though the people had been going to the Temple, offering sacrifices, and keeping the feast days. The reason for this destruction was that they had honored God with their lips, but their hearts had been far from him.

what others say

David Wilkerson

We are not just to intercede [pray] for things we need, but to ask for the things He desires. . . . Often we go to the Lord only to unburden our troubles and sorrows to Him—to seek a supply of strength for the next battle. Of course, that is Scriptural; we are invited to come boldly to God's throne of grace . . . But our praying is not complete if we do not understand God's need! Whereas we seek relief and help from the Lord, He desires fellowship with us—intimacy and communion. Our primary purpose in praying ought always to be fellowship with the Lord. . . . If most Christians subtracted such petitions from their prayer time, there would be little or no prayer left![1]

The motives for why we do something, even something that we assume will please God, are much more important than what we actually do. If we do something only out of habit, our actions are lifeless. If we do something because we want God to bless us, our motives are selfish and not born out of love for him. God knows the motives of our hearts much better than we do. When we read the Word of God, we should be asking the Lord to search our hearts and reveal our true motives. When our eyes are fixed on him and on pleasing him, our gracious God will reveal our true motives to us and help us to walk in love rather than in selfishness and self-centeredness.

How Their Ancestors Could Have Pleased God

> **Zechariah 7:8–10** ***Then the word of the Lord came to Zechariah, saying, "Thus says the Lord of hosts: 'Execute true justice, Show mercy and compassion everyone to his brother. Do not oppress the widow or the fatherless, the alien or the poor. Let none of you plan evil in his heart against his brother.'*** *(NKJV)*

God did not ask their ancestors to fast and mourn at the same time every year, but he did ask them to treat people with compassion and mercy. He wanted these Jews to know that fasting and mourning were necessary if they mistreated people or harbored ill feelings for them.

Many people today leave their Christianity at the front door of the church when they walk out into their daily lives. Attending church on Sunday and then mistreating people on Monday is offensive to God. No amount of work at the church or money we donate to the local charity will cancel out the mistreatment of others. By the same token, no amount of singing in church or attending home group meetings on Wednesdays will excuse the harboring of hatred of another person. If we are giving and sacrificing but are not mindful of what the Spirit is telling us about the motives and conditions of our hearts, God's attention will remain fixed on our hearts rather than blessing our actions.

What Their Ancestors Did

> **Zechariah 7:11–12** ***But they refused to heed, shrugged their shoulders, and stopped their ears so that they could not hear. Yes,***

they made their hearts like flint, refusing to hear the law and the words which the LORD of hosts had sent by His Spirit through the former prophets. Thus great wrath came from the LORD of hosts. *(NKJV)*

Their ancestors had gone through the motions of going to the Temple, fasting, and mourning. They heard what the prophets had to say, but they stiffly refused to obey. They turned their backs, put their fingers in their ears, and hardened their hearts to the commands and warnings. They were determined to do things their own way.

Many churches say they want revival. They schedule a special service and call it a revival. They invite an evangelist to preach and advertise the meetings, hoping new people will attend. True revival, however, is the transformation of the motives of people's hearts. The work of the Holy Spirit moves upon the hearts of people, purifying their motives and revealing truth to them so that they can begin to truly forgive people who have hurt them in the past. When this happens, people's spirits are revived and renewed by the Holy Spirit and the preaching of the Word of God. Compelled by their love for God, they become living expressions of his compassion for other people.

What God Did to Their Ancestors

ZECHARIAH 7:13–14 ***Therefore it happened, that just as He proclaimed and they would not hear, so they called out and I would not listen," says the LORD of hosts. "But I scattered them with a whirlwind among all the nations which they had not known. Thus the land became desolate after them, so that no one passed through or returned; for they made the pleasant land desolate."*** *(NKJV)*

God said he gave them what they gave him. When he called, they turned their backs and put their finger in their ears. Then, when they called, he turned his back and put his finger in his ears. They prayed when the Babylonians were threatening to destroy the nation, but he had refused to listen, had scattered them, and had made their land desolate. The bottom line, however, was that they had brought all this on themselves when they stiffly refused to do things their own way.

Chapter Wrap-Up

- The former exiles were fasting and mourning in the fifth month of every year, but God was not blessing them the way they expected. They sent a committee to Jerusalem to pray and ask the priests if they should continue this practice.
- God told Zechariah to ask the Jews if they were really fasting and mourning for him, or for selfish reasons. To make his point, he reminded them of his dealings with their ancestors.
- God told the Jews that what he had actually wanted from their ancestors was for them to honor him by treating others with compassion and mercy.
- God pointed out that their ancestors had ignored him, hardened their hearts, and refused to listen to the messages sent to them by his Holy Spirit through the prophets. He said that because their ancestors had ignored him, he ignored them when trouble came upon them.

Study Questions

1. Can we get things from God by fasting and mourning?
2. Name four things God wanted from the exile's ancestors.
3. Does God get angry? Does he destroy nations?
4. Are there repercussions for ignorng God?

Zecharia 8
Jerusalem Will Prosper

Chapter Highlights:
- God's Promises
- Israel's Wonderful Future
- Zealous for Zion
- Jesus Will Be Saved

Let's Get Started

After bringing to remembrance the ways in which he had responded to the self-centeredness and rebellion of previous generations, God began to speak about the future. He wanted the Jews to know that his plans for Israel and Jerusalem had not changed. Their ancestors failed, but he would not fail the nation. He would keep his covenants. He would fulfill every promise he had made. Israel has a bright future. The nation will have much to celebrate during the Millennium.

what others say

Warren W. Wiersbe

God's people don't live on explanations; they live on promises. Faith and hope are nourished by the promises of God given to us in the Scriptures. That explains why Zechariah dropped the discussion of the traditions and delivered a message from the Lord. In this message, he focused the people's eyes of faith on the future and shared some wonderful promises to encourage them.[1]

Israel's Wonderful Future

the big picture

Zechariah 8:1–23

Fifteen times it is stated that this is what the Lord of hosts says (vv. 1, 2, 3, 4, 6, 7, 9, 11, 17, 18, 19, 20, 23) and twice it is stated that this is what the Lord says (vv. 3, 17). Six times it is stated that he is talking about Jerusalem (vv. 3, 4, 8, 15, 22) and twice he refers to Zion (vv. 2, 3).

This is what the Lord of hosts says:

- God is jealous for Zion (Jerusalem occupies a special place in God's heart).
- God will return to Zion and dwell in Jerusalem.

truth
John 14:6

holy
Psalm 99:9

- The presence of God in Jerusalem will result in its being called a "City of Truth" (Jesus is Truth).
- The presence of God in Jerusalem will result in the Temple Mount being called the "Holy Mountain."
- The presence of God in Jerusalem will make the city safe.
- The promises about a future Jerusalem were marvelous in the eyes of the Jews who returned to Israel in Zechariah's day.
- God also marvels at what he can do because nothing is too difficult for him.
- God will bring the Jews from the east and west to dwell in Jerusalem.
- The Jews will be God's people, and he will be honest and do the right thing when he deals with them.
- God wanted the Jews who heard these words in Zechariah's day to be strong.
- The Jews in Zechariah's day laid the foundation for the Second Temple.
- Before they built the Second Temple, the Jews in Zechariah's day weren't prospering and didn't have peace, but they had many trials and great division among themselves.
- Times changed when the Jews started building the Second Temple: the rain fell, the crops grew, and the people prospered.
- The Jews have been cursed, but the day will come when God will save them and make them a blessing to all people.
- When the returnees' ancestors provoked God to wrath he decided to punish them.
- He had now decided to bless them.
- He wanted the returnees to be honest, maintain honest courts, treat their neighbors fairly, and not love false accusations.
- The returnees' sad days will eventually be glad days.
- Because God controls the future, people should be honest and peaceful.
- Everyone will want to visit Jerusalem in the future (during the Millennium).

- People will go to Jerusalem to pray and seek the Lord.
- Multitudes of people will pray and seek the Lord in Jerusalem.
- Ten Gentiles will grab the clothing of one Jew and say they will go to Jerusalem with him.
- The Gentiles will say they have heard that God is with the Jews.

weep
Zechariah 7:3

gladness
Zechariah 8:19

The returnees at Bethel had asked God a question, "Should I weep in the fifth month and fast as I have done for so many years?" (NKJV). He didn't answer the question right away, but in this chapter he noted that they were actually fasting four times a year (in the fourth, fifth, seventh, and tenth months). History shows:

- The fast in the fourth month mourned Nebuchadnezzar's destruction of Jerusalem.
- The fast in the fifth month mourned the burning of the Temple.
- The fast in the seventh month mourned the murder of Gedaliah governor of Judah.
- The fast in the tenth month mourned the beginning of Nebuchadnezzar's attacks on Jerusalem.

God's answer was these fasts, which "shall be joy and gladness and cheerful feasts" (NKJV). During the Millennium, Israel will be so blessed that her times of fasting and self-imposed sadness will be replaced with feasts of joy and gladness to celebrate all that God is doing.

Chapter Wrap-Up

- God's promises to Israel were meant to encourage the people of Zechariah's day, but most of what he said will not be fulfilled until the Millennium. Jesus will return, dwell in Jerusalem, make the city safe, be the God of the Jews, bless the Jews, save the Jews, make them a blessing to the whole world, cause the Gentiles to visit and worship in Jerusalem, and more.

Study Questions

1. Where will Jesus dwell during the Millennium? What two things will the place be called?
2. How will God's presence in Jerusalem affect people during the Millennium?
3. What did God tell the Jews of Zechariah's day to do?
4. What will happen to the fast days during the Millennium?
5. Who will the Gentiles seek in Jerusalem during the Millennium?

Zechariah 9 Alexander the Great and the Coming Messiah

Chapter Highlights:
- Alexander the Great
- The First Coming
- The Second Coming
- God's Weapon
- A Powerful Army

Let's Get Started

The last six chapters of Zechariah were given several years after the Temple was completed. They form the third and final major division of his book. There were no chapter and verse divisions when Zechariah wrote his book, but he divided these last six chapters into two parts called "The burden of the word of the Lord." The first burden of the word of the Lord is found in chapters 9–11. The second burden is found in chapters 12–14.

Chapter 9 looks forward from Zechariah's time. When he was prophesying, the Jews were under the rule of the Medes and Persians. The first eight verses of chapter 9 look beyond the empire of the Medes and Persians to the empire of Alexander the Great. They predict Alexander's defeat of Israel's enemies in the north and south. From there, Zechariah prophesied across the pages of history to the first coming and then to the second coming of Jesus. After that, he bounced backward to Israel's struggle with Greece in the days of the Maccabees. Bouncing back and forth over hundreds of years instead of presenting the events in chronological order makes these passages difficult to follow, but Zechariah definitely gave an amazing revelation of world events in advance of the events occurring.

Some of the amazing prophecies in the first burden of the word of the Lord are:

Chapter 9

- The defeat of Israel's enemies in the north and south by Alexander the Great.
- The triumphal entry of Jesus.
- Israel's struggle against Antiochus Epiphanes, and Greece.
- Israel's victory in the days of Antiochus Epiphanes and also over the Antichrist at the end of the age.

Chapter 10

- The end of the drought in Zechariah's day.
- The first and second coming of Jesus.
- The restoration of Israel as one undivided nation at the end of the age.

Chapter 11

- The unfaithfulness of Israel's leaders and the destruction in the Middle East by Rome in AD 70.
- The betrayal of Jesus for thirty pieces of silver.
- Israel's acceptance of the Antichrist at the end of the age.

Israel's Enemies in the Days of Alexander the Great

ZECHARIAH 9:1–8 ***The burden of the word of the LORD against the land of Hadrach, and Damascus its resting place (for the eyes of men and all the tribes of Israel are on the LORD); also against Hamath, which borders on it, and against Tyre and Sidon, though they are very wise. For Tyre built herself a tower, heaped up silver like the dust, and gold like the mire of the streets. Behold, the LORD will cast her out; He will destroy her power in the sea, and she will be devoured by fire. Ashkelon shall see it and fear; Gaza also shall be very sorrowful; and Ekron, for He dried up her expectation. The king shall perish from Gaza, and Ashkelon shall not be inhabited. "A mixed race shall settle in Ashdod, and I will cut off the pride of the Philistines. I will take away the blood from his mouth, and the abominations from between his teeth. But he who remains, even he shall be for our God, and shall be like a leader in Judah, and Ekron like a Jebusite. I will camp around My house because of the army, because of him who passes by and him who returns. No more shall an oppressor pass through them, for now I have seen with My eyes.*** *(NKJV)*

This is the judgment that God declared upon Hadrach, Damascus, Hamath, Tyre, Sidon, and four of the Philistines' most important cities: Ashkelon, Gaza, Ekron, and Ashdod. The first five areas were to the north of Israel. The four Philistine cities were to the south of Israel. This is truly a remarkable prophecy because Zechariah revealed the conquest of these places before the events occurred in a literal sense. Alexander the Great fulfilled the prophecy after the Battle of Issus in 333 BC. The identity and location of Hadrach are somewhat of a mystery, but authorities believe it was in Syria. Hadrach and Hamath are both connected with Damascus in this passage, and no one doubts that Damascus was in Syria. In the beginning, the city of Tyre was on the mainland, but it was badly damaged in a thirteen-year siege by King Nebuchadnezzar. The city was rebuilt on an island in the Mediterranean Sea and many authorities thought it was impregnable. Then, Alexander the Great came along, pushed the debris of the old city into the sea, used it to build a causeway out to the city on the island, and conquered it. Sidon simply gave up without a fight. The four Philistine cities were taken. Judah was not taken. God camped around it, and Alexander bypassed it on his way to Egypt. In fact, he bypassed it several times. It is intriguing that Zechariah would mention the king (Alexander the Great) passing by, amazing that it literally happened, and even more amazing that, in the next verse, he would mention a King who wouldn't pass by. The city was preserved for the King that was coming. Along with that, the men of God had prophesied many other events that would be fulfilled there as well.

Although they are amazed at the accuracy of this prophecy, a few scholars do not believe it has been completely fulfilled. Some think Alexander the Great conquered only part of the territory mentioned here. They suggest that the areas north and south of Israel will be conquered again at the end of the age.

Because these events were future to Zechariah and some liberal scholars do not believe it is possible to predict the future with the kind of accuracy found here, some want to assign the book of Zechariah to a later date. They contend that this book of the Bible is a book of history that was written by a second writer who used the name Zechariah. Conservative scholars do not contest the date and believe that the degree of prophetic accuracy is possible because God knows all.

The King Is Coming

ZECHARIAH 9:9 ***"Rejoice greatly, O daughter of Zion! Shout, O daughter of Jerusalem! Behold, your King is coming to you; He is just and having salvation, lowly and riding on a donkey, a colt, the foal of a donkey.*** **(NKJV)**

King
Matthew 2:2; 27:37

Jesus
Matthew 21:1–11; John 12:14–15

Artaxerxes
Nehemiah 2:1–8

This verse is a contrast with verses 1–8. Notice the following:

- Verses 1–8 mention the king that would pass by Israel, but this verse mentions the King that would enter in.
- Verses 1–8 mention a reason for Israel's enemies to weep (their destruction), but this verse mentions a reason for Israel to rejoice (their salvation).
- Alexander the Great was a ruthless conquering king who rode a great stallion, but this verse mentions a humble King who would ride a donkey.

This prophecy was literally fulfilled by Jesus many years later when he made what is commonly called his triumphal entry into Jerusalem.

what others say

Charles H. Dyer

According to some scholars, Jesus rode into Jerusalem exactly 173,880 days after Artaxerxes issued his decree to Nehemiah. Jesus entered Jerusalem on a colt the way Zechariah said the Messiah would come (Zechariah 9:9).[1]

Peace on Earth

Zechariah 9:10 ***I will cut off the chariot from Ephraim and the horse from Jerusalem; the battle bow shall be cut off. He shall speak peace to the nations; His dominion shall be 'from sea to sea, and from the River to the ends of the earth.' (NKJV)***

Here, Zechariah's prophecy skips from the first coming of Jesus all the way over to the Millennium. It skips the Roman occupation, the destruction of rebuilt Jerusalem, the Church Age, the modern-day return of the Jews, the Tribulation Period, and much more. The mention of Ephraim, a major tribe in the Northern Kingdom, and Jerusalem, the capital of the Southern Kingdom, speaks of a reunited Israel at the end of the age. The removal of weapons of war—chariots, warhorses, and the battle bow—speaks of a time of peace on earth. The gentle King who rode in on a donkey the first time will come back as the King of kings and Lord of lords. He will sit on the throne of David in Jerusalem and rule with an iron scepter. He will proclaim peace to all the nations, and his reign will extend over all the earth.

An Unusual Weapon

covenant
Genesis 15:7–17; Exodus 24:4–8

water
Ephesians 5:26

ZECHARIAH 9:11–13 ***"As for you also, because of the blood of your covenant, I will set your prisoners free from the waterless pit. Return to the stronghold, you prisoners of hope. Even today I declare that I will restore double to you. For I have bent Judah, My bow, fitted the bow with Ephraim, and raised up your sons, O Zion, against your sons, O Greece, and made you like the sword of a mighty man."*** *(NKJV)*

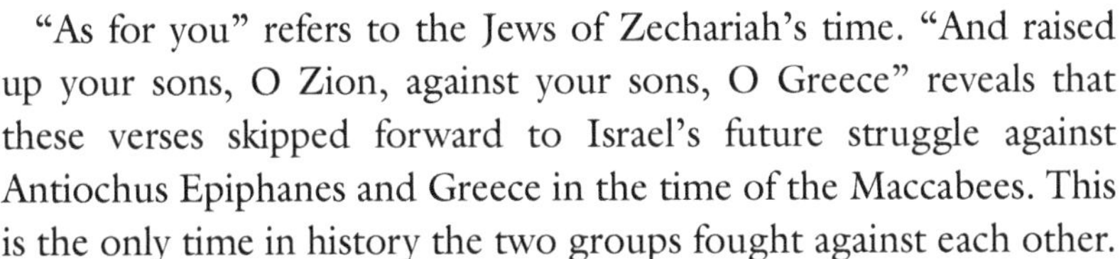

"As for you" refers to the Jews of Zechariah's time. "And raised up your sons, O Zion, against your sons, O Greece" reveals that these verses skipped forward to Israel's future struggle against Antiochus Epiphanes and Greece in the time of the Maccabees. This is the only time in history the two groups fought against each other.

God was promising to return the Jews to the land in Zechariah's day on the basis of the blood covenant he had with the nation. There is some ambiguity about which blood covenant is meant here. It could be the blood covenant God made with Moses when he gave the Jews the Ten Commandments at Mount Sinai, but it is most likely the blood covenant he made with Abraham after he moved to the Promised Land. God was promising to restore the nation and bless the land on the basis of one of his covenants. He promised to make the land a fortress for those who were prisoners in foreign lands without the water of the Word.

But there would be problems between the sons of Zion and the sons of Greece in the future. The Jewish people would be God's weapon of war against Greece.

what others say

Thomas Edward McComiskey

We learn now how Zion will come to prominence and power among the nations: Yahweh will use her as a war bow. He will do this "for himself"; that is, Zion cannot depend on weapons of war (9:10) or conquer on her own; it is only as God uses her as an instrument of war for himself that he will advance Zion's cause in the arena of nations.[2]

The Secret Behind Israel's Great Warriors

ZECHARIAH 9:14–17 ***Then the LORD will be seen over them, and His arrow will go forth like lightning. The Lord GOD will***

blow the trumpet, and go with whirlwinds from the south. The LORD of hosts will defend them; they shall devour and subdue with slingstones. They shall drink and roar as if with wine; they shall be filled with blood like basins, like the corners of the altar. The LORD their God will save them in that day, as the flock of His people. For they shall be like the jewels of a crown, lifted like a banner over His land—for how great is its goodness and how great its beauty! Grain shall make the young men thrive, and new wine the young women. *(NKJV)*

Israel's army would see the Lord hovering over them when they went out to fight against Antiochus Epiphanes and Greece. He would signal the attack, accompany the troops in battle, and protect them from harm. Israel's army would overcome her enemies, they would celebrate, the bloodshed would be great, and the death of Israel's enemies would be like the death of an animal sacrificed to God.

"In that day" is a phrase Zechariah uses over and over again in reference to the Tribulation Period. He was revealing the fact that Israel's struggle against Antiochus Epiphanes and Greece foreshadows their struggle against the Antichrist at the end of the age. God will save his people and look after them like a good shepherd looks after his flock. The Jews will sparkle in the Promised Land like precious jewels in God's crown. Gentiles will admire them. They will prosper by feeding on the Word and drinking from the Holy Spirit.

Chapter Wrap-Up

- Zechariah predicted God would cause the defeat of powerful enemies to the north and south of Israel. Then the Lord raised up Alexander the Great to conquer Syria, the Phoenicians, the Philistines, and others.
- Zechariah predicted the triumphal entry of Jesus into Jerusalem at his first coming with gifts of righteousness and salvation.
- Zechariah predicted the second coming of Jesus will bring peace on earth.
- Zechariah predicted God will remember his blood covenant with Israel, he will restore the nation, and will use Israel to defeat his enemies.
- Zechariah predicted God will appear over the Israeli army at the end of the age, judge his enemies, accompany the Israeli army into battle, and give the army overwhelming victories. He also predicted that would cause the Jewish nation to stand out in the world, to be admired, to feed on his Word, and to receive his Spirit.

Study Questions

1. What did Zechariah see in the future of the armies to the north and south of Israel? Who caused this?
2. What did Zechariah see in the future of Jerusalem that was worthy of great rejoicing?
3. When will peace come to Israel and to all the earth?
4. What will be the basis of Israel's return to the Promised Land at the end of the age? What weapon will God use to destroy his enemies?
5. Who will protect Israel's army at the end of the age? What will cause the Jews to prosper?

Study Questions

3. Where will peace come to Israel and to all the earth?

Zechariah 10 Israel to Be Scattered and Regathered Again

Chapter Highlights:
- Just Ask
- To Kinds of Shepherds
- Restoration Is Coming

Let's Get Started

Chapter 9 revealed that Israel has a glorious future. Chapter 10 reveals that their glorious future cannot arrive until there is a return of the leaders' hearts to God and a massive return of the people to the land. This chapter talks about the importance of having the right kind of leader and how the scattered people will be regathered. It reveals that Israel would go on a roller coaster of blessings and promises, but God will never give up on her, and he will ultimately bring her to repentance and the point he intended all along.

Just Ask

ZECHARIAH 10:1 ***Ask the LORD for rain in the time of the latter rain. The LORD will make flashing clouds; He will give them showers of rain, grass in the field for everyone.*** (NKJV)

drought
Haggai 1:9–11

latter rains
spring rains in March or April

Israel's three greatest needs are peace with God, peace with her neighbors, and water. Very long dry summers with a limited supply of precious water puts the nation at risk just as much as Israel's rebellion against God and the presence of wicked neighbors. Knowing this, God told the people to pray for the **latter rains** to come. He makes the clouds, sends the rain, and causes the plants to grow. But he also wants to hear the prayers of people who believe. In this case, he told them to ask him for rain, not for idols or diviners.

In the days of Moses, God told the Hebrews that he would send the rain when they were obedient and he would withhold the rain when they were disobedient. The former rain, Israel's spring, usually fell in our fall (October–November) and the latter rain, Israel's fall, usually fell in our spring (March–April). When the returnees went back to Israel from Babylon, they started work on the Temple and then stopped. In response, God sent a drought. At the time of this passage, Israel had rebuilt the Temple so God was saying, "Pray and get ready to receive water and good crops." Obedience is followed by blessings, but disobedience is followed by hard times.

what others say

Charles L. Feinberg

God's blessings on Israel are compared to rain (Hosea 6:1–3); here are included all material blessings, emblems of the spiritual ones. The lightnings which precede the rain will assure her of the rain, and God will give her torrential rains to supply the need of every heart in Israel. Our God is a bountiful Giver, but He must be entreated and trusted implicitly.[1]

Two Kinds of Shepherds

ZECHARIAH 10:2–5 ***For the idols speak delusion; the diviners envision lies, and tell false dreams; they comfort in vain. Therefore the people wend their way like sheep; they are in trouble because there is no shepherd. "My anger is kindled against the shepherds, and I will punish the goatherds. For the LORD of hosts will visit His flock, the house of Judah, and will make them as His royal horse in the battle. From him comes the cornerstone, from him the tent peg, from him the battle bow, from him every ruler together. They shall be like mighty men, who tread down their enemies in the mire of the streets in the battle. They shall fight because the LORD is with them, and the riders on horses shall be put to shame.*** *(NKJV)*

Following his call for the returnees to pray to him for rain, God talked about the futility of what the shepherds (leaders) of their ancestors did that had played a big part in God's letting Babylon destroy Judah. The nation's past shepherds prayed to idols, but, since idols can't send rain, the answers their ancestors said they received were the worthless product of their own imaginations. They used diviners, but, since demons can't forecast the weather, their demonic predictions were only a guess. They dreamed dreams and attached authority to them, but these were the product of their own wicked creativity and not the inspirations of God. The result of these practices was a false sense of comfort, hope, and security. In response to all this, God eventually destroyed the nation.

Another and far more serious result was that the Jews wandered like confused sheep having problems, but having no shepherd. This angered God and provoked a promise to hold these false shepherds and the goatherds that followed them accountable for their faulty lives. Why? Because God is like a true shepherd who looks after the well-being of his flock, and he intends to turn his true sheep into a warhorse that will trample upon his enemies. From the God of Israel would come:

- ***The cornerstone***—the most important stone or the one upon which all other stones are dependant. It sets the direction of two walls. This means that Jesus would be the way, the truth, and the life.
- ***The tent peg***—the large nail that was driven into the center support post of a tent to serve as a hanger for the owner's valuables. It means everything of value would hang or depend upon Jesus.
- ***The battle bow***—the weapon that would destroy all of God's enemies. It means Jesus would have the power to overcome all opposition to Israel or God.
- ***The rulers***—true shepherds who will follow the Lord as mighty men trampling upon powerful enemies as though they were mud in the streets. With God's help Israel would one day easily defeat the exalted armies who oppose them.

cornerstone
Matthew 21:42; Ephesians 2:20; 1 Peter 2:4–8

peg
Isaiah 22:25

enemies
Psalm 45:5

what others say

Norbert Lieth

What she [modern Israel] still lacks is the Good Shepherd. The "shepherds" of today's Jews are not leading them in the direction God wants them to go. This refers to the political and religious authorities (rabbis) and it is a tragedy.[2]

Restoration Is Coming

Zechariah 10:6–12 ***"I will strengthen the house of Judah, and I will save the house of Joseph. I will bring them back, because I have mercy on them. They shall be as though I had not cast them aside; for I am the Lord their God, and I will hear them. Those of Ephraim shall be like a mighty man, and their heart shall rejoice as if with wine. Yes, their children shall see it and be glad; their heart shall rejoice in the Lord. I will whistle for them and gather them, for I will redeem them; and they shall increase as they once increased. I will sow them among the peoples, and they shall remember Me in far countries; they shall live, together with their children, and they shall return. I will also bring them back from the land of Egypt, and gather them from***

Gilead
the Golan Heights

Assyria. I will bring them into the land of Gilead and Lebanon, until no more room is found for them. He shall pass through the sea with affliction, and strike the waves of the sea: all the depths of the River shall dry up. Then the pride of Assyria shall be brought down, and the scepter of Egypt shall depart. So I will strengthen them in the LORD, and they shall walk up and down in His name," says the LORD. (NKJV)

Because God wants to be merciful, the house of Judah—representing the Southern Kingdom, and the house of Joseph—representing the Northern Kingdom, will be fully restored so the two kingdoms can jointly share in the coming blessings as one nation. The Jews will not hold God's scattering of the nation against him. They will act as though that never happened. He will be their God and answer their prayers. They will become a mighty nation with much to rejoice about. God will speak to the hearts of those in foreign lands and they will return to Israel. But their return will not be just to the land because, in due time, they will remember their God and return to him. He will bring them from foreign lands, from Egypt and Syria, to **Gilead** and Lebanon, a great population so that the borders of the nation will be greatly expanded. They will encounter many problems and be opposed by Syria and Egypt, but their enemies will be disgraced, God will strengthen them in his ways, and they will walk with him.

Notice, what God will do for Israel in the future and how the Jews will respond:

- I will strengthen the house of Judah.
- I will bring them back.
- I will hear them.
- I will whistle for them and gather them.
- I will redeem them.
- I will sow them among the peoples.
- I will bring them back from the land of Egypt and gather them from Assyria.
- I will bring them into the land of Gilead and Lebanon.
- I will strengthen them in the Lord.
- They shall be as though I had not cast them aside.
- Their heart shall rejoice in the Lord.

- They shall increase as they once increased.
- They shall remember me in far countries.
- They shall live together with their children.
- They shall return.
- They shall walk up and down in his name.

According to the Bible, there will be two main waves of returnees at the end of the age: the first in unbelief prior to the Tribulation Period, and the second in belief at the end of the Tribulation Period. The first is well under way with spiritually blind Israel growing strong and her enemies being defeated over and over again. But judgment will still come because of her unbelief. She will sign a phony covenant with the Antichrist and be weakened and humbled. However, God will perform miracles to preserve her and cause her to repent. Then, all the Jews will turn to Jesus and the second main wave will return in belief.

Chapter Wrap-Up

- God promised clouds, rain, and green grass to Israel in the future, if the people will just ask.
- God was angry with Israel's leaders and punished them because they were worshiping idols, consulting diviners, interpreting dreams, and misleading the people. God promised to make Israel a powerful nation, to bring the Messiah out of that nation, to purge that nation of corrupt leaders, and to be with the people.
- God will return Israel to the land and the Jews will serve him. God will be merciful to them, be their God, and hear their prayers. They will rejoice, prosper, and expand their borders. God will help them with their difficulties, embarrass their enemies, strengthen them in the Lord, and cause them to walk with him.

Study Questions

1. Who controls the weather? Does he form the clouds and send the rain? Why would he send drought or cause poor crops?
2. What caused God to be so angry with Israel's leaders?
3. Why will Israel's army be so powerful at the end of the age?
4. What indication does this chapter give that the Ten Northern Tribes have not ceased to exist?
5. What indication does this chapter give that Israel's borders will be much larger than they are today?

Zechariah 11
Israel, Christ, and the Antichrist

Chapter Highlights:
- The Fallen Trees
- The Forsaken Sheep
- The Forsaken Shepherd
- The Foolish Shepherd

Let's Get Started

The wonderful promises in chapter 10 will be preceded by a dark time in Israel's history, a time future to Zechariah. Most commentators attribute this future time to the Roman invasion in AD 70, but many think what happened back then prefigures coming warfare at the end of the age. What is the problem? After betraying and rejecting the Messiah, Israel will turn around and accept the Antichrist.

Destroy the Trees

ZECHARIAH 11:1–3 ***Open your doors, O Lebanon, that fire may devour your cedars. Wail, O cypress, for the cedar has fallen, because the mighty trees are ruined. Wail, O oaks of Bashan, for the thick forest has come down. There is the sound of wailing shepherds! For their glory is in ruins. There is the sound of roaring lions! For the pride of the Jordan is in ruins.*** *(NKJV)*

trees
Ezekiel 31:1–9; Daniel 4:9–27; Luke 21:29–31

shepherds
Zechariah 10:2–3

pride
Proverbs 16:18

Bashan
Golan Heights

Three areas are mentioned: Lebanon, famous for its cedars; **Bashan**, famous for its oaks; and Jordan, famous for its thick clusters of trees, bushes, and shrubs that grew along the banks of the Jordan River and hid dens of sleeping lions. Trees are Bible symbols for kings and kingdoms. Thus, God is warning the leaders and nations to the north and east of Israel, the nations called Lebanon, Syria, and Jordan. He warns them of an invading army that will destroy them as they pass through their land on the way to Israel. This army will move across Lebanon, over the Golan Heights, and south toward the Jordan Valley.

Shepherds are Bible symbols for spiritual leaders. The shepherds in these areas will suffer the same fate as their kings because they have misled the flock. Pride, haughtiness, and unfaithfulness will precede their destruction.

It's difficult to deny the devastation that took place in this area during the Roman invasion in AD 70, but other prophecies reveal that a more and greater devastation is expected at the end of the age.

sheep
Psalm 44:22

Lebanon, Syria, Jordan, and the unfaithful leaders in Israel will all come under the judgment of God.

what others say

Peter C. Craigie

The scene is suggestive of the violence and warfare that would precede the Kingdom of God. Those great rulers and kings of the world's nations, despite the apparent continuity of their reigns and the seeming invincibility of their strength, would be lamented in their collapse.[1]

Fatten the Sheep

ZECHARIAH 11:4–6 ***Thus says the LORD my God, "Feed the flock for slaughter, whose owners slaughter them and feel no guilt; those who sell them say, 'Blessed be the LORD, for I am rich'; and their shepherds do not pity them. For I will no longer pity the inhabitants of the land," says the LORD. "But indeed I will give everyone into his neighbor's hand and into the hand of his king. They shall attack the land, and I will not deliver them from their hand." (NKJV)***

These verses amplify the actions of the unfaithful leaders in verses 1–3. In similar fashion, they refer to the Roman invasion of Israel in AD 70, but they are also prophecy with an end-of-the-age application.

God told Zechariah to assume the role of a shepherd (representing Jesus) for the purpose of feeding a flock of sheep destined to be slaughtered. This endangered flock represents the common people of Israel. The owners represent the Romans who would slaughter them in AD 70. The sellers represent the Jewish religious and political leaders who would betray their own people for profit. This was a parable suggesting the coming Roman destruction of Israel for its rejection of Jesus as the Messiah. The Jews under the unscrupulous leadership of the Pharisees and Sadducees would reject Jesus and give him over to a cruel slaughter at the cross. He, in turn, would reject them without pity and give them over to cruel treatment by the Romans. In a sense the Romans would be bad, but the Jewish religious leaders would be worse because they would betray their own people for profit.

How this prefigures the end of the age is speculation. The owners may well represent the Quartet (UN, EU, U.S., and Russia) or some other Gentile group that harbors plans for the destruction of Israel. The sellers probably represent modern religious and political leaders seeking to gain wealth and power with offers to give away strategic land on the West Bank and/or control of religious sites such as the Temple Mount. If they cared about the common people, they would extract great concessions from the Palestinians and turn to their true Messiah for peace, but they will willingly overlook the Palestinian threat, cater to the Gentiles, and expose their nation to great risk. Ultimately, they will commit the nation's security into the hands of the false shepherd called the Antichrist and he will slaughter many.

We Don't Like This Shepherd

> ZECHARIAH 11:7–14 *So I fed the flock for slaughter, in particular the poor of the flock. I took for myself two staffs: the one I called Beauty, and the other I called Bonds; and I fed the flock. I dismissed the three shepherds in one month. My soul loathed them, and their soul also abhorred me. Then I said, "I will not feed you. Let what is dying die, and what is perishing perish. Let those that are left eat each other's flesh." And I took my staff, Beauty, and cut it in two, that I might break the covenant which I had made with all the peoples. So it was broken on that day. Thus the poor of the flock, who were watching me, knew that it was the word of the LORD. Then I said to them, "If it is agreeable to you, give me my wages; and if not, refrain." So they weighed out for my wages thirty pieces of silver. And the LORD said to me, "Throw it to the potter"—that princely price they set on me. So I took the thirty pieces of silver and threw them into the house of the LORD for the potter. Then I cut in two my other staff, Bonds, that I might break the brotherhood between Judah and Israel.* (NKJV)

In obedience to the Lord God, Zechariah assumed the role of a shepherd (Jesus). He fed all the sheep, but he took special care of the poor. In those days, shepherds used two staffs (called a rod and a staff) when caring for their flock: one, a rod or defensive club to fight off predators, and the other, a staff or long stick with a hook at the end used for walking and recovering sheep from crevices and steep places on the side of mountains. Zechariah selected two staffs and he began to feed the sheep (common people) like a good shepherd (Jesus)

poor
Luke 4:18

staff
Psalm 23:4

good shepherd
John 10:11

slave
Exodus 21:32

would do. He named one of his staffs "Beauty," meaning favor or grace, and he named the other "Bonds," meaning oneness, united, or tied. These names symbolize the peace Zechariah (Jesus) hoped to achieve for the doomed sheep (Israel) under his care. He loved the sheep and wanted them to survive by gaining the beauty, favor, or grace of God (peace with God). He also wanted them to be bonded, united, or tied together (at peace with the Romans and each other).

In one month, Zechariah got rid of three false shepherds. He (Zechariah/Jesus) loathed the false shepherds and they abhorred him. But their repudiation of him caused him to resign his role as shepherd and repudiate them. They would perish anyway (spiritually without grace), so he would give them up to their enemies who would slaughter them. They would "eat each other's flesh" is a prophecy of cannibalism during the coming Roman invasion. When Titus attacked Rome he cut off the food. Many starved to death. Others turned to cannibalism.

Zechariah took his staff named "Beauty" and cut it in two. This signified Israel's covenant (peace with God) would come to an end with the rejection of the Good Shepherd. The meek and humble of the flock knew that he was speaking for God. They represent those who believed our Lord spoke for God. After his death, burial, resurrection, and ascension, they heard Peter preach and became the nucleus of the church.

Zechariah asked the false shepherds to decide whether he should be paid for his work as a shepherd. He said, "If you want to, you can pay me what I am worth, but if you do not want to, you can just keep your money." They didn't have to, but they chose to show contempt for him by giving him thirty pieces of silver. This was a way of saying they didn't think he was worth any more than an injured slave. It would have been better to not pay him anything than to insult him this way. This deliberate indignity prompted God to tell Zechariah to throw the thirty pieces of silver into the Temple for the potter. He did, but throwing it instead of handing it to the potter was a sign of God's wrath. Then, Zechariah cut in two his staff named "Bonds," signifying the period of Israel's peace with the Romans and with each other would come to an end.

This reveals that the good shepherd Zechariah, who tried to gain peace for his doomed flock, actually symbolized Jesus the Good Shepherd, who was sold out for thirty pieces of silver immediately before he laid down his life for the sheep. It is also a foretelling of what occurred when Judas Iscariot was rebuffed in his effort to return the thirty pieces of silver. He threw the silver into the Temple and the Jews used it to buy the potter's field.

thirty
Matthew 26:14–16

potter's field
Matthew 27:1–10

At the end of the age, traitorous shepherds will sell out Israel again. She will be unable to find peace with her neighbors and will constantly suffer from internal turmoil. This is the result of rejecting their Messiah, the Prince of Peace. A remnant will believe and be saved.

what others say

Charles L. Feinberg

Now we have the language of one whose patience is finally exhausted. When every means of grace had failed to draw them, the Messiah gives over the nation to its own sinful way. The sheep which are dying of pestilence and famine will die. Those of the flock that are to be cut off by war and bloodshed will be cut off, and the rest will be given over to continuous internal conflict. Light rejected always brings greater night.[2]

H. A. Ironside

But before His rejection, our Lord said to the Jews, "I am come in my Father's name, and ye receive me not: if another shall come in his own name, him ye will receive" (John 5:43). He spoke undoubtedly, of the willful king, the personal Antichrist of the last days, whom the Jews will receive as the Messiah when he comes with all power and signs and lying wonders. This dreadful person is who Zechariah is next called upon to set forth.[3]

This Shepherd Is a Fake

ZECHARIAH 11:15–17 ***And the LORD said to me, "Next, take for yourself the implements of a foolish shepherd. For indeed I will raise up a shepherd in the land who will not care for those who are cut off, nor seek the young, nor heal those that are broken, nor feed those that still stand. But he will eat the flesh of the fat and tear their hooves in pieces. Woe to the worthless shepherd, who leaves the flock! A sword shall be against his arm and against his right eye; his arm shall completely wither, and his right eye shall be totally blinded."*** *(NKJV)*

lost
Matthew 15:24

little
Matthew 18:10–14

heal
Matthew 12:9–14

feed
John 21:15–19

Zechariah was told to assume the role of a shepherd a second time, but this time it is the role of a foolish shepherd. Why? Because Israel rejected the Good Shepherd, God intends to raise up a morally corrupt shepherd to gain control over her. This man of sin will not do any of the things a good shepherd would do. He will not care for the lost sheep, seek the little sheep, heal the sick sheep, or feed the healthy sheep. This wolf in sheep's clothing will spend his time feeding on the good sheep and tearing off their limbs. He will be the exact opposite of the Good Shepherd. Commentators call him the Antichrist. Before he gets through with the Jews, they will plead for the Good Shepherd to appear. The judgment of God will come upon the Antichrist. That arm that won't lift a hand to help the sheep and that eye that blinds itself to what is happening to the sheep will be struck. Some commentators associate this with the wounding of the Antichrist in Revelation 13.

Contrasts Between Christ and the Antichrist

Christ	Antichrist
The Good Shepherd (John 10:11)	The worthless shepherd (Zechariah 11:17)
The Holy One of God (Mark 1:24)	The lawless one (2 Thessalonians 2:8)
The Son of God (Luke 1:35)	The son of perdition (2 Thessalonians 2:3)
The Truth (John 14:6)	Will cause deceit to prosper (Daniel 8:25)
The Lamb of God (John 1:29)	The beast (Revelation 13:1)

what others say

David R. Reagan

Using symbolic language, it seems to me the prophet is saying that divine judgment (the sword) will fall upon the Antichrist's power (his arm) and his intelligence (his eye), and that he will suffer complete defeat (the withering of his arm and the blinding of his eye).[4]

Chapter Wrap-Up

- Zechariah predicted a future invasion of Lebanon, Syria, and Jordan. Some writers say this was fulfilled during the time of the Maccabees, some say when the Romans invaded Israel, and some say it is still to come in the future.
- Zechariah assumed the role of a shepherd fattening his sheep for the slaughter to demonstrate that future leaders will sell out Israel to Gentile powers. The Gentile powers will go unpunished, Israel's leaders will gain great wealth, and God will permit it.
- Zechariah made two staffs called "Beauty" and "Bonds" to symbolize external and internal peace. He removed three traitorous shepherds, but the people disliked that and he tired of trying to help them. When he resigned, the people insulted him by paying him thirty pieces of silver. He threw it into the Temple for the potter. He also broke the two staffs. This tells us Israel will suffer external and internal turmoil because they rejected their Messiah. He was betrayed for thirty pieces of silver. Judas cast the money into the Temple and it was used to buy the potter's field.
- Zechariah assumed the role of a foolish shepherd who will gain control of Israel and be the exact opposite of the Good Shepherd. He is the Antichrist and God will judge him.

Study Questions

1. What do trees symbolize? Why should people to the north and east of Israel be concerned about events that will take place at the end of the age? Identify the nations listed.
2. Who will sell out Israel at the end of the age? What will be their motivation? What will the Gentiles want to do to Israel?
3. What do "Beauty" and "Bonds" mean? What is the significance of the broken staffs? Why will this happen?
4. Who does the foolish shepherd represent? What will God do to him?

Zechariah 12 Israel and Jerusalem at the End of the Age

Chapter Highlights:
- **An International Headache**
- **Blind and Crazy**
- **Why Are You Crying?**

Let's Get Started

The second burden of the word of the Lord is found in chapters 12–14. It's a series of awesome predictions about the end of the age. Current events seem to indicate that the world is fast approaching the time when these things will be literally fulfilled. The key phrase is "in that day." It appears five times in this chapter and sixteen times in the last three chapters. The Bible refers to "that day" as the "**Day of the Lord**." The key words are "Jerusalem" and "nations," which occur twenty-two and thirteen times respectively in the last three chapters.

Day of the Lord
Joel 3:9–16;
Zephaniah 1:14–18

Day of the Lord
another name for the Tribulation Period

Some of the amazing prophecies in this second burden of the word of the Lord are:

Chapter 12

- Jerusalem will be a problem for the whole world at the end of the age.
- God will defeat everyone who attacks Jerusalem at the end of the age.
- God will pour out his Spirit on Israel and the Jews will accept Jesus at the end of the Tribulation Period.

Chapter 13

- The Jews will be cleansed at the end of the Tribulation Period.
- Idols and false prophets will be purged from Israel during the Millennium.
- The Jews will realize they killed their Messiah.
- Two-thirds of the Jews in the land of Israel will die during the Tribulation Period.

Chapter 14

- The Tribulation Period will take place and Jerusalem will be attacked, but the battle will be won by God.
- Jesus will come back to the Mount of Olives.

Judah
the southern part of Israel

- Jesus will establish his throne in Jerusalem and rule the world as King of kings.
- The whole world will worship Jesus during the Millennium.

what others say

Thomas Ice and Timothy Demy

The phrase "day of the Lord" is one of numerous terms and phrases used throughout the Bible to refer to both a time of judgment (such as the tribulation) and a time of blessing (such as the millennium). In other words, the day of the Lord will literally be a day or period of time in which Jesus will impose His presence and rule, whether in judgment (the tribulation) or in glorious display (the millennium). In the current state of affairs, the Lord is not exerting His rule in a visible way. Of course, He could if He were pleased to do so, but His plan calls for the current time to be a temporary period in which He lets humanity go its own way (Romans 1:24–32).[1]

An International Headache

ZECHARIAH 12:1–3 ***The burden of the word of the LORD against Israel. Thus says the LORD, who stretches out the heavens, lays the foundation of the earth, and forms the spirit of man within him: "Behold, I will make Jerusalem a cup of drunkenness to all the surrounding peoples, when they lay siege against Judah and Jerusalem. And it shall happen in that day that I will make Jerusalem a very heavy stone for all peoples; all who would heave it away will surely be cut in pieces, though all nations of the earth are gathered against it. (NKJV)***

Zechariah's final message reveals what God said will happen with regard to Israel and Jerusalem at the end of the age. This was preceded by these actions of God:

- He causes the heavens to grow larger and larger.
- He created the foundation of the earth.
- He gives life and breath to mankind.

This is the point. This prophecy should be believed because it comes from the Creator. He intends to make Jerusalem an unsolvable problem for the whole world and to use it as an instrument of judgment for all the nations around her. **Judah** and Jerusalem will be attacked. Eventually, every nation on earth will gather against

Jerusalem, but God will make the city too strong for her enemies and all who attack her will just be harming themselves.

Jerusalem is mentioned more than 1,000 times in the Bible (about 800 by name, and more than 200 in other ways: Holy City, City of God, City of David, Zion, etc.). God plans to put his name on that city and dwell there (2 Chronicles 6:6; Psalm 132:13–14). As far as God is concerned, it is the most important city on earth. The United Nations' desire to make it an international city, the Vatican's desire to exercise control over important religious sites, the Quartet's (UN, EU, U.S. and Russia) desire to divide it, and the Islamic desire to possess it as the capital of a Palestinian state is a satanic effort to take possession away from God. These selfish desires are taking the world to the end of the age's confrontation that is prophesied in these verses.

The word "all" appears three times in verse 3, meaning this attack on Jerusalem will have worldwide support. Whether it is the United Nations, the one-world government of Antichrist, or armies from all over the world is not clear, but the point here is that armies will be going up against God. This means that they will be marching toward their own destruction.

The Battle For Jerusalem

Year	War	Result
1948	Israel attacked by Lebanon, Syria, Iraq, Transjordan, and Egypt.	Israel won.
1956	Egypt blocked Suez Canal and Gulf of Aqaba. Israel attacked Egypt.	Israel won.
1967	Egypt, Jordan and Syria massed troops to attack Israel.	Israel won.
1973	Nine Arab League and four Muslim countries attacked Israel.	Israel won.

what others say

Peter C. Craigie

The God who is the source of creation also has the power to move the created world towards its consummation. And as, in the first acts of creation, order emerged from primeval chaos, so in the move towards consummation there are elements of chaos prior to the establishment of a final order "on that day."[2]

what others say

Tim LaHaye

These events look ahead to the Tribulation period when the Antichrist will invade the land of Israel and bring all the nations of the earth against it. The prophet predicts that this great invasion, which culminates at the Battle of Armageddon, will end in defeat for Israel's enemies because of the supernatural intervention of God.[3]

Dave Hunt

How heavy is this "burdensome stone"? The United Nations has consumed one-third of its time deliberating over Jerusalem and Israel, a small despised nation with one-thousandth of the earth's population. From 1967 through 1989, out of 865 resolutions in the Security Council and General Assembly, 526 were against Israel. The last anti-Arab vote was 57 years ago in 1947. More than 60,000 individual votes have been cast in the UN condemning Israel.[4]

Blind and Out of Their Mind

ZECHARIAH 12:4–9 *In that day," says the LORD, "I will strike every horse with confusion, and its rider with madness; I will open My eyes on the house of Judah, and will strike every horse of the peoples with blindness. And the governors of Judah shall say in their heart, 'The inhabitants of Jerusalem are my strength in the LORD of hosts, their God.' In that day I will make the governors of Judah like a firepan in the woodpile, and like a fiery torch in the sheaves; they shall devour all the surrounding peoples on the right hand and on the left, but Jerusalem shall be inhabited again in her own place—Jerusalem.*
"The LORD will save the tents of Judah first, so that the glory of the house of David and the glory of the inhabitants of Jerusalem shall not become greater than that of Judah. In that day the LORD will defend the inhabitants of Jerusalem; the one who is feeble among them in that day shall be like David, and the house of David shall be like God, like the Angel of the LORD before them. It shall be in that day that I will seek to destroy all the nations that come against Jerusalem. (NKJV)

In that day, when all the nations of the earth gather against Jerusalem, God will step in, disable their weapons, and take over the battle on Israel's behalf. He will instantaneously strike Israel's enemies with confusion, insanity, and blindness. After blinding them, he will open his all-seeing eyes to Judah's plight, show her favor, give her protection, and supernaturally energize the Israelis to do battle with their enemies. Knowledge of God's involvement will make the Jews like a bowl of fire in a pile of dry wood, like a flamethrower in a field of very dry grass. It will empower them to easily and utterly destroy the nations around them.

In that day, one would think that the first victory will come in the fortified city of Jerusalem rather than at the unwalled settlements in the outlying areas of Judah (southern Israel) that are more exposed and have fewer defenders. But this is not so. God will cause the first victories to come in the weakest areas of Judah so that the inhabitants of Jerusalem will know the victory is his doing and not theirs.

In that day, with God's intervention and protection, the most feeble Jew will suddenly possess the strength of the great warrior David, and the average Jew will possess the strength of Almighty God. Under these conditions the armies of the world will be thoroughly trounced and the city of Jerusalem will remain where it is.

what others say

Clarence H. Wagner Jr. and Jim Gerrish

Just as God used Jerusalem and Israel as a standard in days of old to determine if nations understood and supported His agenda for the world, today He is again using a regathered Israel and the city of Jerusalem, now the capital of a re-established Jewish state, as a prophetic test. Sadly, most world leaders are more intent on gaining increased influence, power and wealth as part of a New World Order, and are distancing themselves from what they see as "outdated" Bible passages and promises.[5]

Kenneth L. Barker and John R. Kohlenberger III

In Deuteronomy 28:28, "panic" ("confusion of mind"), "madness," and "blindness" are listed among Israel's curses for disobeying the stipulations of the covenant. Now these curses are turned against Israel's enemies.[6]

Why Are You Crying?

ZECHARIAH 12:10–14 ***"And I will pour on the house of David and on the inhabitants of Jerusalem the Spirit of grace and supplication; then they will look on Me whom they pierced. Yes, they***

pierced
Psalm 22:16;
John 19:34

Megiddo
2 Chronicles 35:22

Spirit of grace and supplication
Holy Spirit

pierced
crucified

messianic age
the Millennium

will mourn for Him as one mourns for his only son, and grieve for Him as one grieves for a firstborn. In that day there shall be a great mourning in Jerusalem, like the mourning at Hadad Rimmon in the plain of Megiddo. And the land shall mourn, every family by itself: the family of the house of David by itself, and their wives by themselves; the family of the house of Nathan by itself, and their wives by themselves; the family of the house of Levi by itself, and their wives by themselves; the family of Shimei by itself, and their wives by themselves; all the families that remain, every family by itself, and their wives by themselves." *(NKJV)*

God is not just interested in Israel's physical salvation. He is also interested in her spiritual salvation. After he supernaturally strengthens the Jews to win this great victory, he will pour out the **Spirit of grace and supplication** upon them. This will cause them to reflect on why God helped them, to pray, and to examine their need for a better relationship with him. When they look to the Lord they will take a look at the One they have **pierced**. They will suddenly realize that their ancestors crucified the Messiah, and that they are guilty too through their own rejection of him . . . This will lead to a period of intense grief such as that of a parent at the loss of an only child. The entire nation will mourn as it did when its beloved king Josiah was killed in the plain of Megiddo. Every individual will go into seclusion to mourn over their own sins.

what others say

Arnold G. Fruchtenbaum

Before Israel will receive the cleansing of her sin and before Christ will return to establish His kingdom, Israel must first look unto the One whom they have pierced and to plead for His return. Once they do this, then, and only then, will they receive their cleansing and begin to enjoy the blessings of the **messianic age**.[7]

Chuck Missler

We have intense sorrow. We're talking private and public, national and individual, personal and family, and the deepest grief always seeks seclusion. And the language, I suspect, refers to every family apart and the wives apart, every family alone, grieving as they realize their predicament, as they repent of the rejection of their Messiah. And this is on a national basis, but down to the individual. Whose doing the work here? The Holy Spirit![8]

what others say

Tim LaHaye

Zechariah foretells Israel's rejection of the Messiah at His first coming and their reception of Him at His second coming. The New Testament attributes this change of heart to the preaching of the "two witnesses."[9]

Chapter Wrap-Up

- At the end of the age, our Creator God will make Jerusalem an international problem and use it to draw all nations into a battle for control of the city.
- God will afflict Israel's enemies, causing them to injure themselves. He will protect Israel, strengthen her troops, and cause them to destroy their enemies.
- The Holy Spirit will reveal Jesus to the Jews as their Messiah and everyone will grieve bitterly as a nation and as individuals.

Study Questions

1. Why should we believe that God can protect Israel?
2. What will God use to draw the nations into war?
3. What will God do when the nations attack Jerusalem?
4. What will cause great weeping in Israel?

Zechariah 13 The Jews Will Accept Jesus and Be Forgiven

Chapter Highlights:
- God's Fountain
- Idols and Prophets
- Shepherds and Sheep
- Two-Thirds and One-Third

Let's Get Started

The current peace process in the Middle East will not lead to peace there. It will lead to the Tribulation Period, which will include perilous times for Israel that will ultimately bring about the national conversion of those who survive. The land will be cleansed and pure worship will be restored.

weeping
Zechariah 12:10–14

what others say

Russell L. Penney

The physical deliverance of Israel (12:1–9) and the spiritual repentance of Israel (12:10–14) will be followed by a spiritual cleansing of the nation (13:1–6). In that day, at Christ's return, a fountain will be opened for the house of David and for the inhabitants of Jerusalem, for sin and for impurity (13:1).[1]

Merrill F. Unger

The prophetic disclosure of Israel's national cleansing meets the supreme need of the Jews throughout the Christian centuries—Their spiritual cleansing and regeneration. The essence of their woe, succinctly summarized by the apostle Paul, has been their ignorance "of God's righteousness" and their "going about to establish their own righteousness," refusing to submit themselves to "the righteousness of God" (Romans 10:3). In this great prophecy they submit to God's righteousness in Christ as they look to the nail-pierced One and believe.[2]

A Fountain Filled with Blood

Zechariah 13:1 ***"In that day a fountain shall be opened for the house of David and for the inhabitants of Jerusalem, for sin and for uncleanness.*** *(NKJV)*

This chapter begins where the last one left off. "In that day" refers to the Day of the Lord. Other Scriptures make it clear that this will take place at the end of the Tribulation Period while Israel is still weeping over her rejection of the Messiah. Instead of the priests hav-

cleansing
Numbers 8:5–11; 19:1–13

names
Exodus 23:13; Psalm 16:4

times of the Gentiles
the period Gentiles rule on earth (the period of time from the Babylonian captivity to the Second Coming)

ing the water of cleansing sprinkled on them for purification, a fountain will be opened for the cleansing of the entire nation. Everything that separates the people from their Messiah will be forgiven.

what others say

Walter C. Kaiser Jr./Lloyd J. Ogilvie

Here would come a repentant Israel, the very thing the apostle Paul had prayed for and desired above everything else in Romans 9–11. The **times of the Gentiles** would have ended, and a repentant Israel would be grafted back on to the very tree from which the branches of the olive tree had been temporarily lopped off (Romans 11:26–27). The people of Israel would now be washed with the washing of the Word and renewed by the inner work of the Holy Spirit (Titus 3:5).[3]

John MacArthur

This has direct reference to the New Covenant of Jeremiah 31:31–34; Ezekiel 36:25–32; Romans 11:26–29. So the storm that broke upon Israel for the crime of Calvary and has raged with unmitigated fury for long, tragic centuries will suddenly end, and salvation will turn sin into righteousness in the gladness and glory of Messiah's kingdom.[4]

Richard Mayhue and Thomas Ice

Old Testament believers anticipated (Hebrews 9:15) Christ's life-giving sacrifice (2 Corinthians 3:6) involving (1) grace (Hebrews 10:29), (2) peace (Isaiah 54:10; Ezekiel 34:25; 37:26), (3) the Spirit (Isaiah 59:21), (4) redemption (Isaiah 49:8; Jeremiah 31:34; Hebrews 10:29), (5) removing sin (Jeremiah 31:34; Romans 11:27; Hebrews 10:17), (6) a new heart (Jeremiah 31:33; Hebrews 8:10; 10:16), and (7) a new relationship with God (Jeremiah 31:33; Ezekiel 16:62; 37:26–27; Hebrews 8:10). This covenant pictures Israel's new betrothal to God (Hosea 2:19–20) initiated by the same divine mercy as the Davidic covenant (Isaiah 55:3).[5]

Banished

ZECHARIAH 13:2 ***"It shall be in that day," says the LORD of hosts, "that I will cut off the names of the idols from the land, and they shall no longer be remembered. I will also cause the prophets and the unclean spirit to depart from the land.*** *(NKJV)*

Verse 1 is about the cleansing of individuals. This verse is about the cleansing of the land. In Old Testament times, speaking the names of idols was forbidden. During the Millennium, the very mention of their names will be banished from the land of Israel. They will be so thoroughly disgraced that they will be forgotten. False prophets and **unclean spirits** will not be found in the land anymore. Should anyone claim to be a prophet, his parents will threaten his life for lying in the name of the Lord. If he prophesies, his parents will kill him.

Spirit
1 Timothy 4:1–2

unclean spirits
demonic spirits

what others say

Charles L. Feinberg

To cut off the names of the idols out of the land, so that their names will no more be remembered, is to destroy their authority, power, and influence upon Israel. God's people will cease to acknowledge them. The worship of God will be fully purified and cleansed.[6]

The Holy Spirit, through the apostle Paul, warned that the teaching of false doctrines will be a major problem for the world at the end of the age. False prophets will be enticed by unclean spirits to do this. Paul said, "Now the Spirit expressly says that in latter times some will depart from the faith, giving heed to deceiving spirits and doctrines of demons, speaking lies in hypocrisy, having their own conscience seared with a hot iron" (NKJV). Idolatry in the form of Antichrist worship will also be a major problem. It will be stopped at the second coming of Jesus.

I Don't Know What You're Talking About

Zechariah 13:3–6 ***"It shall come to pass that if anyone still prophesies, then his father and mother who begot him will say to him, 'You shall not live, because you have spoken lies in the name of the Lord.' And his father and mother who begot him shall thrust him through when he prophesies." And it shall be in that day that every prophet will be ashamed of his vision when he prophesies; they will not wear a robe of coarse hair to deceive. But he will say, 'I am no prophet, I am a farmer; for a man taught me to keep cattle from my youth.' And one will say to him, 'What are these wounds between your arms?' Then he will answer, 'Those with which I was wounded in the house of my friends.'*** *(NKJV)*

Guilt will overwhelm the false prophets. They will be ashamed to speak in public anymore. They will know it is useless to put on a

death
Deuteronomy 13:1–5; 18:20

wounds
1 Kings 18:28

Jesus
Matthew 26:31

prophet's garment
sometimes a cloak of camel's hair, sometimes a mantle of sheepskin or goatskin

prophet's garment to try to deceive people anymore. They will also know that, according to the Law of Moses, false prophets should be put to death, so they will deny they are prophets and try to claim they are farmers. Many false prophets will have self-inflicted wounds from worshiping false gods and idols, and so when they are asked about this, they will claim their wounds were received in the houses of friends. This does not appear to be a prophecy about Jesus as some say. Since he was a prophet, he certainly would not deny being one. Also, he was called the carpenter's son, but never a farmer. He is known for the wounds in his hands, feet, and side—not between his arms. This seems to be a contrast or a transition to the next passage, which is about Jesus.

what others say

The Pulpit Commentary

Such was the mantle of Elijah (1 Kings 19:13, 19; 2 Kings 1:8; 2:13, 14) and of John the Baptist (Matthew 3:4), and it seems to have become the distinctive badge of the prophet, and was assumed by these pretenders in order to inspire confidence.[7]

Walter C. Kaiser Jr.

It is an awesome responsibility to deliver the Word of God. Toying with it, distorting it, or twisting it to fit some subjective idea or loyalty other than to the Lord is extremely serious, since it involves the lives of other people for all eternity![8]

Strike the Shepherd, Scatter the Sheep

ZECHARIAH 13:7 ***"Awake, O sword, against My Shepherd, against the Man who is My Companion," says the LORD of hosts. "Strike the Shepherd, and the sheep will be scattered; then I will turn My hand against the little ones. (NKJV)***

In chapter 11, Zechariah revealed that a sword would strike the worthless shepherd. Here he reveals that a sword would strike the True Shepherd. While Israel is grieving over the rejection of her Messiah, God will show the nation that the death of Jesus was his doing. The Lord of hosts is the One who called for the sword to strike the True Shepherd at the cross. Jesus even applied this verse to himself. This Shepherd is a Man. He is also God's Companion. Notice, that Shepherd, Man, and Companion begin with capital letters. This is a clear indication of the deity of the One to be struck. *"Man"* also speaks of his humanity. He was God in the flesh. "Companion" speaks of the closeness of the Shepherd and the Lord of hosts. They are associates or the Three in One.

The scattered sheep could be a reference to the disciples who deserted Jesus at the cross, or it could be a broader reference to the scattering of the people during the Roman invasion of AD 70. Not everyone would be destroyed or scattered. God promised to turn his hand over to protect a remnant of his flock. Some see this as a prophecy of the church that was driven out of Jerusalem before AD 70.

deserted
Matthew 26:56

deity
a god

Jehovah
God

what others say

John MacArthur

The expression "My Shepherd . . . the Man who is My Companion" speaks of the Lord's anointed One, the Messiah. The Hebrew word for "My companion" can also mean "My equal"—signifying Christ's **deity**. But the most remarkable thing about Zechariah's prophecy is that it is **Jehovah** Himself who calls for the Shepherd to be stricken with the sword.

In summation, the Zechariah prophecy is more evidence from the Old Testament that the crucifixion of Christ was God's plan. He was still in control, even when it seemed from the human perspective that Satan and the forces of evil were in control of the situation.[9]

God's Refinery

ZECHARIAH 13:8–9 ***And it shall come to pass in all the land," says the LORD, "that two-thirds in it shall be cut off and die, but one-third shall be left in it: I will bring the one-third through the fire, will refine them as silver is refined, and test them as gold is tested. They will call on My name, and I will answer them. I will say, 'This is My people'; and each one will say, 'The LORD is my God.'"*** *(NKJV)*

Here, Zechariah's vision shifted from the scattering of the sheep and the protection of his little ones after the first coming of Jesus to the plight of the Jews just prior to his second coming. The disciples who fled at the cross and the church that was dispersed by persecution prior to Jerusalem's destruction in AD 70 are types of what will happen at the end of the age.

flee
Matthew 24:15–16

look
Zechariah 12:10

refining
testing

Holocaust
mass destruction of Jews

During the coming Tribulation Period, two-thirds of the Jews living out in the land of Israel will be killed (note that half of those in Jerusalem will be cut off). The other one-third will flee into the wilderness when the Antichrist defiles the Temple, where they will be supernaturally protected and spared. It is understood that this two-thirds are those God knows will not accept Jesus as the Messiah, and this one-third is the faithful he knows will accept Jesus.

The coming Tribulation Period will be a time of **refining** for the faithful. They will suffer terrible persecution, but it will make them more pure than silver or gold and cause them to look to the Lord Jesus. He will respond to their prayers of confession and repentance by saying, "This is My people." In turn, they will respond, "The LORD is my God."

what others say

Arnold G. Fruchtenbaum

In the **Holocaust** under Hitler one third of the world Jewish population died. Under the fierce persecution of the Antichrist, controlled and energized by Satan, two thirds of the Jewish population will die. This will be the largest and most intense persecution of Jews ever known in Jewish history.[10]

Arno Froese

Now that we have seen that God chose this city, why, we may ask, do Gentiles want it? The reason is very simple: It is the devil who rules the nations of the world! He is the prince of the power of the air, the father of lies. He desires to destroy that which God chose, to pollute that which He sanctified, to make Jerusalem a city of sin instead of a Holy City, the city of lies instead of the city of truth, a city of destruction instead of the city of salvation. It should, therefore, be no surprise to us when we read or hear politicians, religious leaders, and those in elevated positions in this world take offense at Jerusalem.[11]

Chapter Wrap-Up

- At the end of the Tribulation Period a fountain will be opened up for all the Jews, and the entire nation will turn to Christ and be forgiven and cleansed.
- Every idol, false prophet, and spirit of impurity will be removed from the land. Every idol will be forgotten, and anyone who prophesies falsely will be killed by his own parents. The false prophets will be ashamed of their visions, refuse to dress like prophets anymore, deny they are prophets, and lie about the wounds on their bodies.
- God said he would call for the death of his Son and the people would be scattered. He also promised to protect the humble in Israel.
- During the Tribulation Period, two-thirds of those living in Israel will perish. The one-third who survive will be sorely tested. They will be precious to God, be his people, and he will be their God.

Study Questions

1. What is the purpose of the fountain in Israel at the end of the Tribulation Period? What makes this possible?
2. What and who will be banished from Israel when the Jews accept Jesus as their Messiah? After the Tribulation Period, what will happen to false prophets?
3. After the Tribulation Period, what will the false prophets try to hide? Who will cause these things they are trying to hide? Who will be blamed?
4. Who does "my shepherd" refer to? How was he struck? How did this affect the sheep?
5. What portion of the Jews will survive the Tribulation Period? Who will they worship?

Zechariah 14
The Second Coming of Jesus

Chapter Highlights:
- Second Coming
- Meteorological Changes
- Millennium
- God Wins

Let's Get Started

This last chapter is difficult to understand. The problem is in the fact that chapter 12 presents Jerusalem as an impregnable city under the supernatural protection of God, whereas this chapter predicts the fall of half of the city. There seems to be no good explanation for this unless it is that Jerusalem withstands every attack right up until the last day of the Tribulation Period. Then, on the last day, when the forces of the Antichrist finally break through and begin to pillage and to rape, Jesus will return to deliver his people.

forefathers
Zechariah 1:2–6

what others say

Tim LaHaye

In his concluding vision, Zechariah predicts the ultimate triumph of the Messiah at the Battle of Armageddon when the Gentile nations, led by the Antichrist, will be defeated at the second coming of Jesus Christ. Zechariah sees the Lord standing on the Mount of Olives when He returns (v. 4). From the very place where Jesus ascended back into heaven (Acts 1:11–12). He will again return, and this time the mountain shall split in half, creating a rift valley from the Mediterranean to the Dead Sea (v. 8).[1]

It's Coming

ZECHARIAH 14:1 ***Behold, the day of the LORD is coming, and your spoil will be divided in your midst.*** (NKJV)

Some do not like to talk about a Day of the Lord, some don't believe in a Tribulation Period, and some try to spiritualize this event and explain it away, however, no one can deny that the Bible says the Day of the Lord is coming. Christians should not be like Israel's forefathers who did not believe God's true prophets. They refused to repent and perished because of their unbelief. Zechariah said the Tribulation Period is coming. When it does, probably on the last day of that terrible seven-year period, Jerusalem will be at the mercy of

refine
Zechariah 13:8–9

her enemies, the city will be captured and plundered, and the attackers will divide the plunder among themselves.

what others say

Grant R. Jeffrey

Tragically, the city of Jerusalem, conquered twenty-seven times in the past, will fall to its enemies one final time. The enemy soldiers will attack the women and place half the population in captivity. They will loot the riches of the city as the "spoil will be divided in your midst."[2]

Thomas Ice and Timothy Demy

The second half of the tribulation will be characterized by an extreme attempt to wipe the Jews off the face of the earth. Likely, Satan's thinking on this matter is that if the Jews are exterminated, then God's plan for history will have been thwarted. Satan might think this would somehow prevent the second coming. This persecution is pictured in Revelation 12:1–6.[3]

It Ain't Over Until It's Over

Zechariah 14:2 ***For I will gather all the nations to battle against Jerusalem; the city shall be taken, the houses rifled, and the women ravished. Half of the city shall go into captivity, but the remnant of the people shall not be cut off from the city. (NKJV)***

Peace conferences, treaties, and mediation over the future of Israel and Jerusalem will not change the fact that God has already given the Promised Land to Israel, including all of Jerusalem. He did it in the form of a covenant that he cannot break. Many negotiators in the world today are failing to recognize this covenant, which should be their guide. This failure, or refusal, is a tool in Satan's effort to divide the land and give it away. Ultimately, the solution will come at the Battle of Armageddon rather than at the peace table.

God will use the world's efforts to destroy his covenants with Israel to draw the nations into that Great War. This conflict will be the event that God uses to show the world who he is, and it will also be the furnace that he uses to refine the people of Israel. A world army, perhaps the United Nations or a coalition of armies with troops from all the nations, will undertake one last siege of

Jerusalem. They will finally succeed in breaking through the defenses of the city. They will be brutal. Troops will enter the houses of ordinary citizens. They will grab all the valuables they can find and carry. The women who have not managed to escape will be raped. Half the city will be taken, and it will appear that the remainder is doomed.

what others say

John F. Walvoord

In AD 70 the Roman armies surrounded Jerusalem at the time of the feasts and did precisely what this passage predicts. Those who were able to flee from the city were in some cases saved. Others who remained in the city were slaughtered as the Roman armies breached the walls and destroyed the temple as well as the city. This was in sad fulfillment of what Jesus had predicted concerning the destruction of the temple (Matthew 24:2). At the end of the age preceding the second coming of Christ, Jerusalem will be in a similar situation.[4]

Norbert Lieth

Where has the Lord's zeal for Jerusalem gone? Where is the fulfillment of His promises for the future? Jerusalem is the city of the Messiah; it is the city of David's descendants, to whom God has promised that there will never be a lack of a descendant on his throne. Is this a lie, or perhaps only a dream? Isn't the Bible true? Or is it just a book like any other?[5]

David Hocking

Before the peoples of Judah and Jerusalem will be empowered for victory (as in Zechariah 12:6–8; 14:14), the Gentile armies will at first obtain an initial taste of victory in Jerusalem, including the typical characteristics of conquest described here. The fact that "the residue of the people shall not be cut off" implies that the Lord will return to destroy the enemies before their conquest is more than half completed, however.[6]

This Will Be a Battle with God

Zechariah 14:3 ***Then the Lord will go forth and fight against those nations, as He fights in the day of battle.*** (NKJV)

The plunder, rape, and exile of God's people will not last very long because he will defend his people and the city of Jerusalem. Hebrew scholars say the language here indicates that it is going to be a slaughter. The world armies and all their mighty weapons will be no

battle
Revelation 16:14

horses' bridles
Revelation 14:20

heaven
Acts 1:9–12

coming
Matthew 24:3–51

Red Sea
Exodus 14:1–31

horses' bridles
about four feet high

furlongs
about 180 miles

match for the power of Jesus. The book of Revelation calls it "the battle of that great day of God Almighty" (NKJV). It says the blood will flow up to the **horses' bridles** for a distance of 1,600 **furlongs**. God will summon the birds of the air to feast upon the bodies of kings, captains, mighty men, horses, and many people. The Antichrist and False Prophet will be captured and cast alive into the Lake of Fire. Jesus will destroy many and the birds will be filled.

what others say

Charles H. Dyer

Daniel, Joel, and Zechariah identify Jerusalem as the site where the final battle between the Antichrist and Christ will occur. All three predict that God will intervene in history on behalf of His people and will destroy the Antichrist's army at Jerusalem.[7]

The Second Coming

ZECHARIAH 14:4 ***And in that day His feet will stand on the Mount of Olives, which faces Jerusalem on the east. And the Mount of Olives shall be split in two, from east to west, making a very large valley; half of the mountain shall move toward the north and half of it toward the south.*** **(NKJV)**

Jerusalem is a literal city. The Mount of Olives is a literal place. Along with this, the second coming of Christ will be a literal event. He will personally make a visible return to the Mount of Olives. This is the same place he went away from when he ascended up into heaven. It is also the same place where he preached the Olivet Discourse, which is the most famous passage in the Bible about his second coming. As soon as his nail-scarred feet touch the ground, there will be a great earthquake that causes the Mount of Olives to split into two mountains. One half will move to the north, the other will move to the south, and a great divide or valley will be created between the two that will run east and west.

This will be an incredible event. The Mount of Olives is a towering mountain ridge about 2,700 feet high on the east side of Jerusalem. It rises above the other mountains in the area and dominates the Jerusalem skyline. When the Jews fled Pharaoh's army in the days of Moses, God parted the Red Sea so that they could escape. At the end of the Tribulation Period, they will flee the

Antichrist's army and God will part the Mount of Olives so that they can escape. This kind of power is why his people cannot be wiped out and why they will wind up with the Promised Land.

earthquake
Amos 1:1

glory
Matthew 24:30–31; 25:31

armies
Revelation 19:14

what others say

John F. Walvoord

Those who seek to escape Jerusalem will flee by this newly made valley which, apparently, will extend from Jerusalem down to the city of Jericho. This makes clear that the Second Coming is a future event as the Mount of Olives is still intact.[8]

Thomas Ice and Timothy Demy

Christ returns first to Bozrah and rescues Israel from the Antichrist and his armies (Isaiah 14:3–21; Jeremiah 49:20–22; Joel 3:12, 13; Zechariah 14:12–15; Revelation 14:19, 20). After this, Christ makes His victory descent to the Mount of Olives in Jerusalem (Joel 3:14–17; Zechariah 14:3–5; Matthew 24:29, 30). The second coming will be complete at this time.[9]

Run for Your Life

ZECHARIAH 14:5 ***Then you shall flee through My mountain valley, for the mountain valley shall reach to Azal. Yes, you shall flee as you fled from the earthquake in the days of Uzziah king of Judah. Thus the LORD my God will come, and all the saints with You.*** *(NKJV)*

The divide running east and west between the two mountains will provide a way of escape for the Jews in Jerusalem. This valley will extend to an unknown site called Azal. Some scholars say this is the name of a place. Others say it is a symbol of something else. In either case, this divide will run the full width of the mountain and will be long enough to protect all the people. Those who know the Scriptures know that their ancestors fled a great earthquake in the days of Uzziah king of Judah, and they will know to flee in terror at the end of the Tribulation Period. Then, the second coming of Jesus will take place in power and glory with all the armies of heaven, including his church and the Tribulation Period saints. Of course, the angels will come along too.

sun
Isaiah 13:10; Joel 3:15; Matthew 24:29

knows
Matthew 24:36

light
Isaiah 60:19–20

light
John 8:12

Not a Normal Day

ZECHARIAH 14:6–7 ***It shall come to pass in that day that there will be no light; the lights will diminish. It shall be one day which is known to the LORD—neither day nor night. But at evening time it shall happen that it will be light.*** *(NKJV)*

The day of the Second Coming will be unlike any day the world has ever seen. People will say, "The sun isn't shining, but it's not dark, either." Some commentators say this will be the result of bombs, smoke, and burning debris from the battle for Jerusalem. The Bible says that the cosmos will be affected. The sun and moon won't shine, many stars will fall, and the heavenly bodies will shake. God is the only One who knows when this will happen; however, when it does, there will be light at evening time.

Zechariah does not say, but this evening light will probably be the light of Jesus. The weather will probably be affected, and it will last for a thousand years. Jesus will be the Light of the World during the Millennium. Garden of Eden conditions will prevail. The nature and the eating habits of the animals will change. People will live longer, and there will be economic prosperity globally.

what others say

Russell L. Penney

This will also be a unique day in that it will be a day without night (Isaiah 13:10; Jeremiah 4:23; Ezekiel 32:7–8; Joel 2:30–31; Acts 2:16, 19–20). There will be no need for luminaries since the Light of the world will be present, so even in the evening there will be light.[10]

Water in a Dry Land

ZECHARIAH 14:8 ***And in that day it shall be that living waters shall flow from Jerusalem, half of them toward the eastern sea and half of them toward the western sea; in both summer and winter it shall occur.*** *(NKJV)*

The phrase "living waters" is used two ways in the Bible. It can mean pure, clean running water, or it can be a symbol of the Holy Spirit. Here it means literal water. Israel has always had a tenuous water supply. Although the rainfall is increasing there today, also increasing are the population, the need to irrigate crops, and Israel's willingness to share with her neighbors. When Jesus returns, the water supply will no longer be precarious. Instead, living water that does not cease will flow to the east and the west.

wilderness
Luke 4:1–8

This, no doubt, is a reference to the end of the seas turning to blood, famine and destroyed crops, and all the environmental damage that will take place during the Tribulation Period. This dramatic change will take place when Jesus returns. A supernatural stream of life-giving water will flow from Jerusalem to irrigate the crops and impart life to the destroyed seas. It will flow forth abundantly, and will not freeze in the winter or dry up in the summer.

what others say

Arnold G. Fruchtenbaum

While the river will begin in the temple, it is clear from this passage that it will flow southward to the city of Jerusalem where it will be divided in two. The western branch will flow down the mountain and empty into the Mediterranean Sea. The eastern branch will flow into the Dead Sea. The branching out of these waters towards the areas designated for growing food on both sides of Jerusalem will provide the necessary water for the growth of the crops.[11]

King James Bible Commentary

Water is used symbolically throughout the Old Testament to indicate purification and refreshment. The point of the symbolism is that when Messiah returns, spiritual purification and refreshment will be ever spread throughout the land.[12]

King of Kings and Lord of Lords

ZECHARIAH 14:9 ***And the LORD shall be King over all the earth. In that day it shall be—"The LORD is one," and His name one.*** *(NKJV)*

This is what Satan offered Jesus when he tempted him in the wilderness, but Jesus turned it down. When Jesus comes back he will dethrone the Antichrist and be crowned King over all the earth. His reign will put an end to the worship of idols and false gods. People will no longer look to astrologers and horoscopes. When this day arrives, Jesus will be universally accepted and worshiped. The entire world will call him Lord, and he will have no rivals. Even those in

kingdoms
Revelation 11:15

Geba
town and district near the northern boundary of the tribe of Judah, about five miles north of Jerusalem

Rimmon
a town in the area settled by the tribe of Simeon, about thirty-three miles southwest of Jerusalem

heaven will declare, "The kingdoms of this world have become the kingdom of our Lord and of His Christ, and He shall reign forever and ever!" (NKJV).

An Earthly Kingdom

- His kingdom will fill the whole earth (Daniel 2:35).
- "Your kingdom come. Your will be done on earth as it is in heaven" (Matthew 6:10 NKJV).
- "We shall reign on the earth" (Revelation 5:10 NKJV).

The kingdom of God includes an earthly millennial kingdom that will begin at the second coming of Jesus.

what others say

Norbert Lieth

The day is coming during which all religious books will be thrown away and there will be no more founders of religions. The day is coming when no theory, philosophy or ideology will be valid and all idols will be forgotten. This is the day when all people will recognize that there is only one King and only one Name above all names: Jesus Christ, the Messiah of Israel.[13]

Topographical Changes

ZECHARIAH 14:10–11 ***All the land shall be turned into a plain from Geba to Rimmon south of Jerusalem. Jerusalem shall be raised up and inhabited in her place from Benjamin's Gate to the place of the First Gate and the Corner Gate, and from the Tower of Hananel to the king's winepresses. The people shall dwell in it; and no longer shall there be utter destruction, but Jerusalem shall be safely inhabited.*** **(NKJV)**

At this time, Jerusalem and the surrounding area are very hilly, but Zechariah is saying this will change with the second coming of Jesus. The land of Israel will be leveled out into a great plain that will extend from **Geba** to **Rimmon**. Then, Jerusalem will be elevated above the surrounding area. It will remain in its present location and will be inhabited. It is difficult to accurately identify the exact boundaries of the city, but it is plain that many Jews will live there, the city will be a safe place to live, and it will never be destroyed again. This has to be good news for the Jews who are constantly being harassed and who have been driven off the land many times. The day will come when that will no longer happen. The Jews will dwell in peace for the first time in their history, and at the same time, the world will have peace.

what others say

John Phillips

By the time Christ returns, the world at large will be in a shambles. Devastating wars will have been fought and earthquakes and other natural disasters will have wrought havoc. The entire planet will be in chaos, but nowhere will the ruin be more evident than in Israel and Jerusalem. Therefore some far-reaching physical changes will take place when the Lord returns.[14]

John F. Walvoord

Changes in the Holy Land will be in preparation for Israel's possessing the whole area described in Genesis 15:18–21, from the Euphrates River to the River of Egypt. In general, the Holy Land will extend from the north from approximately Damascus, using the Jordan River as the eastern border and the Mediterranean as the western border, and continue south until it reaches the border land of Egypt, the River of Egypt.[15]

A Terrible Plague

ZECHARIAH 14:12 ***And this shall be the plague with which the LORD will strike all the people who fought against Jerusalem: Their flesh shall dissolve while they stand on their feet, their eyes shall dissolve in their sockets, and their tongues shall dissolve in their mouths.*** *(NKJV)*

The focus of the vision shifts back from the reign of Jesus, the climate, the topography, and things like that to those who are guilty of attacking Jerusalem. A series of problems and disasters will beset all of Israel's enemies. The first one mentioned here is a terrible plague. This plague sounds like some type of nuclear or biological weapon because it will strike so fast that the flesh of many enemy soldiers will melt while they are still standing on their feet. While they are still on the battlefield, their eyes will melt in their sockets and their tongues will melt in their mouths. Many people would have thought this impossible 2,500 years ago, but it is different today. It can happen!

what others say

Merrill F. Unger

The stroke of the plague is similar to a horrible leprosy that spreads through the body with such shocking rapidity that the flesh will "rot" or "decay," leaving the victim a mere skeleton, erect upon his feet, with his flesh a putrid mass about him. The "flesh" will rot away because it dared to exalt itself against God; the "feet" because they were swift to shed blood; the "tongue" because it had wickedly blasphemed God; and the "eyes" because they were keen to seek out God's people in order to exterminate them in one final fell blow.[16]

Grant R. Jeffrey

The Bible describes terrible plagues and horrible sores occurring throughout the world's population in the Great Tribulation. The plagues that will destroy hundreds of millions in the last days may include the effects of biological and chemical weapons.[17]

Panic and In-Fighting

ZECHARIAH 14:13 ***It shall come to pass in that day that a great panic from the LORD will be among them. Everyone will seize the hand of his neighbor, and raise his hand against his neighbor's hand; (NKJV)***

This is the second in a series of problems and disasters that will beset Israel's enemies. The sight of people's flesh, eyes, and tongues dissolving while they are standing on their feet will terrify some in this enemy army. Others will be overcome with panic from the realization that they are fighting the Lord. The thought of his second coming will scare some to death. Some will try to flee and others will try to keep them from fleeing. When this happens infighting will break out. Many of Israel's enemies will die at the hands of their so-called friends.

An Army from Judah

ZECHARIAH 14:14 ***Judah also will fight at Jerusalem. And the wealth of all the surrounding nations shall be gathered together: gold, silver, and apparel in great abundance.*** *(NKJV)*

This is the third in a series of problems and disasters that will beset Israel's enemies. Supernaturally empowered Jews from Judah will discover what is happening in the city and will enter the battle on Jerusalem's side. The plague, panic, and infighting among Israel's enemies will make them easy targets. Then, the Jewish troops will do to their enemies what those enemies were doing to Jerusalem: they will plunder this invading army and will seize back the property they had stolen and the property of the invading army. The amount of gold, silver, and clothing that is taken will be enormous.

Judah
Zechariah 12:6–7

plunder
Zechariah 2:8–9

King
Revelation 19:16

Feast of Tabernacles
Ezra 3:4

saved
people who have accepted Christ, received forgiveness and eternal life

Another Plague

ZECHARIAH 14:15 ***Such also shall be the plague on the horse and the mule, on the camel and the donkey, and on all the cattle that will be in those camps. So shall this plague be.*** *(NKJV)*

The great army that moves across the country to attack Jerusalem will use a wide assortment of animals. The animals will experience the same plagues as the troops experienced. Camels are a good indication of Arab or Muslim involvement.

The Millennium

ZECHARIAH 14:16 ***And it shall come to pass that everyone who is left of all the nations which came against Jerusalem shall go up from year to year to worship the King, the LORD of hosts, and to keep the Feast of Tabernacles.*** *(NKJV)*

Those who attack Israel will be destroyed, but many of them will have relatives back home and a few of those relatives will be **saved**. This saved remnant of survivors will compose people from all nations. They will live on into the Millennium and repopulate the earth. Every year they and their descendants will make an annual pilgrimage to Jerusalem to worship Jesus. He will rule the earth as King and Lord. They will also make this annual pilgrimage to celebrate the Feast of Tabernacles.

iron rod
Psalm 2:9; Revelation 2:27; 12:5; 19:15

iron rod
scepter or staff a ruler carries to demonstrate his authority

what others say

David R. Reagan

Jesus is currently a "king-in-waiting." Like King David, who had to wait many years after he was anointed before he became king of Israel, Jesus has been anointed King of kings and Lord of lords, but He has not yet begun to rule. He is currently serving as our High Priest before the throne of God (Hebrews 8:1). He is waiting for His Father's command to return and claim all the kingdoms of this world (Hebrews 2:5–9 and Revelation 19:11–16).[18]

Ed Hindson

The idea of the kingdom of God on earth is central to all biblical teaching. The Old Testament prophets predicted it. Jesus announced it. And the New Testament apostles foretold it again. The psalmist said, "God is my King" (Psalm 74:12). Jeremiah said of the Lord, "He is a living God, and an everlasting king" (Jeremiah 10:10).[19]

No Worship, No Water

ZECHARIAH 14:17 ***And it shall be that whichever of the families of the earth do not come up to Jerusalem to worship the King, the LORD of hosts, on them there will be no rain.*** *(NKJV)*

Because of all the wonderful changes that will take place during the Millennium, someone may think that there will be no problems. Without a doubt, the blessings will be abundant, but Jesus will also rule with an **iron rod**. This means he will put down all opposition to his reign. Those who refuse to worship him will suffer from drought. Their crops will not grow and produce, their animals will have no water, and they will have a series of other problems.

This mystifies some. They expect the Millennium to be peace and prosperity, and for the most part it will be, but it must be remembered that those who survive the Tribulation Period to live on into the Millennium will still be in their original body and will still have a sin nature. Also, many will parent children with a sin nature. Early on in the Millennium, people will remember the Tribulation Period and desire to worship and obey the Lord. After a few hundred years, however, the remembrance of things will wear off and new generations will not have the personal experience that the older generation had. Some will stop making an annual pilgrimage to Jerusalem to worship Jesus. He will deal with it.

Egypt
Exodus 12:31–42

Egypt

ZECHARIAH 14:18 ***If the family of Egypt will not come up and enter in, they shall have no rain; they shall receive the plague with which the LORD strikes the nations who do not come up to keep the Feast of Tabernacles.*** *(NKJV)*

Egypt did not worship the Lord when the Israelites were slaves in their country. They experienced the ten plagues of God when they tried to prevent Moses from leading them to the Promised Land. They should have repented and turned to him when that happened, but they have always opposed him. They are staunch enemies of Jehovah and of the Jews today, and some will continue to be that way until the very end. Many will perish at or before the Second Coming. The good news in this verse is that some of the Egyptians will accept Jesus, survive the Tribulation Period, and enter the Millennium. The bad news is that some of their offspring will stop taking annual pilgrimages to Jerusalem to worship Jesus and he will cut off their rain. Even though there is plenty of rain in the surrounding nations, the Egyptians will not escape the plague. They will only be secure as long as they celebrate the Feast of Tabernacles in Jerusalem.

what others say

Arnold G. Fruchtenbaum

In summary, peace will come between Israel and Egypt by means of conversion. Only when the Egyptians worship the same God as Israel, through Jesus the Messiah, will peace finally come.[20]

Ralph L. Smith

Egypt seems to be singled out for special attention in vv 18 and 19, perhaps because the threat of a plague reminded the author of the earlier plagues of Egypt at the time of the exodus, but also because Egypt would not naturally be affected by the lack of rain because she depended almost entirely upon the Nile for her water supply.[21]

No Favorites

Zechariah 14:19 ***This shall be the punishment of Egypt and the punishment of all the nations that do not come up to keep the Feast of Tabernacles.*** *(NKJV)*

It is God's desire to treat all nations alike and to bless all people. He is good, and his blessings will flow abundantly to all who worship him. Most people will be thankful and they will eagerly show it. But any nation that does not want to worship him will experience his rejection. Any nation that is unwilling to celebrate the Feast of Tabernacles in Israel will experience drought.

When the Jews neglected to build the Temple, God sent a drought upon the land. Those who stray from God will find that he is patient. He will always try to bring them back. But when people refuse to return to him, he will eventually withhold his blessings. When people do not meet his desires, he has no obligation to meet theirs. It was that way in Old Testament times and it will be that way during the Millennium.

Holy, Holy, Holy

Zechariah 14:20 ***In that day "HOLINESS TO THE LORD" shall be engraved on the bells of the horses. The pots in the Lord's house shall be like the bowls before the altar.*** *(NKJV)*

drought
Haggai 1:9–11

Temple
2 Thessalonians 2:4

Satan
Revelation 12:7–9

deceiving spirits
1 Timothy 4:1

lake of fire
Revelation 19:20

bound
Revelation 20:1–3

worship
Zechariah 14:16

During the Tribulation Period, the Antichrist will rule. He will oppose God and defile the Temple. Satan will be cast down to this earth. Multitudes will abandon the faith and give heed to deceiving spirits and things taught by demons. Almost everything will be corrupt, defiled, and unholy. But the situation will be just the opposite during the Millennium. The Antichrist will be cast into the lake of fire burning with brimstone. Satan will be bound and chained. Pure worship will be restored. And almost everything will be holy. The horses that were once instruments of war in an effort to destroy Israel will be set aside for God's service. The common vessels in the Temple will be like the bowls in the Holy of Holies that held the blood of sacrificial animals. In other words, a sense of holiness will prevail on earth during the Millennium, with virtually all people and all things set aside for God's service.

"Holiness to the Lord" was engraved upon a gold plate and attached to the sacred turban worn by the high priest of Israel. This meant that he was special to God. He was set aside to represent the people and bear their sins before God. It is a beautiful picture of Jesus bearing the sins of his people on the cross. During the Millennium almost everyone and everything will be holy to God.

A Big Change

ZECHARIAH 14:21 ***Yes, every pot in Jerusalem and Judah shall be holiness to the LORD of hosts. Everyone who sacrifices shall come and take them and cook in them. In that day there shall no longer be a Canaanite in the house of the LORD of hosts.*** **(NKJV)**

In Old Testament times some pots and pans were holy and some were not, depending upon their use. Vessels that caught the blood of a sacrifice were holy, but not those used for cooking ordinary food. But during the Millennium there will be no distinction between the vessels in Jerusalem and Judah. All will be holy to God and everyone, not just the priests and Levites, who goes to Jerusalem with offerings and sacrifices will use holy things. There will be no distinction between people.

Even the Canaanites will be different. These were unclean people in Old Testament times who merchandised and trafficked in holy things. There will be no buying and selling or money-changing going on in the Millennial Temple.

what others say

John F. Walvoord

Though it is objectionable to some to have animal sacrifices in the millennial scene, actually, they will be needed there because the very ideal circumstances in which millennial saints will live will tend to gloss over the awfulness of sin and the need for bloody sacrifice. The sacrifices offered will therefore be a reminder that only by the shedding of blood and, more specifically, the blood of Christ, can sin be taken away.[22]

turban
Exodus 28:36–39

offerings
Isaiah 66:20–23; Ezekiel 43:22–27; Malachi 3:3–4

sacrifices
Jeremiah 33:18; Ezekiel 46:13

Chapter Wrap-Up

- Jerusalem will be attacked one last time at the very end of the Tribulation Period, half the city will be captured and plundered, and women will be raped. Jesus will return to the Mount of Olives, enter the battle on Israel's side, and the Jews will escape through a new valley in the mountain.
- The weather and heavenly bodies will be affected so that there will be no day or night, except at evening there will be light.
- During the Millennium, water will flow from Jerusalem toward the Mediterranean and Dead Seas, Jesus will rule the earth, and he will be the only One who is worshiped.
- Jerusalem will be elevated, surrounded by a great plain, be inhabited, be a safe place to live, and never be destroyed again.
- Plagues, infighting, and the men of Judah will kill those who attack Jerusalem. The Jews will plunder them. During the Feast of Tabernacles, saved survivors from all nations that attacked Jerusalem will go on pilgrimages to the Holy City to worship Jesus. Those who don't worship Jesus will not receive rain. Sacrifices will be offered, and everyone and everything in Jerusalem will be holy.

Study Questions

1. What part will Jerusalem play at the end of the Tribulation Period? Will there be any human rights violations there? If so, who will do this?
2. Whose side will God be on when the nations attack Jerusalem? How will Israel escape?
3. Who will rule the world during the Millennium? Who will people worship then? Where will they worship?
4. How will the topography change in Israel during the Millennium? Will Jerusalem ever be safe? When?
5. When Jerusalem is attacked, who will be struck with plagues? Will there be plagues during the Millennium?

BE SMART • BE INSPIRED •

Appendix A - The Answers

Ezra 1

1. It means the Holy Spirit influenced Cyrus to do the will of God. Yes. God causes people, especially leaders, to do things so his Word will be fulfilled. (Ezra 1:1)
2. It was a gift from the Lord and it was his responsibility to rebuild the Temple in Jerusalem. (Ezra 1:2)
3. Go to Jerusalem and build the Temple of the Lord. Take up an offering to fund the project. (Ezra 1:3–4)
4. He returned the articles Nebuchadnezzar took from the first Temple. This established a physical connection between the first and second Temples. (Ezra 1:7–11)

Ezra 2

1. This is where God said the ruler of Israel would be born. Joseph took Mary there hundreds of years later and that is where Jesus was born. (Ezra 2:1–63)
2. 42,360. No. It was a small percentage of the 2- to 3-million who were in exile. It tells us that rebuilding the Temple and reestablishing the nation weren't very important to them. (Ezra 2:64–65)
3. 7,337. It tells us that God had blessed the Jews and caused them to prosper even though they were exiles in a foreign land. (Ezra 2:64–65)
4. Carried items, cared for people, cared for animals, etc. (opinion requested, no reference)
5. The house of the Lord and the house of God. (Ezra 2:68)

Ezra 3

1. To offer burnt offerings according to the Law of Moses. No. They worshiped God before they laid the Temple foundation. (Ezra 3:2, 6)
2. Because they were afraid and wanted God's protection, because it was their duty, to praise the Lord, and to give thanks for his goodness and love. (Ezra 3:3–4, 10–11)
3. When they completed the altar, on the Feast of Tabernacles, on the new moons, on the set feasts, and when they completed the Temple foundation. (Ezra 3:3–4, 5, 10)
4. Yes. After going to their hometowns, they quickly returned to Jerusalem, immediately rebuilt the altar, immediately ordered materials to rebuild the Temple, and returned to Jerusalem seven months later to rebuild the Temple foundation. (Ezra 3:1, 3, 7–8)
5. No. The Jews sang, cried, and shouted. (Ezra 3:11–12)

Ezra 4

1. They can try, but it won't work. Israel's enemies made both of these claims, but they were not saved, or else they would not have opposed God the way they did. (Ezra 4:2)
2. They tried to join the Jews to discourage them and they bribed counselors to lobby against them. Yes, construction of the Temple stopped. (Ezra 4:2–5)
3. They called themselves "your servants" and said it was "not proper for us to see the king's dishonor." (Ezra 4:11, 14)
4. Taxes, honor, and territory. Yes, construction of Jerusalem was stopped. (Ezra 4:13–16, 24)
5. He commanded that the city not be rebuilt "until the command is given by me." Yes, it means he could change his mind later on if he wanted to. (Ezra 4:21)

Ezra 5

1. Haggai and Zechariah. Their authority came "in the name of the God of Israel." (Ezra 5:1)
2. They said the original Temple was destroyed because their ancestors angered God. They said they were serving the God of heaven and earth. (Ezra 5:11–12)
3. King Cyrus issued a decree to rebuild the Temple, returned the Temple articles, appointed a governor, and told the new governor to put the articles in the new Temple. (Ezra 5:13–16)

Ezra 6

1. He found that King Cyrus had written a memorandum. It proved the Jews had been properly authorized to rebuild the Temple. (Ezra 6:1–3)
2. The Jews could rebuild the Temple, offer sacrifices, and receive financial help from the royal treasury. (Ezra 6:3–5)
3. Stay away from the Temple, pay the expenses of the Jewish workers, and provide them with what they need for the sacrifices. They would be killed and their houses would be destroyed. (Ezra 6:6–12)
4. He wanted them to offer sacrifices pleasing to God and to pray for the well-being of him and his sons. (Ezra 6:10)
5. They dedicated the Temple. They celebrated the Feast of Passover and the Feast of Unleavened Bread. (Ezra 6:13–22)

Ezra 7

1. The hand of God was upon Ezra. It means the Holy Spirit was working in his life and on his behalf. (Ezra 7:6, 9, 28)
2. He devoted himself to study, keeping, and teaching the Law of Moses. He was to teach everyone who did not know this Law. (Ezra 7:6, 10, 26)
3. He and his advisers gave freely, he authorized freewill offerings in Babylon and among the people and priests, and he authorized Ezra to draw funds from the royal treasury. (Ezra 7:15–16, 20)
4. The laws of God and the laws of the king. Death, banishment, loss of property, and jail. (Ezra 7:26)
5. They were not separated. The king selected Ezra because of his religion, helped finance Ezra's religion, had Ezra the priest appoint magistrates and judges, and told Ezra to punish those who broke the Law of God. (Ezra 7:6, 15–18, 25–26)

Ezra 8

1. Priests, royalty, and common people, but no Levites. (Ezra 8:1–20)
2. Because he told the king that God helps those who seek him and opposes those who forsake him. He proclaimed a fast and asked the returnees to humble themselves and to pray. (Ezra 8:21–22)
3. He weighed and inventoried it before he left, he distributed it to trustworthy men, and he told them it would be checked again at the Temple in Jerusalem. (Ezra 8:25–30)
4. They were holy (consecrated to the Lord) because they had been charged with protecting holy things. (Ezra 8:28)
5. Rested, delivered the treasure, worshiped, and delivered their orders to the political leaders. (Ezra 8:32–36)

Ezra 9

1. Very widespread. It involved the people, priests, Levites, leaders, and officials. (Ezra 9:1–2)
2. Because those who intermarried took up the detestable practices of their neighbors and this was a threat to the purity of the holy race. (Ezra 9:1–2)
3. Ezra tore his clothes, pulled hair from his head and chin, set down for a long time, rose, and fell on his knees with his hands spread and prayed. Others gathered around him in support. (Ezra 9:3–5)
4. He noted that the sin of Israel's forefathers was why God allowed the nation to suffer war, captivity, pillaging, and humiliation. (Ezra 9:6–7)
5. God had been gracious in preserving a remnant, giving them understanding, giving them protection in slavery, not deserting them, letting them rebuild the Temple, and punishing them less than they deserved. (Ezra 9:8–15)

Ezra 10

1. The people proposed a solution through their spokesman, Shechaniah, that called for a covenant with God to send away the foreign wives and their children. (Ezra 10:1–3)
2. A proclamation was issued throughout the land for everyone to assemble in Jerusalem within

three days. Those who disobeyed would lose their land and be expelled from the assembly of exiles. (Ezra 10:7–8)

3. He told them to confess their unfaithfulness and to separate themselves from the non–Jews around them and from their foreign wives. Most obeyed, but not all. (Ezra 10:11, 15)
4. Because many people were involved, because they were standing outside in the rain, and because it would be a mistake to rush this. (Ezra 10:13)
5. The guilty groups included priests, Levites, singers, gatekeepers, and many Israelites. Some of the guilty people had children. (Ezra 10:18–44)

Nehemiah 1

1. In the palace at Susa. The Jews were being persecuted, and the walls and gates of Jerusalem had been destroyed. His brother and others told him. (Nehemiah 1:1–3)
2. He sat down, cried, mourned, fasted, and prayed for several days. (Nehemiah 1:4)
3. Israel had sinned against God by not obeying his commands, decrees, and laws. God will restore those who return to him. (Nehemiah 1:5–9)
4. To grant him favor with this man (King Artaxerxes). Cupbearer to the king. (Nehemiah 1:11)

Nehemiah 2

1. He did not know because he was very sad and very much afraid when he talked to the king. (Nehemiah 2:1–2)
2. Because Jerusalem was in ruins and the city gates had been burned. He referred to Jerusalem as "the place of my fathers's tombs." (Nehemiah 2:3 NKJV)
3. He wanted the king to give him permission to rebuild Jerusalem, to give him letters to governors for safe conduct, and to supply him with lumber from the king's forest. The king granted all his requests and sent troops to protect him. (Nehemiah 2:5–9)
4. Because he had the help of God and he had the help of the king. (Nehemiah 2:17–18)
5. Three leaders in the area started mocking and ridiculing the Jews. (Nehemiah 2:19)

Nehemiah 3

1. More than forty different groups worked on the project, men worked with women, priests worked with non-priests, leaders worked with the common people, goldsmiths worked with perfumemakers, etc. (Nehemiah 3:1–32)
2. No. Some groups repaired two sections. (Nehemiah 3:4, 21; 3:5, 27)

Nehemiah 4

1. Ridicule, insults, and threats. (Nehemiah 4:1–4, 11)
2. One-half. They prayed. (Nehemiah 4:8–9)
3. He prayed, posted guards day and night, stationed people at the lowest points of the wall, had them carry weapons, and kept them inside the wall at night. (Nehemiah 4:9, 13, 16, 22)
4. The workers were getting tired, a large amount of rubble remained, the Jews outside the city kept reporting threats. (Nehemiah 4:10–12)
5. Because they were spread out and the work was extensive. God. (Nehemiah 4:19–20)

Nehemiah 5

1. The people had to mortgage their fields, crops, and homes to buy food; they had to borrow money to pay taxes; and had to sell their children into slavery. (Nehemiah 5:1–5)
2. The problem was caused by rich Jews who were charging their countrymen excessive interest. They were greedy and had no respect for God. (Nehemiah 5:6–9)
3. To stop what they were doing and to return the property and money they had collected. Yes. (Nehemiah 5:6–9)
4. He did not trust them. They took an oath in front of the priests. (Nehemiah 5:12)
5. Twelve years. He did not take his allotments of food, require heavy taxes, or buy land. (Nehemiah 5:14–19)

Nehemiah 6

1. They wanted to meet with him in the Plain of Ono. No. He believed they wanted to harm him and stop the work. (Nehemiah 6:1–4)
2. That Israel was planning a revolt and Nehemiah was planning to be crowned king. A false report said it was true, but Nehemiah denied it and prayed for God to strengthen Israel. (Nehemiah 6:6–9)
3. They hired him to scare Nehemiah into hiding inside the Temple. A true prophet would not defile the Temple by having a layman enter a for-

bidden area. (Nehemiah 6:10–14)

4. Fifty-two days. They believed Israel's God helped them and the thought that they had opposed him scared them. (Nehemiah 6:15–16)
5. Through some of his in-laws who were working on the wall. He was trying to intimidate Nehemiah. (Nehemiah 6:17–19)

Nehemiah 7

1. The gatekeepers, singers, and Levites. Hanani and Hananiah. Keep them closed and barred until the sun was high in the sky. (Nehemiah 7:1–3)
2. Hanani was Nehemiah's brother. Hananiah guarded the palace, was an honest man, and respected God. (Nehemiah 7:2)
3. Jews were to be stationed on the walls, some at selected places and some near their own houses. (Nehemiah 7:3)
4. Because not many people lived inside the city. He used the census Ezra took. They had to prove their Jewish ancestry. (Nehemiah 7:4–73)

Nehemiah 8

1. God had commanded it for Israel. Ezra read it. Everyone who was able to understand. (Nehemiah 8:1–2)
2. They listened attentively. They stood up, lifted their hands, said "Amen," bowed down, and worshiped God with their faces to the ground. (Nehemiah 8:3–5)
3. They had Levites teach those who didn't understand and asked the people to share with those who didn't have anything to eat. (Nehemiah 8:9–10)
4. Weeping and grieving. Celebrate and rejoice. Because it was a sacred day and because they now understood the words that were read to them. (Nehemiah 8:8–12)
5. They built booths. God told them to do it. They built them to dwell in for seven days. It was a reminder of the temporary buildings their ancestors had occupied in the wilderness. (Nehemiah 8:13–18)

Nehemiah 9

1. Fasted, wore sackcloth, put dust on their heads, confessed their sins, confessed the sins of their ancestors, read from the Word of God. (Nehemiah 9:1–3)
2. Half a day (about six hours total). Stand and praise the Lord. (Nehemiah 9:3–5)
3. There is only one God. He made and gives life to everything. (Nehemiah 9:6)
4. The land. Commands, decrees, and laws. (Nehemiah 9:7–15)
5. Their ancestors kept rebelling against God, he would punish them, they would repent, and he would restore them. This gave Ezra hope that true repentance would bring a restoration of the nation. (Nehemiah 9:16–38)

Nehemiah 10

1. To show they were serious about keeping it. (Nehemiah 10:1–27)
2. They bound themselves with a curse and an oath. (Nehemiah 10:29)
3. Intermarry. (Nehemiah 10:30)
4. Let the land rest. Cancel debts. (Nehemiah 10:31)
5. They cast lots. (Nehemiah 10:34)

Nehemiah 11

1. They cast lots, but a few volunteered. Ten percent. (Nehemiah 11:1–2)
2. Judah and Benjamin. (Nehemiah 11:4–9)
3. Priests, Levites, and gatekeepers. (Nehemiah 11:10–24)

Nehemiah 12

1. This is a list of priests and Levites who returned with Zerubbabel and Jeshua. (Nehemiah 12:1)
2. Mattaniah and his associates. (Nehemiah 12:8)
3. The head of a priestly family in the line of Jeremiah during the days of Joiakim. (Nehemiah 12:12)
4. The Jews celebrated with songs of thanksgiving and with the music of cymbals, harps, and lyres. The priests used trumpets and musical instruments. These were used inside the Temple. (Nehemiah 12:27, 36, 40–41)
5. They gave the portions required by the Law. (Nehemiah 12:44)

Nehemiah 13

1. They were reading the Law of Moses and discovered that God had said the Jews were to exclude them because of their mistreatment of the Jews when they were in the wilderness. (Nehemiah 13:1–3)

2. He let a foreigner named Tobiah store his possessions in one of the Temple storerooms. This happened while Nehemiah was out of the country. He threw Tobiah's possessions out of the room, ordered the room purified, and returned the room to its proper use. (Nehemiah 13:4–9)
3. The people had stopped giving the proper offerings. Nehemiah rebuked the officials, returned the Levites to their positions and appointed trustworthy men to oversee the collection and distribution of the tithes. (Nehemiah 13:10–14)
4. People were desecrating the Sabbath by working and doing business. This was something that brought the wrath of God on their ancestors. It didn't work at first because a few merchants set up shop outside the gates, but they moved on when Nehemiah threatened to arrest them. (Nehemiah 13:15–22)
5. They married foreigners. He drove him away. (Nehemiah 13:23–28)

Haggai 1

1. They were saying it was not time to build the Temple. They had their priorities wrong and were using hard times as an excuse. Hard times did not prevent them from building expensive houses for themselves. (Haggai 1:1–4)
2. God advised the Jews to consider their ways. He pointed out that they were working hard but not accomplishing very much. (Haggai 1:5–7)
3. God told the Jews to cut timber for the Temple. He sent a drought because they had left the Temple in ruins. (Haggai 1:8–11)
4. Obedience and respect. God promised to help them. (Haggai 1:12–13)
5. The Jews were encouraged to begin construction. (Haggai 1:14–15)

Haggai 2

1. They realized that the rebuilt Temple was going to be much smaller than the one Solomon built. The covenant God made to be with their ancestors when they came out of Egypt. (Haggai 2:1–5)
2. God's presence. Peace. (Haggai 2:7–9)
3. Sin in the people's life. (Haggai 2:11–14)
4. He wanted the Jews to remember the day their hard times ended and his blessings started. (Haggai 2:15–19)
5. He will overthrow their kingdoms and defeat their armies by causing them to fight each other. (Haggai 2:20–22)

Zechariah 1

1. He would return to bless them. Because they ignored God when his prophets urged them to repent. (Zechariah 1:4–5)
2. The Angel of the Lord and a group of angels that patrolled the earth for him. (Zechariah 1:7–11)
3. Because they were not upset over Israel's affliction and they added to her troubles during the Babylonian captivity. (Zechariah 1:11–15)
4. Return with mercy, cause the Temple to be rebuilt, cause Jerusalem to grow, cause the towns to grow and prosper, and bless Israel in the future. (Zechariah 1:16–17)
5. The four horns represent nations that scattered Judah, Israel, and Jerusalem. The four craftsmen represent God's instruments of judgment that terrify and destroy nations that oppose Israel. (Zechariah 1:18–21)

Zechariah 2

1. To Jerusalem. To measure the city. The city will be greatly expanded in the future. (Zechariah 2:1–2)
2. Jerusalem will outgrow the present wall. By a wall of fire. God. (Zechariah 2:4–5)
3. Those who oppose Israel oppose God. They will reap what they sow. (Zechariah 2:8–9)
4. He will dwell in Israel. Israel and Jerusalem will be his special possession. (Zechariah 2:10–12)
5. Many will serve the Lord. (Zechariah 2:11)

Zechariah 3

1. When the Angel of the Lord rebuked Satan, he said he had chosen Jerusalem. (Zechariah 3:1–3)
2. Joshua's filthy clothes. Joshua was given rich garments and the clean turban of the high priest. (Zechariah 3:3–5)
3. Obey God and keep his commandments. (Zechariah 3:6–7)
4. Angels. Joshua's associates. (Zechariah 3:7–8)
5. After the Branch/Stone removes their sin in a single day. (Zechariah 3:8–10)

Zechariah 4

1. Israel, the Word of God, and the Holy Spirit.

(Answers from Scripture other than this chapter)

2. Because the Jews needed God's help to do God's work. (Zechariah 4:6)
3. A mountain of opposition and problems. The Temple would be started and completed in Zerubbabel's lifetime. (Zechariah 4:7–9)
4. To see that the lampstand (their people, Israel) received oil (the Holy Spirit). The religious and political leaders. (Zechariah 4:11–14)

Zechariah 5

1. Judgments in the Word of God. The third and eighth commandments. Thieves and liars. (Zechariah 5:1–4)
2. The flying scroll applies to individuals who steal and lie. The measuring basket applies to the wickedness of all Jews, regardless of the kind of sin. The measuring basket represented sin, but the wicked woman represented the cause or spirit of sin. (Zechariah 5:5–8)
3. The forgiveness of Israel and the removal of sin, and its causes, from the land at the end of the age. (Zechariah 5:9–11)

Zechariah 6

1. Weapons of war. From the presence of God to the whole earth. (Zechariah 6:1–7)
2. Their mission will appease the wrath of God. (Zechariah 6:8)
3. It signified the coming of a High Priest who will also be a King. It was removed because Joshua was not that coming Priest-King. Displaying it was a reminder that One is coming. (Zechariah 6:9–15)
4. The Branch. A priest on his throne. (Zechariah 6:13–14)

Zechariah 7

1. We might, but why we fast and mourn may prevent us from receiving anything from God. (Zechariah 7:5–6, 13)
2. Administer justice, show mercy and compassion, don't oppress people, and don't think evil thoughts about people. (Zechariah 7:8–9)
3. God gets very angry. He destroyed Israel and Judah. (Zechariah 7:12–14)
4. God destroyed Israel and Judah for ignoring him and said they brought it upon themselves. (Zechariah 7:11–14)

Zechariah 8

1. Jerusalem. The "City of Truth" and the "Holy Mountain." (Zechariah 8:3)
2. Men and women will live longer and it will be a safe place for boys and girls to play. (Zechariah 8:4–5)
3. Tell the truth, require their courts to show true and sound judgments, and treat their neighbors fairly. (Zechariah 8:16–17)
4. God will turn them into festivals. (Zechariah 8:19)
5. The Lord. (Zechariah 8:21–23)

Zechariah 9

1. Zechariah saw their defeat. God used Alexander the Great to overthrow them. (Zechariah 9:1–8)
2. Zechariah saw the humble coming of Israel's King with righteousness and salvation. (Zechariah 9:9)
3. At the second coming of Christ. (Zechariah 9:10)
4. God's blood covenant with Israel. The Jews will be arrows in his bow. (Zechariah 9:11–13)
5. God will appear over them, fight for them, and shield them. The Jews will feed on God's Word and quench their thirst with the Holy Spirit. (Zechariah 9:14–17)

Zechariah 10

1. God. Yes! Because people don't ask and believe. (Zechariah 10:1)
2. Instead of praying to him, they talked to idols, consulted with diviners, and lied about their dreams. What they said was worthless and left the people without leadership. (Zechariah 10:2–3)
3. Because the Lord will be with them. (Zechariah 10:5)
4. Two of the Ten Northern Tribes, Joseph and Ephraim, will be part of the restored kingdom. (Zechariah 10:6–7)
5. There will be too many for the land and some will dwell in Lebanon, an area outside Israel's current borders. (Zechariah 10:10)

Zechariah 11

1. Kings and kingdoms. Because an invading army will come through and destroy their nations. Lebanon, Syria, and Jordan. (Zechariah 11:1–3)
2. Her leaders. Money. Destroy the nation. (Zechariah 11:4–6)
3. "Beauty" and "Bonds" symbolize external and internal peace. Breaking the staffs signified external and internal turmoil. Israel rejected peace when she

rejected her Messiah. (Zechariah 11:7–14)

4. The Antichrist. God will strike him. (Zechariah 11:15–17)

Zechariah 12

1. He causes the heavens to grow, is the Creator, and gives us life and breath. (Zechariah 12:1)
2. The controversy over Jerusalem. (Zechariah 12:2)
3. He will strike their armies with fear, insanity, and blindness; protect and supernaturally energize Israel's troops. (Zechariah 12:4–9)
4. The Holy Spirit will be poured out on the Jews causing them to recognize their Messiah and their sins, and to repent. (Zechariah 12:10–14)

Zechariah 13

1. The fountain will be for the cleansing of Israel's sin and impurity. The death of Jesus on the cross. (Zechariah 13:1)
2. Idols, false prophets, and the spirit of impurity. Their families will kill them. (Zechariah 13:2–3)
3. Their wounds. They will be self-inflicted. Their friends. (Zechariah 13:4–6)
4. Jesus. He was crucified. His disciples, and later the nation, were scattered. (Zechariah 13:7)
5. One-third. The Lord (Jesus). (Zechariah 13:8–9)

Zechariah 14

1. Jerusalem will be attacked by all the nations. Yes! Houses will be plundered and women raped. Troops in the world army. (Zechariah 14:1–2)
2. Israel's. Through a pass created when the Mount of Olives splits. (Zechariah 14:3–4)
3. Jesus. Jesus. Jerusalem. (Zechariah 14:9, 16–17)
4. A large area around Jerusalem will become a plain, Jerusalem will be elevated, and water will flow from Jerusalem toward the Mediterranean and Dead Seas. Yes! After the Second Coming. (Zechariah 14:8, 10–11)
5. All who fight Israel, including their animals. Yes! On those who do not worship the Lord during the Millennium. (Zechariah 14:12–15, 17–19)

Appendix B - The Experts

Arthur, Kay Kay Arthur and her husband, Jack, founded Precept Ministries.

Barker, Kenneth L. General editor of the *NIV Study Bible* and a member of the International Bible Society's Committee for Bible Translation.

Bergen, Martha Editor and author of *Shepherd's Notes.*

Bible Dictionary Written and researched by several Bible scholars.

Bible Expositor and Illuminator Based on the International Sunday School lessons it's one of the best quarterly Sunday school books on the market.

Boda, Mark J. Seminary professor and author.

Booker, Richard Bible teacher and author of several best-selling Christian books.

Breese, Dave Former president of World Prophetic Ministry, and Bible teacher on *The King Is Coming* television program.

Breneman, Mervin Professor of Old Testament at the Seminario Internacional Teologico Bautista in Buenos Aires, Argentina; author of a variety of articles; and has served as assistant editor of *Diccionario de la Biblia.*

Church, J. R. Host of a nationwide television program called *Prophecy in the News* and author of many books.

Colson, Charles Former special counsel to President Richard Nixon, founder of Prison Fellowship Ministries, author of several books and magazine articles.

Cook, David C. Publisher of Christian literature. (Cook Communications Ministries, Colorado Springs, Colorado 80918)

Couch, Mal Founder and president of Tyndale Theological Seminary and Biblical Institute, professor and author of several books. (Fort Worth, Texas)

Craigie, Peter C. Dean of the faculty in Humanities and professor of Religious Studies at the University of Calgary. Author of three books in *The Daily Study Bible Series.* (The Westminster Press, Philadelphia, PA)

Demy, Timothy A Navy chaplain who has co-authored and coedited several books with Thomas Ice.

Dyer, Charles H. Professor of Bible exposition at Dallas Theological Seminary in Dallas, Texas; and author of several books. His home is in Garland, Texas.

Feinberg, Charles L. Dean emeritus of Talbot School of Theology in California, author, lecturer, and recognized authority on Jewish history.

Ernest, Thomas G. Pastor and author of several books.

Fensham, F. Charles Former seminary professor, author, and editor of the *Journal of Northwest Semitic Languages.*

Fields, Don Author for the LifeGuide Bible Studies series.

Ford, W. Hershel Former pastor of several large Southern Baptist churches including First Baptist in El Paso, Texas.

Fruchtenbaum, Arnold G. Founder of Bible Institute in Israel and Ariel Ministries in the United States with fellowships ministering to Jews in several major cities.

Ger, Steven C. Author and director of Sojourner Ministries, a group dedicated to exploring the Jewish Heart of Christianity.

Halley, Henry H. Author of one of the best-known and most-used Bible study guides in the world, *Halley's Bible Handbook.*

Hayford, Jack W. Pastor of The Church on the Way, teacher, composer, author of more than twenty books, and senior editor of the *Spirit-Filled Life Bible.*

Henry, Matthew Former pastor, author, and world-famous Bible scholar.

Hindson, Ed Minister of Biblical Studies at Rehoboth Baptist Church in Atlanta, Georgia; vice president of There's Hope; adjunct professor at Liberty University in Virginia, speaker on *The King Is Coming* TV program, and an executive board member of the Pre-Trib Research Center in Washington, D.C.

Hocking, David Author of many books, pastor, radio host, and director of Hope for Today Ministries.

Ice, Thomas Executive director of the Pre-Trib Research Center.

Ironside, H. A. Famous pastor, lecturer, and author of many books and pamphlets, now deceased.

Jeffrey, Grant R. Best-selling author, conference speaker, and frequent guest on radio and TV programs.

Jensen, Irving L. Professor emeritus of Bible at Bryan College in Dayton, Tennessee, and author of dozens of books with more than sixty currently in print.

Kaiser, Walter C., Jr. Senior vice president of Education, academic dean and professor of Old Testament and Semitic Languages at Trinity Evangelical Divinity School, and author of several books.

King James Bible Commentary A comprehensive and scholarly commentary written by several leading evangelical theologians.

Kohlenberger, John R., III A seminary professor and author of many books.

LaHaye, Tim Founder and president of Family Life Seminars, author, pastor, counselor, television/radio commentator, and nationally recognized authority on Bible prophecy and family life.

Larson, Knute, and Kathy Dahlen Knute Larson is a pastor and puthor of several New Testament Commentaries. Kathy Dahlen is the former director of communications for a large metropolitan church and a freelance writer of several articles for Christian magazines.

Lawson, David A staff member of Precept Ministries, and a former pastor.

Levitt, Zola Before his death, this Christian Jew hosted his own national TV program called *Zola Levitt Presents.* Author of many books.

Levy, David M. Former pastor, author of several books and magazine articles, and associate editor of The Friends of Israel's bimonthly publication, *Israel My Glory.*

Lieth, Norbert Former missionary and author of several books.

Lucado, Max Pastor, radio program host, author, and general editor of many best-selling books.

Master Reference Bible A beautifully illustrated family Bible published under the auspices of the National Sunday School League.

McArthur, John Pastor, author of more than six dozen books, teacher, and conference speaker.

McComiskey, Thomas Edward Prior to his death in 1996, he was presiding fellow of the American College of Biblical Theologians. He was an author and editor of several books.

McGee, J. Vernon Former host of the popular *Thru the Bible* radio program.

Miller, Stephen R. Chairman of Old Testament and Hebrew at Mid-America Baptist Theological Seminary, author, and Bible translator.

Missler, Chuck An expert on Russia, Israel, Europe, and the Middle East, founder of Koinonia House Ministries, and editor of *Personal Update* newsletter.

New Harper's Bible Dictionary, The This eighth edition one-volume dictionary was compiled by scores of first rate scholars.

Phillips, John Retired former assistant director of the Moody Correspondence School, director of Emmaus Correspondence School, professor, radio Bible teacher, and author.

Popular Encyclopedia of Bible Prophecy, The Tim LaHaye and Ed Hindson are the general editors of this prophecy knowledge storehouse containing more than 140 topics by the world's foremost prophecy experts.

Preacher's Outline & Sermon Bible, The An excellent commentary for pastors, teachers, and laymen.

Price, Randall President of World of the Bible Ministries, Inc., and author.

Reagan, David R. Founder and senior evangelist of Lamb & Lion Ministries, host and teacher of *Christ in Prophecy* radio program, Author of several books, and editor of a monthly publication called *The Lamplighter.*

Roberts, Mark D. Senior pastor of Irvine Presbyterian Church in Irvine, California. author and editor of several volumes of The Communicator's Commentary series.

Roberts, Oral Pastor, author of several books, founder of Oral Roberts University, former host of television ministry.

Scharfstein, Sol Author of more than one hundred books.

Scofield, C. I. Famous preacher, teacher, and conservative church leader in the late 1800s and early

1900s. Editor of the 1909 and 1917 editions of the *Scofield Reference Bible.*

Smith, Ralph L. Professor of Old Testament at Southwestern Baptist Theological Seminary in Ft. Worth, Texas. Author of three books in *The Broadman Bible Commentary.*

Stanley, Charles Senior pastor of the 12,000-member First Baptist Church in Atlanta, Georgia; speaker on the radio and television program called *In Touch*, and author of numerous books.

Swindoll, Charles R. President of Dallas Theological Seminary, host of nationally syndicated radio and television program *Insight for Living*, author of more than twenty-five books.

Thomas, Cal Syndicated newspaper columnist, author of books and magazine articles, speaker on radio and television programs.

Thomas, G. Ernest Pastor and author of several books.

Unger, Merrill F. Former professor at Dallas Theological Seminary, and author of many outstanding reference books.

Vereen, Bob A staff member of Precept Ministries, and a former pastor.

Wagner, Clarence H., Jr. International director of Bridges for Peace, editor of *Dispatch from Jerusalem*, editor of *Israel Update Letter*, host of *Bridges for Peace* television program.

Walker, Robert Martin Pastor, author of numerous books, author of several Sunday school lessons primarily in the Cokesbury Adult Bible Studies series.

Walvoord, John F. Former theologian, pastor, author, past president and past chancellor of Dallas Theological Seminary, and past editor of the seminary's theological journal called *Bibliotheca Sacra.*

Wiersbe, Warren W. Writer-in-residence at Cornerstone College in Grand Rapids, Michigan; and Distinguished Professor of Preaching at Grand Rapids Baptist Seminary; former pastor, former general director and Bible teacher for *Back to the Bible Broadcast.*

Wilkerson, David Pastor, author of books, author of The David Wilkerson Times Square Church Pulpit Series.

Williamson, H. G. M. Lecturer in Hebrew and Aramaic at Cambridge University. Author of several books and various articles in *Vetus Testamentum*, *Journal of Biblical Literature*, *Journal of Semitic Studies*, and other publications.

Wycliffe Bible Commentary, The A phrase by phrase commentary on the whole Bible for earnest students by 48 leading American scholars.

Endnotes

Part One: The Book of Ezra

1. Irving L. Jensen, *Ezra, Nehemiah, Esther: A Self-Study Guide* (Chicago: Moody Bible Institute, 1970), 2.

Ezra 1

1. Madeleine S. Miller and J. Lane Miller, *The New Harper's Bible Dictionary, Israel* (New York, Evanston, San Francisco, London: Harper & Row, 1973), 293.
2. Charles R. Swindoll, *The Mystery of God's Will* (Nashville, TN: Word, 1999), 81.
3. Charles R. Swindoll, *God's Masterwork,* vol. 2, *Ezra Through Daniel* (Anaheim, CA: Insight for Living, 1997), 6.
4. Clarence H. Wagner Jr., *Newsletter* (Tulsa, OK: Bridges for Peace, December 1, 1994), 2.
5. Sol Scharfstein, *Understanding Israel* (Hoboken, NJ: KTAV, 1994), 92.
6. John C. Whitcomb Jr., *The Wycliffe Bible Commentary, Ezra* (Nashville, TN: Southwestern, 1968), 424.

Ezra 2

1. Mark D. Roberts, Lloyd J. Ogilvie, gen. ed., *The Communicator's Commentary,* vol. 11, *Ezra, Nehemiah, Esther* (Dallas, TX: Word, 1993), 61.
2. Jack W. Hayford, gen. ed., *Hayford's Bible Handbook* (Nashville, Atlanta, London, Vancouver: Thomas Nelson, 1995), 114.
3. Zola Levitt, *Levitt Letter,* vol. 22, Number 11 (Dallas, TX: Zola Levitt Ministries), 10.

Ezra 3

1. H. A. Ironside, *Lectures on Levitical Offerings* (Neptune, NJ: Loizeaux Brothers), 17–18.
2. Richard Booker, *Jesus in the Feasts of Israel* (South Plainfield, NJ: Bridge), 103.
3. Warren W. Wiersbe, *Be Heroic* (Colorado Springs, CO: Chariot Victor, 1997), 20–21.
4. H. G. M. Williamson, *Word Biblical Commentary,* vol. 16, *Ezra, Nehemiah* (Waco, TX: Word, 1985), 48.
5. Martha Bergen, *Shepherd's Notes, Ezra/Nehemiah* (Nashville, TN: Broadman & Holman, 1999), 24.

Ezra 4

1. *The Pulpit Commentary, Ezra, Nehemiah, Esther & Job,* vol. 7, 44.
2. Kay Arthur, David Lawson, and Bob Vareen, *Overcoming Fear & Discouragement, Ezra/Nehemiah/Esther* (Eugene, OR: Harvest House, 1999), 53.
3. Hayford, *Hayford's Bible Handbook,* 113.

Ezra 5

1. F. Charles Fensham, *The Books of Ezra And Nehemiah* (Grand Rapids, MI: Eerdmans, 1982), 79.
2. Mervin Breneman, *The New American Commentary,* vol. 10, *Ezra, Nehemiah, Esther* (Nashville, TN: Broadman & Holman, 1993), 109.

Ezra 6

1. Jack W. Hayford with Joseph Snider, *Restoring and Renewing the People of God, A Study of Ezra & Nehemiah* (Nashville, TN: Thomas Nelson, 1998), 36.
2. *Bible Expositor and Illuminator* (Cleveland, OH: Union Gospel Press, 1997), 117.

Ezra 7

1. Bergen, *Shepherd's Notes,* 35.
2. Tim LaHaye, *How to Study the Bible for Yourself* (Eugene, OR: Harvest House, 1998), 25.
3. Charles R. Swindoll, Max Lucado, and Charles Colson, *The Glories of Christmas* (Dallas, TX: Word, 1996), 133.

4. Lyle P. Murphy, *Bible Expositor and Illuminator* (Cleveland, OH: Union Gospel Press), June, July, August 1980, 173.

Ezra 8

1. Swindoll, Lucado, and Colson, *The Glories of Christmas*, 122.
2. Roberts, *The Communicator's Commentary*, 131.
3. Williamson, *Word Biblical Commentary*, 119.
4. Ironside, *Lectures on Levitical Offerings*, 51.
5. *Bible Dictionary, Bible Facts at Your Fingertips* (Lincolnwood, IL: Publications International, 1999), 441.

Ezra 9

1. Knute Larson and Kathy Dahlen, *Holman Old Testament Commentary, Ezra, Nehemiah, Esther* (Nashville, TN: Broadman & Holman, 2005), 104.
2. LaHaye, *How to Study the Bible for Yourself*, 30.
3. Swindoll, *The Mystery of God's Will*, 57.

Ezra 10

1. G. Ernest Thomas, *Holy Habits and You* (Nashville, TN: Tidings, 1967), 36.
2. *The Pulpit Commentary*, vol. 7 *Ezra, Nehemiah, Esther & Job*, (Grand Rapids, MI: Eerdmans, 1980), 153.
3. Larson and Dahlen, *Holman Old Testament Commentary, Ezra, Nehemiah, Esther*, 119.
4. Arthur, Lawson and Vereen, *Overcoming Fear & Discouragement, Ezra/Nehemiah/Esther*, 67.
5. Lucado, *Life Lessons with Max Lucado, Books of Ezra & Nehemiah*, 115.

Part Two: Nehemiah

1. Swindoll, *God's Masterwork*, vol. 2, *Ezra, Through Daniel*, 12.

Nehemiah 1

1. Oral Roberts, *Christ in Every Book of the Bible* (Tulsa, OK: Oral Roberts Evangelistic Association, 1977), 31.
2. The Holy Bible, *Authorized King James Version* (Iowa Falls, IA: Word Bible, 1994), 825.

Nehemiah 2

1. Thomas, *Holy Habits and You*, 38.
2. Lucado, *Life Lessons with Max Lucado*, 59.
3. David C. Cook, *Comprehensive Bible Study*, (Colorado Springs: Cook Communications, April 2, 2006), 37.
4. Charles R. Swindoll, *Hand Me Another Brick* (Nashville, TN: Word, 1990), 53.

Nehemiah 3

1. David Hocking, *Reviving the Stones* (Orange, CA: Promise, 1991), 51.

Nehemiah 4

1. Robert Martin Walker, *Thinking About Prayer, Adult Bible Studies, Teacher* (Nashville, TN: Cokesbury, Winter 1999–2000), 44.
2. Don Fields, *Nehemiah, The Courage to Face Opposition* (Downers Grove, IL: InterVarsity, 1994), 18.
3. Hocking, *Reviving the Stones*, 68.
4. Hayford with Snider, *Restoring and Renewing the People of God*, 92.

Nehemiah 5

1. J. Vernon McGee, *Thru the Bible with J. Vernon McGee*, vol. 2, *Joshua–Psalms* (Nashville, TN: Thomas Nelson, 1982), 522.
2. Swindoll, *God's Masterwork*, vol. 2, *Ezra Through Daniel*, 17.

Nehemiah 6

1. Jensen, *Ezra, Nehemiah, Esther: A Self-Study Guide*, 62.
2. Hayford, *Hayford's Bible Handbook*, 120.
3. W. Herschel Ford, *Simple Sermons on Prayer* (Grand Rapids, MI: Baker, 1994), 27.
4. Arthur, Lawson, and Vereen, *Overcoming Fear & Discouragement, Ezra/Nehemiah/Esther*, 93.
5. Ford, *Simple Sermons on Prayer*, 53.
6. John Danielson, *Bible Expositor and Illuminator* (Cleveland, OH: Union Gospel Press), fall quarter *1986*, 163.

Nehemiah 7

1. Warren W. Wiersbe, *Be Determined* (Wheaton, IL: Victor, 1992), 83.
2. Larson and Dahlen, *Holman Old Testament Commentary, Ezra, Nehemiah, Esther*, 211.

Nehemiah 8

1. Emmaus Bible School, *What Christians Believe* (Chicago, IL: Moody, 1951), 11–12.
2. LaHaye, *How to Study the Bible for Yourself*, 26.
3. Emmaus Bible School, *What Christians Believe*, 12.
4. Matthew Henry, *Matthew Henry's Commentary on the Whole Bible* (Peabody, MA: Hendrickson, 1991), 635.

5. Charles R. Swindoll, *Growing Deep in the Christian Life* (Grand Rapids, MI: Zondervan, 1995), 75.
6. Wiersbe, *Be Determined*, 101.
7. Clarence H. Wagner Jr., *Lessons from Sukkot—The Feast of Tabernacles* (Tulsa, OK: Bridges for Peace, October 1995), 2.
8. Booker, *Jesus in the Feasts of Israel*, 106.
9. Zola Levitt, *The Seven Feasts of Israel* (Dallas, TX: Zola Levitt, 1979), 19.
10. Thomas, *Holy Habits and You*, 45.

Nehemiah 9

1. Bergen, *Shepherd's Notes, Ezra/Nehemiah*, 78.
2. Lucado, *The Glories of Christmas*, 116.
3. Grant Jeffrey, *The Signature of God* (Toronto, Ontario: Frontier Research, 1996), 12.
4. Bible Dictionary, *Bible Facts at Your Fingertips*, 380.
5. Fields, *Nehemiah, The Courage to Face Opposition*, 33.
6. E. M. Bounds, *Power Through Prayer* (Midland Park, NJ: Operation Mobilization), 1.

Nehemiah 10

1. Charles Stanley, *Handle with Prayer* (Wheaton, IL: Victor, 1996), 87.

Nehemiah 11

1. Swindoll, *Hand Me Another Brick*, 163–64.
2. *The Preacher's Outline & Sermon Bible, Ezra, Nehemiah, Esther* (Chattanooga, TN: Leadership Ministries Worldwide, 2004), 198.
3. Hayford with Snider, *Restoring and Renewing the People of God*, 139.

Nehemiah 12

1. Swindoll, *Hand Me Another Brick*, 172–73.
2. *The Preacher's Outline & Sermon Bible, Ezra, Nehemiah, Esther*, 204.
3. Stanley, *Handle with Prayer*, 30.

Nehemiah 13

1. Fields, *Nehemiah, The Courage to Face Opposition*, 45.
2. Roberts/Ogilvie, *The Communicator's Commentary*, vol. 11, *Ezra, Nehemiah, Esther*, 295.
3. Swindoll, *God's Masterwork*, 19.
4. Lucado, *Life Lessons*, 117.
5. Wiersbe, *Be Determined*, 146.
6. Breneman, *The New American Commentary*, vol. 10, *Ezra, Nehemiah, Esther*, 272.
7. Ibid., 275.
8. David Wilkerson, *Hell-Shaking Prayer, Times Square Church Pulpit Series, 12-18-2000*, 4.

Part Three: The Book of Haggai

1. Holy Bible, *Master Reference Bible, Family and Library Reference Edition* (Nashville, TN: Good News Publishers, 1968), 800.
2. The Holy Bible (Iowa Falls, IA: World Bible Publishers, 1994), 1453.

Haggai 1

1. Chuck Missler, taped message, *Haggai, Hab/Zep/Hag/Mal-Tape 3* (Coeur d'Alene, ID: Koinonia House, 1997), Side 1.
2. Stephen R. Miller, *Holman Old Testament Commentary, Nahum, Habakkuk, Zephaniah, Haggai, Zechariah, Malachi* (Nashville, TN: Broadman & Holman, 2004), 120.
3. Mark J. Boda, *The NIV Application Commentary, Haggai, Zechariah* (Grand Rapids, MI: Zondervan, 2004), 93–94.

Haggai 2

1. Henry H. Halley, *Halley's Bible Handbook, Large Print Edition* (Grand Rapids, MI: Zondervan, 1965), 377.
2. Boda, *The NIV Application Commentary, Haggai, Zechariah*, 118.
3. Henry, *Matthew Henry's Commentary on the Whole Bible*, 1565.
4. Jensen, *Haggai, Zechariah, Malachi, A Self-Study Guide*, 35.
5. Levy, *When Prophets Speak of Judgment*, 168.
6. Jensen, *Haggai, Zechariah, Malachi*, 13.
7. Hayford, *Hayford's Bible Handbook*, 260.
8. Missler, *Taped Message, Haggai, Hab/Zep/Hag/Mal-Tape 3*, 1997, Side 2.
9. Levy, *When Prophets Speak of Judgment*, 175.
10. Idid., 177.

Zechariah 1

1. Bible Dictionary, *Bible Facts at Your Fingertips*, 490.
2. The Prophecy Bible, *The New King James Version* (Nashville, TN: Thomas Nelson, 1985), 948.
3. Dave Breese, *The Book of Zechariah, Part I* (Colton, CA: World Prophetic Ministries, DB135A), Side 1.

4. Merrill F. Unger, *Unger's Commentary on the Old Testament* (Chattanooga, TN: AMG, Tyndale Theological Seminary, 2002), 1963.
5. Jensen, *Simply Understanding the Bible* (Minneapolis, MN: World Wide Publications, Irving L. Jensen, 1990), 163.
6. David Wilkerson, *Governed by the Word of God*, Part Two of Two Messages, Times Square Church Pulpit Series (Lindale, TX: World Challenge, 5-22-2000) 1.
7. *King James Bible Commentary* (Nashville, TN: Thomas Nelson, 1999), 1099.
8. Ralph L. Smith, *Word Biblical Commentary, Micah-Malachi,* vol. 32 (Waco, TX: Word, 1984), 73.
9. H. A. Ironside, *The Minor Prophets* (Grand Rapids, MI: Kregel, 2004), 238.

Zechariah 2

1. Paul E. Grabill, *Bible Expositor and Illuminator*, (Cleveland, OH: Union Gospel Press), summer quarter, 1985, 157.
2. Wenger, *Bible Expositor and Illuminator*, summer quarter 1985, 147.
3. Dave Breese, *The Tide of Our Times* (Hillsboro, KS: Destiny Newsletter, September 2000), 3.
4. *King James Bible Commentary*, 1103.

Zechariah 3

1. Charles H. Dyer, *World News and Bible Prophecy* (Wheaton, IL: Tyndale House, 1993) 91.
2. Thomas Edward McComiskey, *The Minor Prophets,* vol. 3 (Grand Rapids, MI: Baker, 1998), 1070.
3. J. Vernon McGee, *Thru the Bible with J. Vernon McGee,* vol. 3, *Proverbs–Malachi* (Nashville, TN: Thomas Nelson, 1982) 919.
4. Walter C. Kaiser Jr., Lloyd J. Ogilvie, general ed., *The Communicator's Commentary, Micah–Malachi,* vol. 21 (Dallas, TX: Word, 1992), 326.

Zechariah 4

1. J. R. Church, *They Pierced the Veil* (Oklahoma City, OK: Prophecy, 1993), 187.
2. Smith, *Word Biblical Commentary, Micah–Malachi,* vol. 32, 205.
3. C. I. Scofield, *The New Scofield Study Bible* (New York: Oxford University Press, 1967), 966.

Zechariah 5

1. Steven C. Ger, *Zechariah: Minor Prophet with a Major Message*, Paper Presented to Pre-Trib Rapture Study Group, (Garland, TX: Sojourner Ministries, December 1999), 5–6.
2. Russell L. Penney, *Dictionary of Premillennial Theology, Vision 6: The Flying Scroll* (Grand Rapids, MI: Kregal, 1996), 428.
3. Breese, *The Book of Zechariah, Part I,* Side 2.

Zechariah 6

1. Peter C. Craigie, *Twelve Prophets,* vol. 2 (Philadelphia, PA: Westminster, 1985), 186.
2. Scofield, *The New Scofield Study Bible*, 968.
3. John Phillips, *Exploring the Minor Prophets, The John Phillips Commentary Series* (Grand Rapids, MI: Kregel, 1998), 283.
4. Scofield, *The New Scofield Study Bible*, 968.
5. J. Randall Price, *Why I Still Believe These Are the Last Days* (Oklahoma City, Ok: Hearthstone, 1993), 119.

Zechariah 7

1. Wilkerson, *Prayer That Is Pleasing to the Lord*, Times Square Church Pulpit Series, 2-12-96, 1.

Zechariah 8

1. Wiersbe, *Be Heroic*, 123.

Zechariah 9

1. Dyer, *World News and Bible Prophecy*, 55.
2. McComiskey, *The Minor Prophets,* vol. 3, 1171.

Zechariah 10

1. Feinberg, *The Minor Prophets,* 319–20.
2. Norbert Lieth, *Zechariah's Prophetic Vision for the New World* (West Columbia, SC: Midnight Call Ministries, 2002), 206.

Zechariah 11

1. Craigie, *Twelve Prophets,* 208.
2. Feinberg, *The Minor Prophets,* 327.
3. Ironside, *The Minor Prophets,* 274.
4. David R. Reagan, *The Rise and Fall of the Antichrist, Lamplighter* (McKinney, TX: Lamb & Lion Ministries, November 1998), 4.

Zechariah 12

1. Thomas Ice and Timothy Demy, *Fast Facts on Bible Prophecy* (Eugene, OR: Harvest House, 1997), 64.

2. Craigie, *Twelve Prophets*, 212.
3. Tim LaHaye, *Prophecy Study Bible* (Chattanooga, TN: AMG, 2001), 1099.
4. Dave Hunt, *The Gathering Storm*, Mal Couch, gen. ed. (Springfield, MO: 21st Century Press, 2005), 136.
5. Clarence H. Wagner Jr. and Jim Gerrish, *The Trumpet Is Sounding in Zion* (Tulsa, OK: Bridges for Peace, September, 1995), 5–6.
6. Kenneth L. Barker and John R. Kohlenberger III, *Zondervan NIV Commentary*, vol. 1 (Grand Rapids, MI: Zondervan, 1994), 1536.
7. Arnold G. Fruchtenbaum, *The Footsteps of the Messiah* (Tustin, CA: Ariel Ministries, 1995), 214.
8. Chuck Missler, *Taped Message, Zechariah Chapter 12, Tape 4*, 1997, Side 2.
9. LaHaye, *Prophecy Study Bible*, 1100.

Zechariah 13

1. Penny, *Dictionary of Premillennial Theology*, 432.
2. Unger, *Unger's Commentary on the Old Testament*, 2041–42.
3. Kaiser Jr./Ogilvie, *The Communicator's Commentary, Micah–Malachi*, vol. 21, 408.
4. John MacArthur, *The MacArthur Bible Commentary* (Nashville, TN: Thomas Nelson, 2005), 1071.
5. Richard Mayhue and Thomas Ice, *The Popular Encyclopedia of Bible Prophecy* (Eugene, OR: Harvest House, 2004), 62.
6. Feinberg, *The Minor Prophets*, 335.
7. *The Pulpit Commentary, Amos–Malachi*, vol. 14, 147.
8. Kaiser Jr., *The Communicator's Commentary, Micah–Malachi*, vol. 21, 411.
9. John McArthur, *The Murder of Jesus* (Nashville, TN: Word, 2000), 56.
10. Fruchtenbaum, *The Footsteps of the Messiah*, 197–98.
11. Arno Froese, *Jerusalem Divided*, News From Israel, October 1995, 7–8.

Zechariah 14

1. LaHaye, *Prophecy Study Bible*, 1101.
2. Grant R. Jeffrey, *Prince of Darkness* (New York: Bantam, 1995), 341.
3. Ice and Demy, *Fast Facts on Bible Prophecy*, 221.
4. John F. Walvoord, *Major Bible Prophecies* (Grand Rapids, MI: Zondervan, 1991), 251–52.
5. Lieth, *Zechariah's Prophetic Vision for the New World*, 276.
6. David Hocking, *Visions of the Future* (Tustin, CA: HFT, 2000), 149.
7. Dyer, *World News and Bible Prophecy*, 237.
8. Walvoord, *Every Prophecy of the Bible*, 333.
9. Ice and Demy, *Fast Facts on Bible Prophecy*, 184.
10. Penny, *Dictionary of Premillennial Theology*, 432.
11. Fruchtenbaum, *The Footsteps of the Messiah*, 327.
12. *King James Bible Commentary*, 1135.
13. Lieth, *Zechariah's Prophetic Vision for the New World*, 291.
14. Phillips, *Exploring the Minor Prophets*, 306
15. Walvoord, *Major Bible Prophecies*, 403.
16. Unger, *Unger's Commentary on the Old Testament*, 2058.
17. Jeffrey, *The Signature of God*, 192.
18. David Reagan, *The Master Plan* (Eugene, OR: Harvest House, 1993), 190.
19. Ed Hindson, *Approaching Armageddon* (Eugene, OR: Harvest House, 1997), 279.
20. Fruchtenbaum, *Footsteps of the Messiah*, 352.
21. Smith, *Word Biblical Commentary, Micah–Malachi*, vol. 32, 292.
22. Walvoord, *Every Prophecy in the Bible*, 202.

Index

A

B

C

D

E

F

G

H

I

K

L

M

N

O

P

Q

R

S

T

U

V

W

X

Y

Z

www.ingramcontent.com/pod-product-compliance
Ingram Content Group UK Ltd.
Pitfield, Milton Keynes, MK11 3LW, UK
UKHW052243240325
456661UK00008B/87

9 781418 5100